THE GARDEN
IN COLOR

THE
GARDEN
IN COLOR

By

LOUISE BEEBE WILDER

New York
The Macmillan Company
1937

PRINTED IN THE UNITED STATES OF AMERICA
THE WILLIAM BYRD PRESS, INC., RICHMOND, VIRGINIA

CONTENTS

CONTENTS

Spring

Summer

Autumn

Winter

SPRING

THE GARDEN IN SPRING

SPRING comes to the garden with tentative, indecisive steps. A foot is advanced and withdrawn; but where it has touched, the turf greens or a fragile flower lifts its head. A bird shrills from a pregnant branch and is silent; color creeps up the naked stems of shrubs, awakening them from their winter quietude. From the pond the hylas chant with modern dissonance, and are silenced once, twice, sometimes thrice by the biting cold. The breeze is sharp and tangy, fingering its way about our upturned coat collars. Now and then the sun warms to summer heat, deceiving us.

The very air is charged with suspense; rumors flit from tree to tree and animate the grass. Sap stirs in ancient trunks and in ourselves the blood moves at a quicker pace. Beneath the earth, where roots lie entwined, there is a gentle stretching and straining. The whole natural world is aware of the rhythmic tread of the oncoming army of the Spring. Thwarted by snows, beaten back by storms, this army is never more than momentarily hindered in its inevitable advance. Step by step it moves forward, treading under its frail outposts, and gradually the evidence of Winter's occupation is erased.

And presently there comes a day when the new order seems always to have prevailed. We quickly forget storm and stress. We are conscious only of gentle enticing rains, of the mild airs that wrap us about, of blossoms that lie sunning along dark branches. Sweet scents are tangled in the breeze, and bright flowers flash and sway in beds and borders, while birds mate and make a gay song about it. And we in our oldest and most comfortable clothes, armed with tool kit and innumerable packets of seed, revel in getting as close to the winter-sweetened earth as possible.

In short it is spring.

Now, with a little guile and some industry we can trick Madam Nature into giving us a glimpse of this delectable season some weeks ahead of schedule. In order to enjoy this boon, we cast about for a sheltered situation, a situation the sun will have no trouble in penetrating, and set out there such plants and shrubs and bulbs as are most helpless before the soft blandishments of "the fire that severs day from night." If we do this we shall not have to wait for May to spill her horn of plenty upon the earth. In May it is not difficult to have a lovely garden. Nature herself is then our handmaiden, ready to do our bidding, and doing much besides on her own initiative. But little odd snatches of pure spring may be found in any garden, great or small, during March and April if we plan for them. And come upon unexpectedly—they always seem unexpected, however carefully we have contrived them—these off-the-record bits of spring do more to lift the spirit than all the largess of the later year.

If there are no naturally sheltered regions in the garden, it is no trick to contrive them. A windbreak of evergreens on the north and east sides is perhaps the easiest way to bring about a snug and weatherproof refuge for early-flowering plants. And Hemlock makes a good and sightly hedge for this purpose. If for one reason or another this is not a practicable idea, a close-knit fence will do, or a wall, dry or otherwise. Leaf-losing shrubs provide some shelter but not much. A gardener, however, who goes about hunting for sheltered situations will doubtless find them. There is always the south side of the house or other building; or perhaps the conformation of the ground, sloping to the south or southwest, makes for security against angry weather.

There is one more point that must be thought of where early blossom-

[4]

ing is being considered—the soil. The soil should be what gardeners term "warm." A clay soil, remember, is cold and discourages early awakening, whereas a warm soil is as good as an alarm clock. If a clay soil, however, is all you have, its deleterious qualities may be remedied by deep digging and the addition of generous amounts of old rotted manure and sharp sand. Such situations, too, will nearly always need special attention later in the year. If they are warm in spring they are warmer and dryer in summer, and the plants will suffer unless we take the matter in hand and water them freely and often.

It is a matter of considerable pride to be able to gather flowers from the outdoor garden while our neighbors are still buying them from the florist. And a small nosegay "picked fresh" and tendered a housed and ailing friend means far more than a much grander bouquet of hothouse flowers. It carries a message of hope and reassurance.

❦ Leafless Branches and Freshening Grass Sprigged with Snowdrops (Plate 1)

Only spiritually sightless eyes are unaware of the earliest approaches of the young year. On every hand she seeks to attract our attention. How sad it is to miss these timid advances! There is, for instance, the beauty of still leafless branches seen against the sky or reflected in clear water. Leafless the branches may be, but every twig to the seeing eye is inspired with life. We do not need the language of leaves to know that the whole tree is tingling with vitality. Often the bark has subtly changed its hue, often buds are suddenly in evidence, though tightly closed. The grass below has put off its drab winter coat and is slipping on a green one. And if we have taken a hand and planted the grass thickly with Snowdrops the autumn before, we have played a good part in the drama of the Coming of Spring.

[5]

Where there is water, a placid pond or a stream, the situation should be taken advantage of to make a spring picture: a carefully placed group of trees—Birches with their white stems, Beeches with gray satin bark, a few Dogwoods *(Cornus florida)* for the sake of their spreading grace, an Alder or two—and in the background some brushy material, wild briers, Viburnums, low Dogwoods, Elders, and the like, massed for the sake of the soft color their awakened stems lend the little scene. The trees should never be so closely planted that the individual "handwriting" of their twigs against the sky or reflected in the water is lost or confused. They are far more beautiful and more eloquent in their nakedness than when clothed with leaves.

In the grass may be scattered broadcast Snowdrops *(Galanthus nivalis)*, Scillas *(S. sibirica)*, and many another small and early-flowering bulbous plant, while along the brushy plantation little eager white Violets—*Viola blanda*, a native which loves the proximity of water and blooms early and fragrantly—will weave a fabric of leaves and flowers that we shall willingly go forth to see on a brisk March day. Here Hepaticas, with their furry buds and pink, white, or blue flowers, may also be encouraged, and blithe Spring Beauties; and if a hardy Skunk Cabbage or two thrust up their furled inimitable greenery, so much the better—and the fastidious can always hold their noses.

Galanthus nivalis with *Eranthis hyemalis* (Snowdrops with Winter Aconites) (Plate 2)

If advantage is to be taken of a springy hillside falling away to the north or shaded by high-branched trees or a scattering of bushy shrubs, no better way could be found than to plant it thickly with Snowdrops and Winter Aconites. Early in the year these will weave a lovely white and yellow and green pattern on a groundwork of brown leaves and skim ice. And if such a sight does not draw you from your snug fire I am no judge of gardeners.

There are many kinds of Snowdrops to be had, but the kind that loves the conditions here described is the commonest and least expensive, *Galanthus nivalis*. Of Winter Aconites, too, there is more than one kind; but here again the most familiar, *Eranthis hyemalis*, is the best for our purpose. But there is one point to be remembered about both of them which is of the utmost importance, particularly in the case of the Aconite. They must be put into the ground *early*, late in August if possible, early in September certainly. Otherwise there will be little show in the spring, possibly no show at all, for kept out of the ground they quickly lose their viability and either rot away over the winter or come up in a sadly debilitated state. Plant them early, and plant them close together. They are sociable and like to mingle their roots below ground as they do their flowers above it. Left to themselves, they will increase rapidly once they are established, and crowd about the boles of the trees and forgather merrily beneath the bare stems of the shrubs, and ramble this way and that, sometimes far afield. Surely none should forgo this easy pageantry of swinging snowy bells and yellow upheld cups.

The Snowdrops grow from small tunicated bulbs. They should be planted three times their own depth in the soil and an inch or two apart. The Winter Aconites spring from tubers dark and dour, most unpromising to the eye. But out of these come, surprisingly, golden buttercuplike flowers surrounded by a green ruff and later charming leaves that carpet the ground until the seed is matured, when they attend briskly to the sowing and then retire with the foliage of the Snowdrops until another spring calls them forth.

They may be left absolutely alone, neither transplanted nor mulched. But if for any reason you must move them, dig them up, either Snowdrops or Aconites, in little sods while in bloom and transplant them at once without disturbing the roots to the situations where they are wanted.

✤ *Erica carnea* with *Primula acaulis* (Winter Heath with English Primrose) (Plate 3)

The Winter Heath is a law unto itself. Certainly weather has no terrors for it, and it flowers when the notion takes it. Often, if a thick blanket of snow is turned back, the pretty bells of the Winter Heath will be found all rosy and ready to ring out the good tidings that spring is somewhere in the near offing.

Erica carnea (E. herbacea) is a native of the mountains of central and southern Europe, where it carpets wide tracts. It is a delightful plant to use for covering open hillsides or for forming thickets in the rock garden. It is very hardy, very sturdy and does not require the highly acid soil so necessary to the majority of its family. It is a dwarf plant, some six or eight inches high, very bushy, and its wiry ascending stems are thickly clothed with very narrow, blunt bright green leaves about half an inch long. The flowers are crowded along the upper part of the stem in a raceme two inches or more long. They are narrow-mouthed bells inflated near the calyx. The calyx is red, as are the short individual stems, and from the constricted mouths of the bells protrude brown anthers and long reddish filaments. The blossoms are delicately fragrant, and in the type are a pleasing pinkish purple, but there is a white-flowered form and a number of named varieties not generally available in this country, with bells of various tones of carmine, dark red, purple, and pink. One of these, Queen Mary by name, is an invariable and especially lusty winter bloomer.

They all flower off and on throughout the cold months, but their festive season is early April, when they are joined by the Primroses, Daffodils, and sweet English Violets.

[*8*]

The best soil for this Heath is a good sandy loam with a generous admixture of peat or humus, and water should be given in dry weather as it suffers from drought. Full sun or partial shade suits it equally well, and it may be set out in spring or early autumn. Sometimes the winter suns burn the foliage a little; then the disfigured parts should be cut away so that the fresh effect will not be spoiled.

Set a foot apart, the plants soon grow together and form a close furzy covering for the earth. They may be clipped over occasionally when out of bloom to keep them in shape.

A good collection of Winter Heaths provides many a winter and early spring bouquet for which we are grateful.

Adonis amurensis (Amur Adonis) (Plate 4)

Perhaps the most impatient plant in the spring garden is the Adonis. One watches with anxiety its round knobs appearing above ground despite the most inclement weather. Once they have broken ground they edge upwards daily at a pace that is astonishing, and, before we know it, its great yellow suns are shedding a golden glow over the garden, unmindful of whipping winds and frosty nights. The flowers on sturdy stems about eight inches tall come first; then as these begin to fade a lovely exhibition of ferny leaves takes place. A well grown clump occupies a good deal of space—eighteen inches or two feet across when in full leaf—so that it is necessary to be careful not to plant bulbous things or small plants where they would be injured by its lush shadow. After seed has matured the whole plant dies away until another spring, and lightly rooting annuals such as Sweet Alyssum, Candytuft, or California Poppies may be sown above it to hide the blank it leaves.

This Adonis comes from Manchuria and may be used in the rock garden with fine effect or in the borders. Once established, it may be left in peace

[9]

to grow more and more rotund year by year. It never fails to flower with the utmost generosity and is one of the sights of the spring garden. It is a favorite plant of the Japanese of which they "make constant use in their exquisite toy gardens that compress a dozen miles of mountain or shore into the compass of a salver." But it is only in its earliest stages that it is suitable for this purpose; when the leaves expand, it no longer fits the picture.

It is not a plant particular as to soil, and sunshine or light shade suit it equally well. The double form is perhaps the most splendid but the single is pretty enough. Flowers that bloom with it are Snowdrops, *Scilla sibirica*, *Tulipa Kaufmanniana*, Winter Heath, *Crocus biflorus* and *C. Imperati*.

❦ *Daphne petraea (D. rupestris)* (Plate 5)

The Mountain Garland Flower, as it is called, "dwells high and far in the Southern Alps, confined to one small district, and there haunting hot and terrible cliff-faces of rose-gray limestone fronting the full radiance of the Italian sun." Reginald Farrer's word picture gives us some insight into the proper treatment of this small bit of loveliness if we are so lucky as to become its possessor. I do not know that I have ever seen it offered in this country, but it is well to be prepared. It grows, it seems, in very narrow crevices between great rocks, sending masses of fat roots, yellow and hungry, far down into "nothing, with only the lime of the rock to feed them." And out into the light from a thick neck emerges a little plant, with small glossy evergreen leaves along elfin branches that are held close to the rock face. And presently at the ends of these little branches appear heads of several pink tubelike blooms, a most luscious and lovely pink and deliciously fragrant. Strangely enough, for a plant from such austere surroundings, it is said to do very well in cultivation—in the rock garden, of course, at its highest point between stones, in full sun and with a soil that is full of lime for the roots to ramble in. M. Correvon states that he grows it in his garden in "an east and west position facing a limestone wall, where it flowers well but never seeds . . . I have a twenty-year-old tuft which hardly measures twelve centimeters in diameter." Truly a gem for the rock garden. M. Correvon says that it has been called the king of Daphnes, which only goes to show that kings need not be large to be great. It flowers in May and June.

Other Daphnes suitable for use in the rock garden are *D. Cneorum*, the Garland Flower, *D. Collina (D. sericea)* and *D. Blagayana*. The last is native to the eastern Alps, bears clusters of white flowers at the ends of its little shoots, and gives off the most exquisite fragrance.

✻ *Daphne Genkwa (D. Fortunei)* (Plate 6)

This is the quaintest of little shrubs, a Chinese and Japanese species which, I read, has some economic value in its home lands in the making of paper. I have found it a little tender; and indeed, looking at it, one knows instinctively that it needs shelter and care. Its appearance is altogether frail and a little wavering. It is not an evergreen, but quite early in the spring its soft brown branches are strung with little bunches of lilac flowers, not at all unlike miniature trusses of true Lilacs, but without the fragrance. For this is one of the few Daphnes that have little or no scent. The bush grows finally to a height of about three feet, but it takes time. The leaves are grayish and add little to the elegance of the shrub, for they seem to droop and fade as if in self-effacement. Altogether, it has no "presence" at all and makes no splurge even when in full bloom; but it is nice to have, and one can visit it when one is not feeling too adequate.

This species is hardy as far north as New York and probably may be retained in even colder climates if given some protection from cold winds and a mulch of leaves over the roots after the ground is frozen. Unlike many of the Daphnes this species likes a partially shaded position, and it thrives in a light well drained soil that has some lime in it.

✤ *Daphne Mezereum* (Mezereon) (Plate 7)

All the Daphnes have charm, however modest their port, and the Mezereon is not the least in this attribute. Like *D. Genkwa* it is a deciduous shrub blossoming before the leaves appear in early spring. It is a stiff little shrub that will grow in time four feet tall. With the first softening of the weather the erect branches wrap themselves in bloom, soft purplish pink or white, and they exhale a fragrance that carries for a great distance and is not unlike that of Violets. The flowers are said to be followed by red berries, but this further gift has not been vouchsafed by my bushes. It is pleasant to carpet the ground about the Mezereon bushes with sweet English Violets, purple, mauve, and white; they flower at the same time and like the same conditions of partial shade and a sheltered position.

William Robinson calls it a wild plant in English woods, but I believe it is a doubtful native. It does grow wild in many parts of Europe and Siberia, however, and its bark is of some medicinal value. It is quite easily raised from seed, and as it is hardy it is curious that it is not more often seen. On cold soils it grows more slowly than under milder conditions, and it is rather difficult to transplant, so that it is better to begin with small plants. If this Daphne is raised from seed the seed should be sown as soon as ripe, for it quickly loses vitality. A little thicket of the Mezereon on a bleak spring day is a heart-warming sight.

⚜ *Bulbocodium vernum* (Spring Meadow Saffron) (Plate 8)

Very early in the year—indeed, soon after the Snowdrops—there springs up in the garden, if you are so lucky as to possess it, a curious flower something like a Crocus, something like a Colchicum. It is neither. It is the Spring Meadow Saffron, belonging to the Lily clan, and the only member of its genus in cultivation. When we first behold its pinkish flowers our thought is that it is a rather untidy-looking individual, for it does not possess either the sleekness of the Crocus or the vaselike form of the Colchicum. Commonly, a single well grown corm produces two flowers; and they are prettier in the bud, when they have a certain svelte elegance. The leaves develop after the flowers have matured, and grow to a height of about five inches before they, too, fade away to await another spring.

The corm is blackish and covered with a sort of wool which is indicated by its name (*bolbós*, a bulb, + *kódion*, wool). And this woolly covering is an indication of its preference for a warm situation in light soil, gritty and so well drained. It is very slow of increase, but the corms finally become crowded; when this is the case they should be dug up any time from July to September and planted in fresh soil, three or four inches apart. To companion the Spring Meadow Saffron one will not go wrong in choosing Snowdrops, Leucojums, the pretty Greek Anemone (*A. blanda*) and the sky-blue *Scilla bifolia*.

Bulbocodium vernum is a native of the Alps of Europe and seems to be quite hardy, if a little slothful.

⚜ *Jasminum nudiflorum* (Naked Jasmine, Winter Jasmine) (Plate 9)

Very few Jasmines are hardy in the North, but the Winter or Naked Jasmine does very well in cold gardens. It is half climber, half shrub, a scrambler that resents training. Indeed, it should not be too severely trained but may be fastened here and there to trellis or wall and allowed to shower outwards at will. Or it may be planted at the top of a bank and left free to trail downwards, throwing itself about, this way and that, and rooting where it comes in contact with the soil. It may also be kept cut back like a little shrub when it is nice to use at the base of taller shrubs, hiding the bareness of their unsightly nether limbs.

Its great point is its early flowering. Any time from February onwards the naked whiplike branches may string themselves with yellow stars which are a delight in the cold spring garden. These stems with their eager buds may also be cut and brought indoors in December and January; a few days of genial warmth will serve to make them flower.

It is perhaps safest to give the Naked Jasmine a northern or western exposure to save the buds from premature activity with consequent loss from snappish frosts. But on the other hand it is delightful to have plants in all exposures, for we thus prolong the gay flowering, and if perchance a sudden freeze spoils the bloom of those on the south we still have those on the other aspects to look forward to.

Any good garden soil satisfies its needs. Each spring it will probably be necessary to go over the plants and remove the branches that have died, or to thin them out where they have become congested. No other pruning is necessary.

Jasminum nudiflorum is native in China and Japan, and is quite hardy in the vicinity of New York. It has not the fragrance of other members of its race. Because of its habit of rooting itself so easily there are always plenty of young plants to give away or to transplant elsewhere.

✠ *Crocus Tomasinianus* (Plate 10)

There are a great many desirable Crocus species. They differ from the more usual spring Crocus, forms of *C. vernus*, in their smaller and more fragile flowers, their gentle charm, and their earlier flowering. Some, indeed, flower in the winter. The one here illustrated is a native of Dalmatia and thereabouts, and it is one of the easiest to please, being exceptionally hardy and free of increase in any sunny well drained situation. In parts of my garden it has almost become a nuisance, for it both seeds and increases by little corms until presently it has formed a thick sod that discourages any other vegetation.

It blooms usually early in March. The segments of the flowers are tightly furled like "a smart new umbrella," and they are, in the typical form, a pale silvery lilac in color, almost gray. But with a little urging from a warm spring sun they open and display the lovely amethyst interior. There are several forms; an exquisite white one is to be especially cherished. Some of the Dutch Crocuses have *Tomasinianus* blood in their veins, and *Tomasinianus* charm in their features. These are Margot, a chaste bluish lilac with the characteristic pale exterior, and Maximilian, a rare beauty, of a richer tone of lilac than Margot. Both have rather small flowers, and so are best planted with the wild Crocuses which they resemble, rather than with the fat Dutch varieties.

Crocus Tomasinianus is lovely on tableland in the rock garden or in any sunny, well drained spot. It was named by Dean Herbert, one of England's great gardeners, for his friend Signor Tomasini of Trieste. A further selection of wild Crocuses would include *C. Imperati, C. Sieberi, C. biflorus, C. versicolor, C. etruscus, C. minimus,* and *C. susianus.*

Crocuses may be planted any time in September or October a few inches apart and about three inches deep in the soil.

❀ Crocus with Primrose (Plate 11)

Crocuses do not always linger on to companion the Primroses, but when they do some very nice associations are made possible. The plate here (Plate 11) shows *Primula acaulis rubra (P. vulgaris)*, a red or reddish orange form of the common Primrose, with an orange-yellow Crocus of the Dutch persuasion. It will be seen that here is a true Primrose with one flower to a stem, instead of the heads of flowers that we find in the Polyanthus Primroses, Cowslips, and Oxlips. The leaves are rough, somewhat tonguelike, and stemless; the whole plant grows no more than three inches high.

There are many colored varieties; the typical Primrose has given its name to a lovely pale yellow, but there are now Primroses in every tone from palest pink to deep rose and red, from yellow to orange, lilac, purple, and even a true blue, as well as white. Harbinger is a lovely early-flowering white variety. A partially shaded bank or dampish copse is the place for Primroses; here they will flourish, especially if the soil is deep and rich.

It is said that Primroses are meant to be gathered, as this relieves the plants of a too heavy burden; so we make a charming virtue of expediency. Little glass bowls of Primroses are a delight indoors. Old tufts should be taken up after flowering, separated, and replanted at once in newly enriched soil. And in our dry climate they should be kept well watered until they are safely established and again flourishing.

❀ *Iris reticulata Cantab* (Netted Iris) (Plate 12)

All the *reticulata* Irises have a definite charm, first because of their early flowering, then by reason of their lovely coloring and their butterfly poise. *Reticulata* means "reticulated" or "netted" and refers to the small ovoid

[*16*]

Plate 1. LEAFLESS BRANCHES AND FRESHENING GRASS SPRIGGED WITH
SNOWDROPS BY THE WATERSIDE

Plate 5. *Daphne petraea (D. rupestris)* (ROCK GARLAND FLOWER)

Plate 6. *Daphne Genkwa (D. Fortunei)*

Plate 7. *Daphne Mezereum* (MEZEREON)

Plate 8. *Bulbocodium vernum* (SPRING MEADOW SAFFRON)

Plate 9. *Jasminum nudiflorum* (NAKED JASMINE)

Plate 10. *Crocus Tomasinianus*

Plate 11. CROCUS WITH PRIMROSE

Plate 12. *Iris reticulata* CANTAB

Plate 13. *Iris Tauri (persica* VAR. *Tauri)*

bulb that is covered with a sort of fibrous netting. These bulbs should be put into the ground as early as they can be procured. This is of the utmost importance, as they quickly lose their vitality. They require a warm situation and an open, nourishing, pervious soil to be at their best. Against a warm rock in the rock garden is an ideal situation for them. When the bulbs become crowded they may be dug up in July and replanted in freshly enriched soil, and so the stock is increased.

No one searching for early blooms could find anything more charming than *Iris reticulata* and its various forms and hybrids. In February curious narrow dark leaves with horny tips force themselves through the ground and grow quickly to a height of eight or ten inches, forming a sort of protective stockade about the blossoms that appear in late March in great profusion. These in the type are a rich purple, velvety in texture, and with gold markings on the falls. They have a fragrance of Violets, and a few brought into the house will scent a large room. They bloom with the earliest Crocuses and should be given the sunniest positions possible. They are natives of Asia Minor and perfectly hardy.

The variety shown here is *Cantab*, which originated in the lovely garden of Mr. E. H. Bowles, in England, and received an award of merit and a first-class certificate when it was shown. It is only about three inches high at flowering time, and its soft atmospheric blue is delightful. These Irises are available in this country, though at quite a price, and make splendid pot plants, a half-dozen to an ordinary bulb pan, coming into flower at least a month before those in the garden. The leaves after blossoming grow nearly eighteen inches long and then die away entirely.

Eden Phillpotts is a well known novelist, but too few persons are acquainted with his perfectly delightful works on gardening. In "My Garden" he strongly recommends growing a dozen bulbs of *Iris reticulata* in pots "for people who are in the habit of getting seedy and low-spirited at Christmas time; place these budding things beside your suffering friends, and the reward will be great."

⚜ *Iris Tauri* (Plate 13)

This little beauty is much too small to be left to the hazards and accidents of the open garden and should be given a snug corner in the rock garden. And if a blanket of snow falls upon it and remains during the winter, so much the better. It comes from the alpine pastures of the Eastern Taurus at an elevation of 6,500 feet; also, according to Mr. Irwin Lynch, "from the upper wooded regions in forests of *Juniperus excelsa* at a height of 4,550 feet, where it blooms on the melting of the snow." It is a lovely thing, as may be seen from the plate (13), and is of fairly recent introduction. It belongs to the Juno group and has ovoid bulbs from which depend long stout roots. The leaves, of which there may be six or seven, are bright green and taper to a blunt point. The flowers are produced in succession, usually three to a bulb, and are of the most lovely light violet color, about three and a half inches across; the standards are an inch long, waved and upturned at the sides, and on the spreading falls is some lovely gold and white and deep purple embroidery.

The flower is a little like *Iris reticulata* in form but of somewhat more substance, and lasts splendidly in the garden even in the face of inclement weather. You may do some hunting about before you come upon this Iris in America, but it is well worth looking for and coddling to the best of your knowledge and ability when you find it.

Primula acaulis (P. vulgaris) and *Hepatica triloba* (Plate 14)

The English Primrose lends itself to so many lovely associations in the early spring. Its pale coloring is a complement to almost any other flower color, and its gentle mien fits it to associate with the most lowly. Choose a dampish hillside or low partially shaded swale, or make use of a situation low in the rock garden and on the north side, and plant there as many clumps of the common English Primrose as you like, associating with it tufts of our own Hepatica, particularly those of blue coloring. Thus we shall have an example of international amity that would be hard to better.

Hepaticas come in pink, white, lilac, and a deep blue. The blue ones are the prettiest, and a little selecting as we go abroad in spring, scouting in the woods for signs of spring, will enable us to collect a number. It is almost our earliest spring flower and used to be common in every bit of woodland. But it is fast disappearing, and so perhaps the advice should be given to *buy* your plants instead of collecting them. If you receive white or pale pink ones the effect is almost as good, for the mild hue of the Primrose is in no way combative. Hepaticas do especially well in cultivation, where they are removed from the pressure of wild life about them, and their furry buds and unfolding leaves are a most heartening sign of spring. *Hepatica acutiloba* is a southern species that differs little from *H. triloba* of our northern woodlands.

Primula Sibthorpii (Plate 15)

This is the Caucasian form of the common Primrose, *Primula acaulis;* it is also found in Greece and northern Persia. "But the point of interest," says John Macwatt, who has written an invaluable book called "The Primulas of Europe," "lies in the fact that this plant is unquestionably the original source of varieties in colour of the Primrose, or, in other words, *P. Sibthorpii* is a parent of all our coloured Primroses. The colour of the flowers ranges from purple to rose and reddish pink."

How grateful, then, should we be to this little flower from the far-away mountains of the Caucasus, which through its versatility gives us Primroses of almost every hue! It is a type that flowers very early; and, while in the garden it should be given a partially shaded place, it should also be sheltered from the colder winds, either by a rock or by a small sturdy evergreen. It sometimes goes by the name of *P. acaulis rubra.*

❦ *Primula acaulis caerulea* (Blue Primrose) (Plate 16)

One of the most enchanting flowers that grow is the blue English Primrose. If we get a good strain—they are not all good—we have a flower of purest blue (not the sky-blue of the plate) with a golden eye to set it off. It is one of the earliest to flower and a plant which draws the attention of all visitors to the garden. Blue is not a very common color among flowers, and when we find it we rejoice. It is said that hybridists in their effort to introduce new colors, or shades of color, in some particular plant, have the most difficulty when they try to accomplish a blue form. And so the blue Primrose in a manner of speaking is a triumph. This prize was long striven for, and it was as recently as 1889 that Mr. G. F. Wilson, of Oakwood, Wisley, England (who introduced *Phlox subulata* G. F. Wilson), produced it. It is said that Mr. Wilson worked with a Primrose of purplish coloring to produce Wilson's Blue Primrose; and the fact that the earliest plants had a purplish ring at the base of the corolla lends color to this belief. The ring, in the best forms, has been wholly eliminated, and nothing could exceed the innocence and the purity of the round blue flowers as they smile upwards from their nest of rough green leaves. By raising the

[*20*]

plants from seed you may still get forms with purplish or even reddish flowers, as well as some blue ones. Perhaps the best way is to see them in flower in some nursery and select plants that have not this trend, and increase your stock by division of these.

There are now Blue Polyanthus Primroses as well, but I have not found these bunch-flowered types as pure in color as the true Primrose.

Varieties of *Primula acaulis (P. vulgaris)* Common Primrose (Plate 17)

Looking at Plate 17, one is enchanted by the wide range of colors to be had in the common Primrose. One covets such a rainbow of display. The little pale yellow usual form is lovely enough, but why not have all these others as well—nearly all the tones from pink and rose to scarlet, violet, lavender, pure blue, and snowy white. Nothing is easier. But there are several quite reasonable points that require attention.

In the first place fresh seed must be acquired; old seed takes a year or often more time to germinate, and one is impatient. It is well to buy this seed in the early autumn from reliable firms, specifying that the seed *must* be fresh. Then one or more cold frames, according to one's Primrose appetite, are necessary.

At the bottom of the frames should be placed several inches of drainage material, broken stones or what not, and on top of this a layer of sod, grass side down. Then prepare a quantity of soil in this wise—the recipe of a famous Primula grower: "One part of fibrous loam, one of leaf soil or peat, and about a half of silver sand." This should be well mixed and put through a quarter-inch sieve, and heaped into the cold frames up to within six inches of the top. Reserve a little of this choice mixture for covering the seed. Press the soil down firmly with a smooth board, and you are ready to put in the seed. Choose a fine windless day in November—in October if you have the seed—and sow it thinly in shallow drills; or, if you prefer, mark off your frame into squares, and sow one kind of seed in each square, which is marked in the center by a label. Labeling is important, for one might as well know where to lay one's hand upon the different colors. Then sift over the whole enough soil to cover the seed, and again press it down with a board lightly. The soil in the frame should have been watered the day before. Lower the sash, and dream all winter of your Primroses.

With the first warm days of March a delicate green embroidery will appear upon the soil, and presently you will have plenty of lusty seedlings to do with as you wish. During the winter the frames will not require watering; but open the frames when the snow falls and let it in. Snow water is a wonderful spur to recalcitrant seeds. The young plants, when they are large enough to handle, may be transplanted to other frames where they will have more room, or placed in partially shaded beds of rich soil outside until they are large enough to be moved to their permanent places. They will bloom freely the following spring if they are cared for and watered during hot dry weather.

❀ *Primula acaulis*, double form (Plate 18)

The double Primrose has been in cultivation a long time, but it is a rare plant, seldom seen in American gardens and none too plentiful abroad. Many persons in Europe, in England particularly, spend their lives poking about old gardens in search of double Primroses. Looking at the plate (18), can one wonder? But they are not easy, and they are assuredly not for hot dry climates. They revel in cool conditions and do best in a moist climate where the rainfall is ample. However, something can be done, with the watering can freely used.

[22]

The best place for these choice plants is on the shady side of shrubbery or on the north or west side of a rock garden. The soil should be rich. Every second year the plants should be taken up and divided and planted in fresh soil just after flowering. This does much to keep them in health. A free and hearty development of foliage in the spring is important, and this may have to be promoted by copious artificial waterings and with applications of weak manure water in the case of backward plants. Newly set plants should be kept shaded for a few weeks until they have "taken hold."

Double Primroses are old-fashioned plants. Early works on gardening give long lists of them. In John Rea's "Flora" (1665) he says: "The common double Garden Primrose is so well known, that it is sufficient only to name it, but were it not so common in every Country-womans Garden, it would be more respected, for indeed it is a sweet and dainty double flower, and the chiefest of all our English kinds." Long lists are given in some of the early books, and some of the flowers are quaintly described as the "double green," "brownish-rose," "dove-color," "hair-color," and "the color of an old buff coat"; but "the scarlet Primrose is of the most esteem." The double white and the lovely double lilac are at present available in this country.

❦ *Primula Juliae* in a Rock Garden (Plate 19)

Primula Juliae is a floriferous and accommodating plant. It belongs to the same section, the Vernales section, as the common English Primrose, but it is an Asiatic. It is very low-growing, and the indubitably magenta flowers are borne in the greatest profusion in mid-April. They have a bright golden eye to set them off. A cool and rich soil suits these plants best and will cause them to reward the grower with great generosity. They should be taken up occasionally and divided.

[*23*]

Many hybrids of this prolific plant have been raised, some better than others. One of the best is called Wanda; it is somewhat redder in tone than the type; *P. Juliae* Gloria is superb with large flowers of a rich claret crimson color.

After it has flowered it makes a vigorous mass of leaves, which die away as winter approaches. In mild climates the bright blossoms may appear off and on throughout the winter, but these in no way abate the crimson enthusiasm of the spring display. It comes from the Himalayas.

✤ *Primula rosea* in a Rock Garden (Plate 20)

What a superlatively brilliant small thing is *Primula rosea*. To say that it is pink utterly fails to describe it, for it is pink raised to a pitch of fiery splendor that leaves one utterly speechless before it. This is a bog Primula from the Himalayas, and there is more than one form of it; one called *grandiflora* has taller stems than the type.

In our heat-ridden gardens there is no use trying to grow it anywhere but in a wet situation, or where its roots can quickly reach down to moisture, as at a streamside; if it has plenty of moisture it will endure full sun. It will even grow with its roots right in water and be the happier. The amazing rose-carmine blossoms are borne in loose clusters that fix the eye from the far side of the garden. They are held above a neat tuft of glossy leaves, and in time the plants form generous masses that may be divided at will. It blooms in early April, and certainly nothing can vie with it in sheer sparkle.

It is available in this country, and it is easily raised from seed if the directions under Plate 17 are followed. But secure fresh seed without fail.

❦ *Cytisus praecox* (Warminster Broom) (Plate 21)

There are few more lovely spring-flowering shrubs than the Warminster Broom. It is said to be a hybrid between *C. albus* (*Genista praecox*) and *C. purgans*. It makes a dense bush of whiplike branches that may in time reach a height of five feet. At the time of its flowering in late April or May these branches are completely hidden beneath a cloud of soft sulphur-colored bloom. And when they are bare they are still attractive by reason of their bright green color. It is a shrub to use freely in making groups in the garden; the plants are slow to become "leggy," but they should never be crowded together or crushed in among other shrubs, for thus the full measure of their grace is lost, and there is no rain of radiant flowers from the slender shoots.

It is one of the very best shrubs for planting high upon the rock garden where the branches may spray out in all directions and fall down over the stones. In such a position it never fails to evoke the admiration of all beholders. Besides the pale yellow form there is a pure white almost, if not quite, as lovely. Like all the Brooms it loves sunshine and a soil that is on the dry side, a little sandy. Although fairly hardy it should be planted where it will be sheltered from high winds that fling about the whiplike branches, marring the perfection of the blossoms.

It is said that this plant seldom comes true from seed and is best raised from cuttings which strike easily. Its name, Warminster Broom, comes from the place of its origin.

A vast number of Brooms suitable for growing in American gardens are generally neglected. They are easily satisfied with soil and site and provide a welcome change from the kinds of shrubs generally planted.

❦ *Acer Trautvetteri* (Plate 22)

Nearly all the Maples are handsome in their fruiting. Our own Red or Swamp Maple, *Acer rubrum*, is one of the ruddiest and most effective, giving the swamps an autumn tone in April when they hang out their crimson "keys" from every twig and branchlet.

> The scarlet maple-keys betray,
> What potent blood hath modest May.

And James Russell Lowell wrote, "The Maple crimsons to a coral reef."

The species depicted in the plate (22) is a Caucasian form, but appears not to be behind our native species in the brilliance and size of its "keys." It has cordate leaves, deeply cut into five lobes, five to seven inches across, glaucous and slightly hairy when young, a lustrous dark green above and of large size. It grows finally to a height of about 45 feet but, while hardier than some Caucasian species, is not wholly to be relied upon in cold climates.

❦ *Alyssum saxatile* (Golden Tuft, Basket of Gold) (Plate 23)

Beauty is easily created in any rocky situation by the free use of *Alyssum saxatile*. Its masses of small golden flowers make their appearance in late April or early May. After the flowering is past the plants should be cut over with a sharp pair of shears, removing the unsightly seed-heads, when the soft gray leaves of the plant again make it a conspicuous ornament.

This Alyssum, perennial relative of the well known Sweet Alyssum, *A. maritimum*, is one of the easiest rock plants to grow. A packet of seed will produce plants enough to cover a fair-sized rock garden. But they

[*26*]

want a sunny situation in well drained soil. On heavy soil they tend to die out quickly. In any case old plants become leggy and should be replaced. Where seeding is allowed there will be many youngsters to take the place of those that have seen their best days. There is a variety *compactum* which differs little from the type, but another variety *A. s. citrinum* is greatly superior. Its color, instead of the somewhat acid yellow of the type, is a soft creamy primrose, which blends with any color of its season. It is lovely as a foreground to the small *Tulipa Clusiana*, the Lady Tulip. This variety, however, is a little tender, and should be given the warmest and sunniest aspects and the most impeccably drained soil. Also it is well to keep a few young plants coming on to take the place of those which go down before the rigors of winter. I have not known this kind to self-sow.

To make a show with the Alyssums are numerous gay and easily grown plants of the spring. By their use alone a rocky hillside may be retrieved from dullness to the utmost brilliance. Among these are the double and single Rock Cress (Arabis), Aubrietias in many tones of mauve, purple, rose, and carmine, the Hardy Candytuft (Iberis) and the many kinds of Creeping Phlox (*P. subulata*) including Vivid, Camla, G. F. Wilson, and Apple Blossom.

Alyssum saxatile is a native of Russia and a hardy and vigorous plant. It is sometimes used as a foundation planting for beds of Early Tulips, but its somewhat sharp color makes it a little difficult to harmonize unless the hues of the Tulips are carefully chosen. It is peaceful enough with white Tulips, but with orange-colored ones the effect is gorgeous.

⚘ Phlox and Iberis in a Dry Wall (Plate 24)

One of the most valuable adjuncts to a garden is a dry wall, that is, a wall laid up without cement, with earth between the crevices instead. Such a wall, when being built, should be slanted backwards a little so that rain will be drained back into the pockets for the benefit of the plants. This also prevents the frost from throwing the stones out of place during the winter.

All sorts of things like to grow in a well built dry wall. The accompanying plate (24) shows a soft-colored Broom at the top, probably *Cytisus praecox*, and then a riot of variously hued Creeping Phloxes and Candytufts. In the foreground are some Tulips.

The Candytuft is probably *Iberis sempervirens* or its more compact variety Little Gem. But *Iberis gibraltarica*, with masses of heads of soft rose-lilac flowers, might well be added. The Candytufts are all easily raised from seed and delight in the comfort of a sunny wall-face. After flowering they need to be well cut over in order to keep shapely.

The Creeping Phloxes are many today. One has a choice of a vast number of colors as well as of forms. Some are as close-creeping as moss (this is true of *P. Nelsonii*); others are springy and grow five or six inches high, as does the lovely G. F. Wilson. Most discriminating persons have discarded the old magenta kind, still distressingly in evidence in humble gardens and conspicuously displayed in the small rockeries of hot-dog stands and gas stations. Here is a list of really lovely kinds that may be planted with every expectation of enjoyment: Apple Blossom, blush pink; Blue Hill, compact, pale lavender-blue; Brilliant, carmine-red; Brittonii, fine foliage, white starlike flowers with dark centers; Camla, glistening salmon-pink, long-flowering; Fairy, pale lilac, purple eye; G. F. Wilson, pure lavender, long flowering; June Jane, white-tinted pink with faint pink eye; Leuchstern, compact salmon-pink; Maischnee, pure white; Ronsdorf Beauty, compact with brilliant salmon-pink flowers; Nelsonii, compact, white; Schneewittchen, neat mounds covered with white flowers; Vivid, warm salmon-rose, slightly more upright than many of the others.

[*28*]

❦ Scene in Garden with Tulips, Alyssum and Phlox (Plate 25)

In Plate 25 we have a charming garden scene that might be duplicated in the smallest garden: the simple pergola at the back with a comfortable seat, the dry walls overflowing with spring flowers, *Alyssum saxatile citrinum*, Phlox, Iberis, and the like; the band of Tulips at the back with the dark hedge as a setting and flowering shrubs beyond it; the little statuette to give life to the scene, and across the smooth grass path Box-bordered beds of Tulips in pink and creamy tones. It will be noticed that the stone steps leading to the pergola are crammed with green things, Thymes, Sedums, what not. Every inch of space has been used, yet the effect is not crowded nor heterogeneous, but harmonious and restful.

A band of trees in young leaf incloses the whole as if the little garden had been carved out of woodland. The variety of treatment of the two sides of the path is a relief from the usual uniform verges. The whole thing is distinctly gay and pleasing.

❦ *Tulipa Kaufmanniana* (Water-Lily Tulip) (Plate 26)

The Water-Lily Tulip is the earliest of the species to flower in the garden, if we except those two small members of the tribe, *T. biflora* and *T. turkestanica*, which sometimes catch it up, but which are not often seen outside the gardens of specialists. It flowers usually towards the end of March or at latest the very first of April; it is one of the most beautiful of the species, and though often exposed to beating winds and rains it is seldom injured. Its stems are short and sturdy enough to withstand the angry blasts, and even frosts do not often trouble it.

Tulipa Kaufmanniana comes from Turkestan. The type has narrow cherry-colored buds that open wide to show a creamy interior that becomes yellow as it reaches the base of the petals, or segments. These segments turn back a little giving the flower the appearance of a Lily. Though the plants are no more than eight or ten inches high their effect is graceful and brilliant. *T. Kaufmanniana* is the most thoroughly reliable of the wild Tulips, thriving under ordinary garden conditions and reappearing year after year—increasing, too, with praiseworthy generosity. It is perfect for a low plain in the rock garden and it likes the sandy, well drained soil of this region.

Nowadays we are not confined to the type, though this is lovely enough to satisfy the most fastidious taste. We have *T. K. aurea*, a golden yellow flower with a cherry exterior that flashes in the sunshine; we have Gaiety with silvery white flowers on stems so short that one has to look sharply for the cherry-colored stripe on the outer segments after the flower has opened. Brilliance flowers late and is conspicuous for its dark foliage and the cherry-red coloring of its flowers; Händel is taller than the others, and its cream and carmine blooms are gifted with a circular band of rose-red in the center of the flowers; coccinea is fiery red and very telling, and Primrose, one of the loveliest, a soft primrose color throughout save where at the base of the segments the color becomes a rich yellow.

One can safely plant *Tulipa Kaufmanniana* in mixture; all the kinds blend and seem to set each other off. A large plantation of them on a bright spring day is a softly brilliant spectacle.

✷ Scene in Rock Garden Showing Spring Flowers (Plate 27)

Purple is one of the most coördinating colors in the garden. It harmonizes all other hues and wipes out their differences of opinion, making them appear on the friendliest terms. Unfortunately there are not many pure

[*30*]

purple flowers—some Irises, some Campanulas, a few others, but most going under the name have that wicked tinge of magenta which invariably makes for trouble rather than for peace. But Aubrietias give us many purple varieties for use in many localities, both of garden and of rock garden. Streaming over rocks, either at a wall top or in a rock garden proper, Aubrietias are particularly happy, as the plate (27) shows. In our hot climate they require conscientious watering to keep in good condition; and if, after they are through flowering, they are cut over with a pair of sharp shears, they will live long and prosper.

The Aubrietias are a delightful group of rock plants from the mountains of southern Europe. Most of the kinds we grow today in our gardens are developed from the species *deltoidea*. Hybridists have been busy with them, and forms with large flowers have been evolved: some have a more lax and spreading habit than others, some are close and compact. And besides the rich purple-flowered ones that are the subject of our sketch, there are pale blush-colored ones and others picking out the scale all the way to the most burning crimson, as well as lilacs, mauves, and lavenders in abundance.

Among the best of the true purples are Dr. Mules, *graeca*, *Hendersoni*, Duke of Richmond, and Violet Queen. The new varieties have much larger flowers than the old *A. deltoidea*, and they are all easily raised from seed, germinating readily in flats or a cold frame. Innumerable uses will be found for them.

To make a brave show with the Aubrietias in the early days of May, or late April, we have Arabis, Iberis, Yellow Alyssum, and the many small Irises of the *pumila* type, and such bulbous things as *Tulipa Clusiana*, Muscaris, Narcissus Queen of Spain and *N. juncifolius*.

✠ *Saxifraga oppositifolia* in a Rock Garden (Plate 28)

There are numerous forms of this variable and attractive rock plant. They are found in nature all over the northern and Arctic regions, choosing as a rule for their homes rocky hillsides. In their natural habitat they flower soon after the snows have melted. The flowers are usually some shade of rose or heather-purple, though there is a white form with very small flowers perhaps not worth struggling with. For struggle one must in this climate with this Saxifrage. It does not like our hot dry summers, nor our summer and winter humidity, nor our alternate freezing and thawing. In England it positively ramps; in America it sulks. Perhaps you will not think it worth the effort it demands. Yet there is something very attractive about those flat, spreading mats of wiry, evergreen stems with the fattish, opposite, evergreen leaves and the masses of bright blossoms so early in the year.

Then what is to be done about it! First, of course, it must grow in a rock garden, perhaps down a western slope; then it must be given a top-dressing of leaf-soil and gritty loam every year, either in the very early spring or just after it has flowered. This prevents its going dead in the middle of the mat, and so is of the utmost importance. It normally wants a soil that may be called a light gritty loam, or you can try it in the scree, if you have this useful adjunct to your rock garden.

Saxifraga oppositifolia is found in many parts of the Alps, sometimes at an altitude of twelve thousand feet, but also much lower. It is found also on England's much more modest peaks. A well flowered plant will set its stemless blooms so closely as almost to hide its lush greenery. On the whole it is worth trying for, and, if you live in a mountainous district where the air is pure and keen and the snows lie long in winter, you will probably meet with success.

[*32*]

Plate 14. *Primula acaulis* AND *Hepatica triloba* (ENGLISH PRIMROSE WITH HEPATICA)

Plate 15. *Primula Sibthorpii*

Plate 16. *Primula acaulis caerulea* (BLUE PRIMROSE)

Plate 17. *Primula acaulis*, VARIETIES OF (PRIMROSES)

Plate 18. *Primula acaulis*, DOUBLE FORM

Plate 19. *Primula Juliae*, IN A ROCK GARDEN

Plate 20. *Primula rosea*, IN A ROCK GARDEN

✿ *Anemone nemorosa Allenii* (Allen's Wood Anemone) (Plate 29)

Anemone nemorosa, the European Wood Anemone, first cousin to our meek little Wood Anemone, *A. quinquefolia*, flowers into a number of enchanting forms. Perhaps the most beautiful of these, though it is difficult to choose, is the one named *Allenii*. It grows six inches tall, has the usual delicate palmate leaves, and bears large lavender flowers, of the most exquisite and subtle lavender-blue. They bloom later than the other *nemorosas*, which is an advantage, for anything that prolongs the delightful flowering of the Wood Anemones is a boon for which we should give thanks. Like others of its kind, its blossoms are wide open only when the sun shines full upon them; when the sun fails they modestly droop their heads. In the center of these blue salvers is a brush of golden stamens.

Lovely, too, among these Wood Anemones, is *A. n. Robinsoniana*, very large and very pale. And there is Blue Bonnet, dwarfer in height but much deeper in color, and Blue Beauty, with a silvery reverse side. Then there is the pure white form, sometimes tinged with palest rose, and the little double *nemorosa alba fl.-pl.* that looks like a fairy's powder puff. They are as common in the woods of Great Britain as scentless Violets here; and they are found over most of Europe and in parts of Asia, always in woodlands, always swaying and dancing in the wind which caused Pliny long ago to give them the name of Windflower. They grow from small tuberous roots and should be planted in the autumn in shaded, not too dry situations; if satisfied they will increase in the most gratifying manner until one has literally thickets of these delicate flowers. Let them alone; they can take care of themselves admirably, so long as heartier perennials are kept from pressing in upon them. They flower with the Primroses, Violets, Spring Beauties, Celandines, and the earliest of the Azaleas. That is late in April and into May.

[33]

🌸 *Gentiana acaulis* (Gentianella) (Plate 30)

Perhaps this is the most spectacular of a spectacular race. Mr. Farrer says it is rare in distribution, being found only "at *great elevations*, first of all in the far South of Spain, on the Sierra Nevada, then along the Pyrenees into the Graian, Cottian, and Maritime Alps, and on into the South-western fringe of Switzerland."

There are various forms of it, and some are kindlier to their would-be growers than others. Their shining leaves differ in size and shape; the habit of some is tight and stunted, of others more spreading. In fact, there are said by authorities to be five definite species grown in gardens under this name. No wonder there is so much heartburn and disappointment where this flower is concerned. For sometimes there appear the great grandiose trumpets of purest blue, and sometimes these are absent, do what we will, and our reward is nothing but leaves.

The trumpets arise right out of the flat masses of leaves very early in the year. In England it edges borders, careless of its company, and flops about in paths; but here it must grow in a rock garden and demands the fleshpots. Here is a menu said to please it (and prayer may perhaps help):

No richness is too great for it; if the best is to be desired of it some part of its beds and borders should always be remade every five years, a trench being dug some two feet deep and filled up for a foot or two with every kind of pig trough garbage you can think of, and mown lawn grass . . . and every possible enrichment; then on top of that, the fattest loam with abundance of lime, and then the Gentians planted firmly.

Though they like fullest sun they demand a continual supply of water at all times; so prepare to work overtime for this flamboyant flower, if you think it worth the trouble. Inside the trumpets, if you care to look, you will find flecks of green, but more than likely the size and color of the flower itself will have sufficed and you will look no further.

[*34*]

✠ Tulips, Hyacinths, Hellebores, Omphalodes, Arabis and Primroses (Plate 31)

Here in Plate 31 is a medley of flowers which is quite harmonious. It might appear in any little garden. In fact such an assemblage belongs in a small garden, where the owner has a catholic taste and an ardent appetite for flowers. In a large garden they would be dispersed over a wider area. But this arrangement is pretty and undoubtedly gives pleasure. As most of the flowers in it are treated elsewhere in these pages, it seems best to concentrate on the one that is not—on Blue-eyed Mary, *Omphalodes verna*, the one-time favorite of Queen Marie Antoinette, which the illfated queen probably remembered with tenderness spraying the rocks about her old home. It comes from the eastern ranges of Europe's mountains. It is a trailing creeping plant with shining heart-shaped leaves and sprays of brightest pure blue flowers on three-inch stems very early in the spring, late April or the first of May. There is a white variety *alba* which is attractive but less showy, and both are among the easiest and most amenable plants, preferring, if asked, a light loamy soil in partial shade where they can ramble far and wide at their own sweet will. Your stock is easily increased by simply pulling divisions from the parent mat and starting them off elsewhere. A rock garden is the best place for it, as it is a small thing and needs a setting.

Blue-eyed Mary belongs to the great family of the Borages, which is so richly endowed with pure blue flowers: Borago, Anchusa, Forget-me-not, Bugloss, and the like. It goes by the common name of Navelwort.

Such an easily pleased plant it is surprising not to find more often offered by nurseries or in rock gardens.

The Hellebore pictured is one not often seen in this country, *Helleborus viridis*, the Green Hellebore, a plant of the European mountains, and perhaps more interesting than beautiful.

[35]

✤ *Prunus baldschuanica* (Plate 32)

This charming spreading shrub flowers on its still unclothed branches early in May. It is allied to the Flowering Almonds and the lovely double-flowered *Prunus triloba*, and has the same uses. It is not too tall or too wide-spreading for use in the borders among Tulips, Hyacinths (particularly blue ones), Bleeding Hearts and *Anchusa myosotidiflora*. And here it is especially useful as carrying the color higher up, against wall or hedge or fence, or whatever forms the background of the border. In a long border several of the bushes may be used at intervals. The flowers are single and of an especially delicate and delectable tone of pink. The shrub comes from Turkestan, and an allied species is *Prunus Arnoldiana*, which differs from it chiefly in having pure white flowers. They are hardy as far north as Philadelphia, possibly in more northern latitudes.

Groups of these pink-flowered shrubs add much to the foreground of the shrubbery, or look well against evergreens, or in simple dooryards before white houses.

✤ Flowering Broom and Other Plants in Dry Wall (Plate 33)

The garden suddenly seems to change its appearance when the Cream or Ivory Broom bursts into bloom. The flowers cover the many wandlike branches, and where there are a number of bushes they create a sort of illumination that blends all other colors.

This is *Cytisus praecox*, said to be a cross between the tall pale Spanish Broom and the low-growing Spanish-French Broom, *C. purgans*. It has been known approximately since 1867. According to a Mr. Wheeler it seeded itself in the garden of his grandfather and was first described by the well known dendrologist Bean. As would be expected from its name, *praecox*, it is an early-blooming shrub. It flowers at the same time as *C. pur-*

[*36*]

gans, but later than *C. multiflorus (C. albus)*, its other parent. *C. albus* sometimes grows to a height of eight feet, so that the low stature of *C. praecox* has been brought about by the blood of the dwarfer *C. purgans*, which is about twenty-one inches tall when full-grown. *C. praecox* is hardier than either parent or than the Scotch Broom as well. Nevertheless it may flourish through many winters and then be taken unexpectedly by a bitter cold snap. Like all Brooms it thrives in poorish soil in a sunny well drained position. It is easily raised from seed but should be transplanted when small as, when once established, it does not remove easily. With it in the picture (Plate 33) are to be seen Aubrietias of the reddish tones, Tulips, the soft haze of Cerastium not yet in bloom.

�֎ *Rhododendron impeditum* (Plate 34)

Perhaps no little shrubs are so fascinating as the small Rhododendrons, those that are fitted for the rock garden. They are fairly numerous if one begins to look about, but they are still expensive in this country. One of the very prettiest for the rock garden is *R. impeditum* (Plate 34), and it is also at home in small beds, either alone or with Heathers (Ericas and Callunas). It forms a tidy little bush with shining green leaves and a profusion of lavender-purple flowers in April or May. These flowers have the fluffy appearance of *R. fastigiatum*, caused by the conspicuously protruding stamens. It is very easy to grow in an open situation in soil made up of leafmould and rather heavy loam (no lime, please!), and in our climate the blossoms last longer if there is shade for part of the day, either from high-branched trees at a little distance or from a wall, or even a good-sized rock.

It is said to be easily raised from seed, cuttings or layers, and two-year-old plants are in such a hurry to show what they can do that they often burst into flower. These are so small that a hand can cover them.

Rhododendron impeditum was introduced from western China, where it is native, by Mr. Forrest, in 1911. It was found in open peaty pastures in Yunnan, at an altitude of 15,000-16,000 feet. Despite its high habitat this little shrublet is said to be of doubtful hardiness. It probably misses its warm blanket of snow, of which the substitutes given it at lower altitudes do not take the place. However, it is as yet too rare and too little tried out in this country to be accurately placed.

❦ *Rhododendron hippophaeoides* (Plate 35)

The rock garden stands in great need of comely small shrubs. The little Rhododendrons are the white hope of this area for their irregular growth and gay floriferousness make them especially valuable. It is generally conceded that one of the best is *Rhododendron hippophaeoides*, seeds of which were gathered in western China by Mr. Forrest "in five districts of Yunnan at altitudes ranging from 10,000 to 14,000 feet. Mr. Kingdon Ward also collected this species in 1913 in the Chung River Valley, Yunnan." It is not so genuine a dwarf as some others of its race, for it grows in time to a height of three or four feet. Its evergreen leaves are small, and a well grown specimen is so blossomy that the small trusses, not unlike a miniature form of *Rhododendron catawbiense*, touch each other, and nearly obscure the foliage. It flowers in April and May, and the flowers have the advantage over many of the small-bloomed Rhododendrons in that they last a long time in good condition. It is a much-branched twiggy shrub and might for the sake of good form be a little more compact. It is quite easily raised from seed, and there is a good deal of variation among the seedlings, the best of them being quite blue in tone, the worst leaning towards magenta.

In cultivation it likes the usual Rhododendron mixture of peat and loam, minus lime, and wants a good deal of moisture. Thus if it is planted in the rock garden it should be low down, and water should be given it in

dry weather. It is a newcomer, and little is known about its ultimate for-
bearance of our climate. But Mr. Clement G. Bowers, who does not seem
to admire it, though British writers extol it to the skies, says that it is grown
here in southern Pennsylvania by Joseph B. Gable, and in New Jersey by
G. G. Nearing. Probably the time has not yet come to pronounce upon
its excellencies and failings.

⚘ *Hyacinthus orientalis* Grand Monarque (Plate 36)

This lovely and fragrant bulbous plant belongs to the Lily order. It is
a genus of well known plants commonly used for spring bedding. It has
rounded tunicated bulbs from which spring the strap-shaped leaves and
spikes of bell-shaped flowers. There are Hyacinths in various parts of the
world, but our garden Hyacinths all spring from *Hyacinthus orientalis*,
native of the Mediterranean region. "In 1734," writes John Wistar, "just
a hundred years after the Tulip mania, Hyacinth growing reached the
height of its popularity in Holland." It did not reach the status of a mania.
There were, however, many fine kinds developed, new colors, stronger
stems, larger flowers, some doubled, etc. Today we have many to choose
from; the yellow tones were the last to be brought into being. The blues,
in several tones, are perhaps the most attractive, but there are many pink
ones, of different tones, crimsons, reds, pure white and the new yellows,
with double forms in each color group.

In planting Hyacinths, give them a sandy soil enriched with old, well
rotted manure or, failing this, plenty of good humus. The best time for
planting the bulbs is during September and October; set them four or five
inches deep and six or seven inches apart. In very cold climates, though
the bulbs are quite hardy, it is the part of wisdom to cover them with a
little brush or leaves. The soil should be well dug and deep for the best re-

sults. After Hyacinths have been in the ground for several years they grow more slender and willowy of stem, and though this may be heresy it is then that they are at their most charming.

For countless generations Hyacinths have been used to fill geometrical beds on lawns or in parks, their uniform height and rotund girth fitting them especially for this purpose. But forget this tradition and scatter them about the borders in groups as we do Tulips and Daffodils, and know a new thrill during the wraith days of April. They are delightful combined with the shrubs and plants that bloom at the same time; with the pink and white Flowering Almond, with *Prunus triloba* and *Prunus tomentosa*, with Bridal Wreath, Arabis, Creeping Phlox, Iberis, *Anchusa myosotidiflora* and Primroses. They appear happy released from the bondage of straight lines and calculated curves.

For colors I should suggest among the blues the following: Grand Maître, lavender-blue; King of the Blues, dark blue; Myosotis, pale; Queen of the Blues, soft porcelain blue. Among the pinks and reds: Norma, pale pink; Panama, tall spikes of bright rose-pink; Lady Derby, a lovely tone; La Victoire, strong spikes of bright carmine-rose. Of yellow kinds there are City of Haarlem, Yellow Hammer, and King of the Yellows; of white kinds the best are perhaps La Grandesse and L'Innocence. But there are many more.

❦ *Viola tricolor maxima* (Pansy, Heartsease) (Plates 37 and 38)

The Pansy is a flower about which our tenderest thoughts will always cling. However magnificent it may become, however rich in blotches, streaks, and frills, it is always a simple flower, appealing to our gentler sentiments.

The story of the Pansy is worth telling. More than a hundred years ago

Plate 21. *Cytisus praecox* (WARMINSTER BROOM)

Plate 22. *Acer Trautvetteri* IN FRUIT

Plate 23. *Alyssum saxatile* (BASKET OF GOLD)

Plate 24. CREEPING PHLOX IN DRY WALLS WITH IBERIS, BROOM AND TULIPS

Plate 25. SCENE IN GARDEN WITH TULIPS, ALYSSUM, PHLOX AND OTHER SPRING FLOWERS

Plate 26. *Tulipa Kaufmanniana* (WATERLILY TULIP)

Plate 27. SCENE IN A ROCK GARDEN SHOWING SPRING FLOWERS

Plate 28. *Saxifraga oppositifolia* IN A ROCK GARDEN

Plate 29. *Anemone nemorosa Allenii*

Plate 34. *Rhododendron impeditum*

Plate 35. *Rhododendron hippophaeoides*

two enthusiastic gardeners, Lord Gambier, who lived near Uxbridge, Middlesex, England, and the daughter of the Earl of Tankerville, living at Walton-on-Thames, turned their attention to the "little western flower," which was *Viola tricolor*, a flower that had no resemblance to the Pansy of the present day. There followed the usual story of careful cultivation and rigid selection over a period of many years. The work of these two was taken up and systematically carried on for more years (the vision must have been very clear); every improvement in form was seized upon, every advance made the most of. This work began at the end of the eighteenth century, but more than thirty years after that, while there had been some improvement in marking, a blotch of sorts having been accomplished, Lord Gambier's gardener (a man by the name of Thompson, who became known as "the father of the Heartsease") sized up the flowers' defects by saying that they "were lengthy as a horse's head. Nothing daunted, he resolved to persevere, and was at last rewarded by obtaining 'rich colouring, large size, and fine shape.'" Thereafter a great race of Pansy growers sprang up in England, in France, in Belgium, and later in America. Gradually we were given the English Show Pansy, the Fancy Pansy, and the vast number of varied beauties that we have today. The Pansy flowers into an infinite number of forms and colors; even brown is not strange to it; and for bedding or for winter flowering by florists there is none to surpass it. It was a chance predilection and unswerving industry that brought us this sweet and pleasant flower in all its present-day finery. The flowers we enjoy today have no resemblance to "a horse's head" but many of them are as round as a dollar, the petals are broad and overlap, the blotch has spread to both upper and lower petals, and in some of the kinds the petals have a mere selvage of contrasting color, while some may be flat and others prettily frilled and fluted.

Some one has said that "the raising of seedlings of any plant is always interesting because it is from seed that most varieties are obtained, therefore the amateur has a chance, provided he is growing a good strain, of obtaining some new color or form." The owner of the smallest garden, the most modest equipment has the chance to become a creator.

Perhaps Pansies are among the most useful plants at our command. They appear to be at home in the smallest garden, the window box, the pot on the sill, or the estate of noble proportions. They make a perfect floor for Tulips, for their infinite tints and tones may be brought to harmonize with the varied hues of the Tulips. Take a brown Pansy, for instance, as floor to an orange-hued Tulip, a white one below some of the luscious pink Tulips, and so on.

It appears that in this country California and New Jersey produce the finest Pansies, and few from any locality are finer. Certain winter-flowering varieties will flower out of doors all winter in mild climates. "A strong strain with flower stalks to ten inches, and large flowers, has also been distributed recently with great success."

Pansies like moist cool conditions. Drought and heat weaken the plants and diminish the size of the plants. They should be raised from seed every year, and picked regularly, as seed-forming does them no good. Seeds are best started in a frame and kept moist by means of a fine rose spray, and shaded during the heat of the day. Seed should be sown in July or early in August. Or they may be sown in the early autumn. In any case they must remain in the frames over the winter, and the frames covered with warm mats when the weather becomes seriously cold. The seedlings may be planted out in the spring where wanted. Before they are removed from the frames, the sash should be lifted daily on mild days and the mats removed, in order that the plants may gradually become accustomed to the more intense conditions.

⁘ *Euphorbia epithymoides (E. polychroma)* (Spurge) (Plate 39)

Few Euphorbias are beautiful, and as most of them are poisonous they are seen chiefly in botanical collections, or those of the inveterate specialists. The one under consideration (Plate 39) has considerable claims to pulchritude. It is a herbaceous plant from Europe flowering very early in the spring. It has leafy stems rising to a height of about eighteen inches, each one crowned by a broad head of yellow, faintly green flowers. It has one admirable point which is not generally shared by its hardy brethren; it does not seed wildly in all directions nor spread by underground roots. It gradually forms self-respecting and generous clumps in the position assigned it.

This Spurge may be used to advantage in several ways. It may be planted for early green and bloom in the herbaceous border. It may with very fine effect be set at the top of a dry wall, with Aubrietia or lavender Phlox cascading below it. Seen against the sky thus, it is very lovely. Or it may be given a high tor in the rock garden of ample size. There it will reappear year after year and give no trouble.

If it is desired to increase the stock, the plants may be dug up and cut apart with a sharp knife or spade and replanted. I do not know if this plant shares the poisonous qualities of its family, but there have been no ill effects from handling it. One of its good points is its ample height at a season when most of the plants in the garden hug the ground.

The Spurges are an enormous family, embracing hardy annuals, stove annuals, greenhouse annuals and perennials, hardy evergreens, and hardy herbaceous plants.

❀ *Anchusa myosotidiflora (Brunnera macrophylla)* (Plate 40)

Certain plants are born to confound the elegance and stolidity of certain others. If they did not exist we should miss them sadly. Of such is the Siberian Bugloss or Alkanet, a plant of somewhat recent introduction from Siberia and the Caucasus. It is a charming thing, appearing a little like a giant Forget-me-not. It bears large heart-shaped leaves along the lower part of the somewhat hairy erect stems, with narrower and more tapering leaves towards the upper part of the stems. The plant is a hardy perennial that grows from twelve to eighteen inches high and will thrive in both sun and partial shade, with a definite liking, I should say, for dampish places. At the time when the May Tulips are beginning to flower it bursts into ardent and gracious bloom; the flowers are borne in panicled racemes and form a deep sky-blue cloud above the rich dark leaves. It is a vigorous plant where happily situated and self-sows widely, and one must keep in mind the fact that, while it is comparatively reserved and conservative in its youthful stages, the large leaves expand with lush freedom when the flowering is over, and the plants take up considerable room.

It is a charming accompaniment to Tulips of almost any tint or tone, clothing their nether stems and giving them a most becoming setting. Even the queer off tones respond to its gentle influence. Fawn-colored Tulips of the Breeder type are especially susceptible to the harmonizing powers of this light and graceful plant. Other happy associations for it are with Bleeding-Heart *(Dicentra spectabilis)*, a most exquisite pink and blue arrangement; with Marsh Marigolds *(Caltha palustris)*, for it will stand the damp which these flowers love. And it is charming against bushes of Bridal Wreath and pink Flowering Almond. If you have hitherto failed to grow it successfully, try it in a low part of the garden where the conditions are apt to be damp.

❦ Scene in a Rock Garden with Kew Broom Predominating (Plate 41)

Here in Plate 41 we have a scene in a rock garden in all its spring exuberance. What could be prettier? The lovely Kew Broom, *Cytisus kewensis*, a hybrid raised at Kew, having an unusually graceful habit, forms the focal point. About it are all sorts of delightful things, but the success of the picture is due to the placing of the Broom and the background of trees and broad-leaved evergreens.

Contributing to this gay assemblage are the orange-scarlet flowers of Geums, the pale primrose of *Alyssum saxatile citrinum* in generous masses, matching the Broom, the more acid yellow of *Alyssum saxatile fl.-pl.* in the foreground, a patch of the pure white of *Achillea macedonica* (*Anthemis macedonica*) a neat and tidy species, the silken *Potentilla chrysocraspeda* with large yellow flowers on short stems, from the Alps of the Levant, and a wide spread of Aubrietia in the foreground.

Any rock gardener could thus set forth his rocky slopes as colorfully without going to any great trouble. In looking at this plate it is worthy of note that it is the scarlet flowers of the Geums that bring the whole scene to life. They are not many, but they are deftly placed; and without them we should have insipidity instead of sparkle. Earlier in the year, a clump of such a high scarlet Tulipa as *praestans* or *Kaufmanniana* Brilliant will do the same thing for the pale flowers of the young year if placed on a high mound. And many a dull and conventional border is amazingly enlivened by a scarlet flower or two placed where it will do the most good. Plate 41 also exemplifies how many types of flowers with their differing hues and the various textures of their foliage may be crowded together in a rock garden without bringing about disharmony. A rock garden is like a mosaic, and ordinarily fighting colors may usually be placed together without causing suffering to the fastidious eye.

[45]

✥ Children's Garden with Forget-me-nots, English Daisies, and Other Spring Flowers (Plate 42)

Children usually love flowers, but they do not love order and precision. When it comes to their gardens they like a jumble of the flowers that appeal to them, and they do not care in what juxtaposition they are. What children like are simple homely flowers, and here in this naïve little garden patch we have many simple flowers arranged as artlessly and thoughtlessly as a child would dispose them. Here we have a band of pretty English Daisies across the path from another band of Pansies. A few stepping-stones enable the child to get about easily without stepping on his treasures. Forget-me-nots are obviously favorites, for there are a great many—perhaps they have self-sown from the year before after the manner of their generous habit; then there are Wallflowers, Violas, a few Primroses, and other things. Later there will doubtless be Marigolds, Cornflowers, Zinnias, Sweet Alyssum, and Candytuft.

When summer time comes with its long hot days the child will tire of his garden, and it will doubtless be left to the sun and the rain, and many weeds will creep in, unless he has sown his seed so thickly that there is no room for them. But do not force him to bend his young back over the weeding and the obviously needed staking when the old swimming hole calls. Let him neglect his garden if he is so inclined. If you do not, the memory of a hateful duty will cause him to turn away from the growing of flowers in his maturity, when it could be a source of joy or a refuge in time of stress. Scars go deep in young minds, deeper than we think, and gardening is something that we should let them have as an unsullied pleasure and relaxation.

✿ *Phlox subulata (setacea)* Vivid (Moss Pink) (Plate 43)

Among the most amiable and comely of rock plants are the Creeping Phloxes, those kinds that are commonly listed under the specific name of *subulata*. Reginald Farrer wrote in one of his books: "The day that saw the introduction, more than a century since, of *Ph. subulata* ought indeed be kept as a horticultural festival." This little native plant and its near kin have filled our gardens with beauty. All the Creeping Phloxes known under the specific name of *subulata* do not derive from that species, and there is considerable diversity of form among them, as well as confusion as to their botanical titles. The names *setacea*, *stellaris*, and a number of others have, I believe, no official standing. The numerous kinds we have in cultivation today usually derive from *P. subulata*, *P. nivalis*, *P. bifida*, and *P. Brittonii*. It is not necessary here to probe the minute differences of these species— they all have a good deal in common; that is, they are of creeping habit, with small narrow evergreen leaves, and an exuberant cheek-to-cheek flowering, with either a mosslike habit of clinging to the earth or a somewhat more springy and taller growth and spreading manner, though none attain a height of more than a few inches. Some, however, spread into mats considerably more than a foot across. These so-called Moss Pinks are widely spread in the northern and southern states, and *P. bifida*, at least, is found west of the Allegheny Mountains. They are quite hardy in the northern states—all save the derivatives of *Phlox nivalis*, which is more southerly in its range than the others; its hybrids may inherit a weakness which will stand them in ill stead when an exceptionally bitter winter comes along.

The natural habitat of *Phlox nivalis* is "dry, thin Oak or Pine woods" and occasionally damp meadows. The soil it grows in is usually

[47]

a mixture of sand and clay, often rich in humus but at times rust colored from the presence of hydroxides . . . the whole aspect of its habitats suggests sterility, and its depressed habit, woody stem, and small persistent leaves mark it as a moderate xerophyte.*

Phlox subulata occurs "in the Coastal Plains only northward to western North Carolina to southwestern Michigan and central New York."

The characteristic habitat . . . is a bare, sunny slope, where the soil is sandy or gravelly and rock ledges lie near the surface. Humus may be present in considerable amount, but it is often lacking; moisture is usually very sparse. . . .

Like other members of the section *Phlox bifida* is an occupant of relatively sterile sandy or rocky soil. It is found chiefly on bare cliffs, where it often forms great festoons, and on sandy banks and doons. . . . *P. bifida* ranges through the interior low plateaus, and Central Lowland provinces, from northern Tennessee to southeastern Kansas, eastern Iowa and southern Michigan.*

All this about the little plants we know as Creeping Phloxes or Moss Pinks tells us that they are easy to grow in the garden. No plants that we set out in the rock garden, along the border edge, or in our dry walls so certainly reward us with sturdy growth and a prodigal flowering of stars of various hues. The variety pictured in Plate 43 is Vivid, a plant not too hardy, rather slow of growth, compact, and neat. Its color gets away from that of the common Moss Pink, that undesirable weak magenta, and becomes decisively and brightly pink. And here are some others well worth gathering in your garden: Appleblossom, with large blush pink flowers; Blue Hill, with dark foliage and a generous number of lavender-blue blooms; Brilliant, a really fine crimson, with no hint of magenta; Brittonii, said to be the most drought-resistant of all (its foliage is fine and needlelike,

*Dr. Edgar T. Wherry.

Plate 36. *Hyacinthus orientalis*, GRAND MONARQUE

Plate 37. *Viola tricolor maxima* (COMMON PANSY)

Plate 38. *Viola tricolor maxima* (YELLOW PANSY)

Plate 39. *Euphorbia epithymoides (E. polychroma)*

Plate 40. *Anchusa myosotidiflora* (SIBERIAN BUGLOSS)

Plate 41. SCENE IN ROCK GARDEN WITH KEW BROOM PREDOMINATING

Plate 42. CHILDREN'S GARDEN

and the flowers are small, profusely borne, and either skimmed-milk blue or a deeper tint); Camla, a striking salmon-pink, large-flowered and long-blossoming; Fairy, a dainty plant with flowers of light lilac and meek purple eyes; G. F. Wilson, an old kind, growing somewhat taller than the others and of springy habit, with a cloak of lilac blossoms in late April and early May; June Jane, a beauty with white flowers faintly tinged with pink and a delicate pink eye; Leuchstern, of compact habit and warm salmon-pink flowers; Maischnee, which makes a carpet of pure white, close and gleaming; Ronsdorf Beauty, a handsome salmon-colored kind; Nelsonii, white-flowered and close-growing; Schneewittchen, a little more springy and taller than the others, bearing masses of pure white flowers. And there are many more that the curious searcher may bring to light. They are all valuable, and there is no need to plant the ordinary magenta Moss Pink.

⚘ Muscari Heavenly Blue (Grape Hyacinth) (Plate 44)

This is thought to be a form of *Muscari conicum*, a natural hybrid, perhaps, found growing in the neighborhood of Trebizond. A few bulbs of it were gathered by George Maw, of Crocus fame, and brought back to England, where they were given to J. E. Elwes and the Rev. Harpur Crewe, both enthusiastic bulb growers. Ultimately six bulbs found their way to Peter Barr, and these six bulbs are the progenitors of the thousands upon thousands of Heavenly Blues that now grace the gardens of the world.

Probably no small bulb is so freely planted, and certainly no bulb known to me takes so efficient a hand at spreading itself as this one. It sows its seed and spreads from the bulb until from a handful one has many hundreds in a short space of time.

The Heavenly Blue Grape Hyacinth is a most valuable plant. Where it grows in close colonies it seems to stain the ground with its deep blue,

[49]

and there is no situation, seemingly, where it will not grow. Its hue is vivid, and the tight-lipped bells clothe the upper stalk with a svelte trimness that is very attractive. Moreover it has a scent, not unlike that of the Carnation, that literally pervades all the garden during its blossoming. There are a thousand ways to use it. Plant it beneath Apple or Cherry, or Crab-Apple trees to form a blue carpet for their falling petals; edge your beds with it; plant it among mats of *Phlox subulata* of whatever color; clump it between the fat Peony plants, where its blue flowers look very well with the young red Peony shoots; scatter it at the edge of woodland. But keep it always in the sun, and do not admit it to the rock garden if you expect eventually to have anything else in that special region. For, once in, the little onionlike shoots come up in all directions, and getting them out becomes a life work. Moreover, after the flowering is past its seedpods and flopping lush foliage are very unsightly; and its spread is strong enough to kill many a small royalty—indeed, I have known a few seedlings that made a most innocent début in a large patch of *Iris pumila*, itself no weakling, to completely annihilate the whole plantation in a few years.

So plant Heavenly Blue where it can do no harm; but be sure to plant it, for we should sadly miss its lovely color and truly heavenly scent when the spring comes round. It is nice for cutting, too, with bunches of yellow Polyanthus as companions.

⚜ *Orobus vernus (Lathyrus vernus)* (Spring Vetchling) (Plate 45)

The Spring Vetchling is an erect member of this frequently scandent, tendriled tribe. It is a European plant growing about twelve inches high, perhaps a little more, and bearing in early spring many-flowered clusters of pea-shaped blossoms on short stems. They are purplish blue upon first opening, with delicate red veins faintly outlined, and a green keel. The

[50]

leaves are opposite and light green. The habit of the plant is quite erect and it is useful either in the border or in fairly large rock gardens. It is quite hardy and has been used in gardens since 1629. Orobus is an old Greek name used by Theophrastus and has nothing to do with the present genus, which is a vast one.

This plant is easily raised from seed planted either in a cold frame in the autumn or in drills in the spring, and it is well to remember that it will grow under trees, or on the shaded side of the rock garden. There is a variety *purpurescens*, and also a white variety which I have never seen. This is not one of the choicest plants, nor is it particularly showy; but it is a good-tempered stand-by such as we cannot well do without.

Narcissus, Golden Spur (Plate 46)

This lovely Daffodil, seen in Plate 46 naturalized beneath the naked branches of Beech trees, has been grown in gardens for many years. It is the earliest of the trumpet varieties to flower, and gladdening indeed is a swaying mass of it on an early April day. "To say that any new seedling is 'as good or earlier than Golden Spur' would be high praise indeed."

It is not the largest nor yet the most spectacular of trumpet varieties, but there are few to surpass it in richness of color—it is a rich self-yellow —in sturdiness of constitution or in form. The trumpet is large and spreads at the mouth with the brim gracefully rolled back; the perianth spreads like an open fan behind it.

It is easily forced in pots for use indoors, and has few equals for naturalizing, when it seeds freely, thus increasing its numbers appreciably. It is lovely planted among the gray satin trunks of Beech trees, as seen in the plate. For a scene of fairylike beauty, broadcast Golden Spur among the white trunks of White Birches. The delicate young leafage of the Birches,

[*51*]

their willowlike drooping twigs and slender white trunks, combined with the golden flowers make a scene that is difficult to surpass. Just one Birch tree and a dozen Golden Spurs will give ineffable pleasure.

Now that there are so many new varieties of Daffodils, it is easy to forget some of the old favorites; but Golden Spur is one that should not be omitted from any collection, for it has hardly been surpassed.

Buy many of them and plant them early in September—all Daffodils like early planting—in the borders, beneath the trees, wherever there is space for glowing beauty.

Cervantes is also a very early flowering variety of the Princeps type. Its color is soft primrose. Like Golden Spur, it can be brought into flower in the house by Christmas.

When planting Daffodils in a natural manner beneath trees, put them in a basket and walk about throwing them out by the handful; then plant them where they have fallen. Only thus can you get a truly natural and unstudied effect.

❧ Doronicums and Tulips Along Canal (Plate 47)

The association of water and flowers is always delightful. The narrow canal shown in Plate 47 is an especially effective way of introducing water into a garden, even a small garden. On either side flowers and low shrubs are massed, and in the distance are a few trees in young leaf.

The flowers in the left foreground are Doronicums, commonly called Leopard's-Bane. There are numerous kinds of them, showy daisylike flowers of vigorous growth blooming early in the spring. Almost any soil suits them, and they are frequently used for planting rough banks and other unpropitious places where little else will thrive. All are native to Europe and there is little to choose among the different kinds. *D. austriacum* and *D.*

[52]

caucasicum are neat but showy border plants growing about eighteen inches high, the latter a slightly coarser and slightly taller plant. *D. plantagineum excelsum* is the tallest of all and makes a great show where the soil is rich and not too dry. It is a fine plant for the second row of the herbaceous border and often produces a second crop of its immense yellow "daisies" in the autumn. *D. Pardalianches* is a less refined plant, but it grows three feet tall and flowers after the others have had their day. It is a good plant for naturalizing in rough places. A much smaller species, *D. Clusii,* is admirable in the rock garden, and it is as easily grown as the others.

The plants are bushy and increase rapidly, the flowers are borne on long stems which makes them suited for cutting. A good thing to know about them is that they will grow under the shade of not too dense trees and that they also do not pine in a damp situation.

Doronicums may be easily raised from seed and just as easily increased by division of the roots. The latter operation is best carried out immediately after the plants have finished flowering; each division or crown will produce a good plant for the following year. The vigorous young growths from the outer side of the clump will make the best plants, and so are the best to choose for replanting in prominent situations. They should be separated at least every three years.

Along the little canal they are particularly well grown and make a charming display. With them are a few bright-colored Tulips of the early type, some bushes of red Japanese Maple and clumps of *Anchusa myosotidiflora.* The color of the Doronicums when compared with that of Daffodils appears faintly greenish; so it is best to keep these two spring flowers out of each other's neighborhood.

✠ *Ribes sanguineum* (Red Flowering Currant) (Plate 48)

This Crimson-flowered Currant is a very old shrub in gardens, so old that in the superabundance of new introductions it is often overlooked. In Europe nurseries offer many varieties of it, but here we have only the common kind that grows wild in California. This shrub should not be neglected for its dangling racemes of rose-red flowers that hang until the leaves are well out are a lovely and affecting sight and should place it in the forefront of spring-flowering shrubs for the garden. At present it is known and loved in cottage gardens but ignored elsewhere.

Growing wild from British Columbia to California, its one fault in cold gardens is that it is not of ironclad hardiness; but, given a sheltered position, it will probably come through a considerable degree of cold. It flowers in April, and when the leaves appear they are broad, five-lobed, and whitish beneath; the young growth is slightly hairy. It was discovered, according to Mr. Hottes, by Archibald Menzies, a doctor in the British navy, when on a voyage round the world. This was in 1787, near Nootka Sound. He later sent seed back to England but it was left to that energetic and intuitive young Scotchman, botanist and explorer, David Douglas, for whom so many plants in our country are named, to send seed of it to the Horticultural Society at Chiswick. Its beauty was soon realized and it found its way from garden to garden, until now it is a common thing in an alien land, while neglected in its home.

The bush grows ultimately to a height of ten feet and will thrive, it is said, beneath trees. A bloomy blue-black fruit follows the flowers. It appears best when grouped with a number of its kind, and the ground about it may be carpeted with Grape Hyacinths, early Daffodils, and the like.

[54]

⚑ *Ribes Gordonianum* (Hybrid Flowering Currant) (Plate 49)

This is a species of garden origin, a hybrid between *Ribes sanguineum* and *R. aureum*, the sweet-scented Buffalo or Missouri Currant. It is a charmingly graceful bush with broad-lobed leaves, and is hung all over in April with the characteristic racemes of dangling flowers. It creates a lovely glowing effect, for the flowers are reddish without and creamy-yellow within. And it has taken from its hardier parent, *Ribes aureum*, its sturdy constitution and ability to withstand cold, which enables it to be grown in colder localities than can the Red Flowering Currant.

It is said to have been raised in the beautiful gardens of Shrublands Park, near Ipswich, by Donald Beaton, a well known gardener of his time, about 1837. It shares with both its parents a very real charm, and groups of it would be an addition to any garden.

⚑ *Epimedium Musschianum* with Prostrate Juniper and Sagina (Plate 50)

The association of different types of foliage often brings about as pleasing an effect as do harmonizing flowers. Here in Plate 50 we have the rough sprawling growth of the Canadian Juniper, the soft and tender leaves and little white flowers of the Barrenwort (Epimedium), and the mosslike covering of the earth below them made by the Sagina. Even without the flowers of the Barrenwort we should have a picture worth looking at and emulating. But it should be noted how well placed they are among the rocks—not in a haphazard manner, but so that each may show its full value and quality. The Juniper spread over the pale rock is perfectly arranged. The Barrenwort tucked in below against the floor of mosslike Sagina could not be better situated.

[55]

The Creeping Juniper goes under many names. It is a native plant found from British Columbia, western Canada, and Nova Scotia south to Massachusetts, New York, Minnesota, and Montana. It is valuable as a ground cover among rocks and in exposed situations. It is usually called *Juniperus horizontalis*, and is variable in its forms.

The Epimediums are delightful spring-flowering plants, remarkable for their pretty fresh leaves and for their ability to beautify situations in the shade. They are delightful for shaded corners of the rock garden that we do not know just what to do with, pleasant companions along shaded paths, nice for massing on tree-shadowed banks. There are a number of species, but they all look much alike save for their flowers, which may be white, rose, or yellow—the latter are among the prettiest. They all hail from Japan, the Caucasus, or Persia save *E. alpinum* and *E. hyemalis*, which are European. Our own *Vancouveria hexandra* that comes out of the West might be their blood brother, but is not. In any cool place the Barrenworts are of the most perfect amiability; they live long and prosper, and deserve more notice than they commonly receive.

The Saginas are all of the utmost value for carpeting the earth in any open soil and situation. They could hardly press closer to the ground, hardly cover themselves more ungrudgingly with a Milky Way of tiny white stars. This happens about midsummer. This invaluable little plant will often be found in catalogues under "*Arenaria caespitosa*," and sometimes under "*Spergula pilifera*." But, under whatever name you have it, make free use of it to clothe the spaces between rocks in the rock garden, to cover the ground where grow precious little bulbs, or to clothe the base of small evergreens, and outline the chinks in paved paths. Walking upon it does not disturb it.

Plate 43. *Phlox subulata* VIVID

Plate 44. MUSCARI HEAVENLY BLUE (GRAPE HYACINTH)

Plate 45. *Orobus vernus (Lathyrus vernus)* (SPRING VETCHLING)

Plate 46. NARCISSUS, GOLDEN SPUR

Plate 47. DORONICUMS AND TULIPS ALONG CANAL

Plate 48. *Ribes sanguineum* (FLOWERING CURRANT)

Plate 49. *Ribes Gordonianum* (HYBRID FLOWERING CURRANT)

Plate 50. *Epimedium Musschianum* WITH PROSTRATE JUNIPER AND SAGINA

Plate 51. *Uvularia grandiflora* (BELLWORT)

Plate 52. TULIPS AND SPRING FLOWERS ON GARDEN TERRACE

Plate 53. SPRING FLOWERS IN A DRY WALL, WITH TULIPS IN THE FOREGROUND

Plate 54. TULIPS AND *Euphorbia helioscopia* AGAINST APPLE
BLOSSOMS

Plate 55. TULIP KEIZERSKROON

☫ *Uvularia grandiflora* (Bellwort) (Plate 51)

The Bellworts are among the prettiest and least noticed of our wild flowers. They are modest members of the Lily family and have a certain pride of carriage despite their drooping heads. One or other of them is to be found over a wide area of the eastern and central states, usually where the soil is rich and somewhat sandy in woodlands, and where moisture is not wholly lacking.

Nothing could be more effective for a congregation in some wild garden, or in a section of the rock garden where a little wildness may be allowed. *Uvularia grandiflora* is an erect perennial plant, springing from a hardy rootstock. Nothing more graceful in all nature could be found than the slender flexuous stem. It grows from six to twenty inches high with one or two leaves low on the stem and a cluster of them near the top which have the curious effect of being pierced by the stem. They are long and slender and have a sort of folded appearance. At the apex the stem droops, and from the end between the long narrow leaves hangs the flower, solitary and lovely. It is long, at least an inch and a half, narrowly bell-shaped and soft lemon-yellow in color. The perianth segments are six in number and dispose themselves rather carelessly, as who should say, "I am a Lily, and those who do not know it do not count."

Other members of the genus are less effective. There is the Small-flowered Bellwort, *Uvularia perfoliata*, fairly common in the coastal regions of New York State and in other sandy localities, and *U. sessilifolia*, found from the province of New Brunswick south to Georgia and Arkansas, in moist woods and thickets. The flowers of this kind are smaller and have a greenish tinge.

☗ Tulips and Spring Flowers on a Garden Terrace (Plate 52)

A paved terrace close to a house offers an opportunity for all sorts of treatments. In Plate 52 we have what might be termed an informal formal treatment. The focal point is the rectangular pool, with its graceful jet of water flanked by simple flower pots. About it are narrow borders of spring flowers, Tulips, Iberis, Arabis, and others in pleasant contrast to the soft-colored stone. On two sides runs a low dry wall which has not been planted save at the top along the house, where broad-leaved Evergreens and Arabis make a pleasant setting. The house is built on simple lines, and the bird houses and shadowing trees, the glimpse of the comfortable porch, all add to the pleasurable informality of the scene. A more pretentious terrace would have been out of keeping with the general surroundings and the dwelling.

The gayly planted flower beds are in plain sight of the windows of the house, and one feels that this terrace is enjoyed by the family both indoors and out.

☗ Spring Flowers in a Dry Wall, with Tulips in the Foreground (Plate 53)

A steep slope always offers difficulties to the gardener or landscape gardener. An admirable way to treat such a slope is to step it down in narrow terraces walled up by dry walls, which may be planted with all sorts of attractive plants, and at the rear a well cared-for evergreen hedge will shut off this formal design from the natural woodland behind it. Such a problem that has been worked out after this manner we have in Plate 53. Narrow paths of paving stones run along the terraces, and at the foot is a gay planting of Tulips, which will later be replaced by some other genial

[*58*]

bedding plant; and flanking this border at either end is a well clipped evergreen to lend finish to this rather formal composition. The walls are crammed with all sorts of spring flowers. One recognizes Alyssum, Iberis, Aubrietia, Arabis, Cytisus, Thrift, and all manner of other pleasant spring visitors. And the narrow beds in front of the walls are also overflowing with Tulips, Wallflowers, and many of the plants that grow also in the walls.

A seat is wanted at the foot where one may rest and gaze up at the masses of flowers, but one is grateful for the dark hedge at the top and for the old Cedar at the far left end which throw all this frivolity into relief and yet seem to keep it within proper bounds.

It is interesting to note how vigorously the plants grow in the crevices of the dry walls, seeming to revel in the situation and to be at their very best. The simple coping along the top of the wall also serves to give this lively planting definition and some dignity. There are many estates in America where such a plan and a like planting could be resorted to with marked success.

🎠 Tulips and *Euphorbia helioscopia* Against Apple Blossoms (Plate 54)

A crooked old Apple tree with its branches low-hung invites the companionship of other flowers. Plate 54 shows a cottage garden most informal and somewhat heterogeneous in its planting, yet distinctly appealing and not wholly thoughtlessly assembled. There is first the gnarled old Apple tree. This at once provides a point of departure. So on the sunny side in a free and easy fellowship are gathered together a mass of scarlet early Tulips (in "The Winter's Tale" are the words, "And let's be red with mirth"), and the mirth of the Tulips certainly sets alight the soft yellow masses of the Spurge, *Euphorbia helioscopia*, a European plant which has much the appearance of *E. epithymoides* and *E. polychroma* (Plate 39). In the background we detect a few crowned heads of the Crown Imperial, *Fritillaria imperialis*, and there are other things.

There is no formal bed; the plants are set where it is convenient for the housewife to set them, and back of them billows the orchard with its clouds of pale pink bloom. The ground must be good, for the plants are obviously flourishing. Perhaps a little manure is allowed from the farm for the housewife's garden patch. At all events it is a pleasant scene, and such an one as we should oftener come upon in our farming districts. Probably later there will be Iris and Tiger Lilies and old purple Phlox, and perhaps a Dahlia or two, and the house plants will be set out to sun and air during the summer in the small area that will be cared for out of the scant leisure of a busy woman. Thus does beauty grow where least expected and least tended, but where it is wanted above all things.

❦ Tulip Keizerskroon (Plate 55)

Certain Tulips still grown in gardens today are veritable antiques. Of these is the somewhat garish old Keizerskroon. "This well-known red and yellow early Tulip is described in the Dutch catalogues of a century and a half ago, and shows no loss of vigor." It has lost something, however, in popularity, for the vast number of more beautifully caparisoned Tulips of recent introduction have caused fastidious persons to turn away from its tawdry coloring.

It is said to be one of the oldest of known hybrid Tulips, "a favorite since the eighteenth century." Its flower is large, and each segment has upon it a broad scarlet flame edged conspicuously with yellow. Whatever else may be said of it, good or bad, Keizerskroon is one of the best stayers in the garden of this somewhat ephemeral race. Year after year it hoists its

[*60*]

red and yellow banners, flouting the more recent beauties. It is said that it will even thrive in grass—a test indeed!

It may be easily forced in pots among other precocious kinds for house decoration, and it is perhaps in winter that we are best able to stand its uncompromising coloring. Other good early Tulips that may be easily forced are King of the Yellows, Mon Trésor, pure yellow; Prince of Austria, yellow, netted over with brown, giving an orange effect, richly fragrant; Fred Moore, almost brick-red, also exquisitely scented; Vermillon Brillant, a dwarf scarlet kind; Van der Neer, a low-growing plum-purple; Proserpina, tall and a gentle crimson in color, and the Duc van Thol group. This group contains yellow, scarlet, violet, white, and rose-pink kinds. The scarlet is the best. They are suitable only for forcing, and they may be seen in the florists' shops at Christmas time. Or any one may force them in a sunny window for this season.

🌷 Tulip, Double-Flowering (Plate 56)

Double Tulips are no longer in the mode. They have been put out of date by the slim beauties that we know as Cottages, Darwins, Breeders, and the like. But they have a quaint charm of their own, an opulence, that makes them deserve some attention when so many Victorian ornaments are regaining their status. They are unsurpassed for bouquets, and the modern ones have not the fault that worked against the popularity of the older kinds. Their stems are strong, and the flower is held upright with all its ruffles displayed to the sun, whereas the heavy heads of the earlier types bowed the stems to the earth, often subjecting them to besmirching by mud during storms. It was necessary to plant them where their heads could nod upon clean grass.

The modern double Tulip, whether of early or late variety, makes a

[*61*]

splendid bedding flower and may also be scattered in groups through the perennial borders among the perennials.

Some of the best of the double "Earlies" are Mystery of India, apricot-bronze, tinged with pinkish lights; Orange Nassau, orange-red with brownish sheen; Vuurbaak, bright orange-scarlet; Murillo, a lovely pink and white; Peachblossom, bright pink and white; Triumphator, a fine pure pink tone; Azalea, soft pink flushed with a deeper tone; Golden Giant, immense semi-double pure yellow flower; Maréchal Niel, amber-colored; Mr. Van der Hoef, very full and shining gold; Yellow Rose, an old kind that we still love despite its weak stem for the sake of its delightful scent; Tea Rose (Safrano), primrose and apricot; Schoonoord, white; Boule de Neige, very double white and like a Peony.

Of the May-flowering kinds we have Allegro, fine purplish red; Rose van Saron, reddish with a white edge; Negus, like wine-colored velvet; Snowball, white and very double, long-lasting; Coxa, lovely shade of apricot-red, with orange edges; Uncle Tom, dark red with blackish shadowings; Pavo, small flower, Tyrian pink; Avondson, an immense orange-colored flower, sweetly scented; Cherry Blossom, sweet-scented and of a delicious tone of soft rose-red; Ottawa, fine pure yellow; Lord Derby, soft red, feathered into white at the edges; Hermer, pink; Trixy, bright pomegranate-purple; Epicure, peach-red; Livingstone, rose-red with three flowers to a stem; Mount Everett, purplish red; Bleu Celeste, purplish; Pensée Rose, reddish and of enormous size; Delardier, cherry; Mt. Takoma, semi-double, white, a good stayer; Baltimore, soft cherry with darker shadings.

These late-flowering double Tulips come into bloom between the "earlies" and the Cottages and Darwins, bridging the gap.

⚑ Tulip, Raphael (Plate 57)

Raphael is a representative of a race of Tulips that we know as Darwins. They are probably the most popular Tulips today. It is said that they are Flemish in origin, and that the first Darwin Tulips were exhibited by the firm of E. H. Krelage & Son at Kleinen, in 1886. They are characterized by tall, strong stems and cup-shaped flowers made up of firm-textured rounded petals, distinctly square in outline, or what the growers call "shouldered," to distinguish them from the slender vaselike forms, such as the Cottage varieties, some of which have a distinct waist and never open up wide save under the hottest suns. They are the favorites of the Dutch growers, who like their sturdy, cupped forms and stiff stems, but they are less graceful than the Cottage Tulips though they are more satisfactory for bedding. Until recently the Dutch people were the only large growers of Tulips, and so it was these stout fellows that were grown and marketed to the world in large quantities, to the neglect of the lovely and gracious English Cottage Tulips.

Darwin Tulips are self-colored; but when one has said this one has said little, for they abound in superbly rich tones. There is every tint of pink from pale to deepest cherry and on through the blood-reds, maroons to almost black. There are lilacs and mauves and purples and warm violets; there are blends of rose and apricot and a number of dazzling white varieties. But there are no yellow-flowered kinds among the true Darwins, while the English Cottage Tulip is rich in yellow and orange shades.

Raphael is turned out in two tones of lilac, deep and pale, and is one of the Tulips that look particularly lovely with Apple blossoms, or grouped with clumps of Bleedingheart.

❦ Tulips with Violas and Other Spring Flowers (Plate 58)

In Plate 58 we have a gay assemblage of spring flowers set out in a rocky situation. Scarlet and white early Tulips dominate the scene, but a fine mass of Bergenia (Megasea), or what we know as the large-leaved Saxifrage, with its dense panicles of rose or lilac flowers raised well above the leaves, occupies considerable space and lends stability to the planting. Around and among these important plants are crowded Violas, Violets, English Daisies, Periwinkles, and Primroses. And in the background one sees the swordlike leaves of Irises promising later color. It is all very informal and pretty, and one can well imagine a rocky hillside in sunshine where just such a planting would exactly suit the situation.

The Bergenia is a perennial plant with a thick rootstock from which develop masses of large shining leaves, thick and waxy, that are almost, if not quite, evergreen. The plants spread quickly into wide colonies. When the Tulips and more ephemeral plants have had their day the large-leaved Saxifrage is there to make a green show and companion the Irises, though its own blossoms will have departed. It is a Siberian plant and very hardy, and not at all particular as to soil; but to encourage early flowering it should be given a sheltered position where the frosts will not spoil the great heads of blooms. It makes a very good plant for use at the turn or angle of a border where a continuous display of handsome greenery is desired.

❦ Border of Early Tulips and Aubrietia along a Paved Path (Plate 59)

This is purely a spring picture. Later bedding plants may be used to fill the border now occupied by the Tulips and Aubrietia. A few Japanese Maples are there perhaps for stability, perhaps for their ruddy color, and will last through the season. At the back is a dry wall closely planted, and a dark evergreen hedge which gives a rich setting to the riot of color.

[*64*]

Plate 56. TULIP, DOUBLE-FLOWERING

Plate 57. TULIP, RAPHAEL (DARWIN)

Plate 58. TULIPS WITH VIOLAS AND OTHER SPRING FLOWERS

Plate 59. BORDER OF EARLY TULIPS AND AUBRIETIA ALONG PAVED PATH

Plate 60. MAY TULIPS IN BORDER WITH STANDARD LILACS

Plate 61. BORDER OF IBERIS AND AUBRIETIA

The Garden in Color

The Tulips are evidently a mixed planting of early varieties, pinks and reds, a few violets, and white. Between them are scattered plantings of *Alyssum saxatile citrinum* and English Daisies. The Aubrietia is exceptionally well grown, and makes a lovely binding ribbon for the cheerful Tulips.

Aubrietias are plants of the southern European mountains and come in many tones of mauve, purple, violet, rose, and crimson. European catalogues are full of named varieties, but we must be content with a few. They are easily raised from seed but do not always come quite true to color when obtained in this manner. Seed may be planted in the late autumn or early winter in cold frames and set out in spring when the young plants are large enough to handle. They may flower a little the first year, but their best showing will be made in the second spring. After they have bloomed they should be cut over sharply with a pair of garden shears; they will then make new growth and frequently give a few charming flowers during the autumn. Besides being excellent as an edging plant they grow well in walls, on rock gardens, or in any rocky situations. In our hot dry summers they should be given plenty of water during times of drought.

May Tulips in Border with Standard Lilacs (Plate 60)

Tulips and Lilacs positively ask to be planted together. This, however, is rather a stiff little scene, the dooryard of a simple white house. The Tulips in the border are of Cottage varieties, pink and yellow, and the bed is edged with low Begonias. In front of the house and beneath the Lilacs is a mass of Pansies. The green lawn is restful, and the little bare tree lends a certain grace to the planting.

Later in the season bedding plants, Ageratum, Petunias, Vincas, Verbenas, low Marigolds, and Zinnias, will doubtless fill the beds.

[65]

⚏ Border of Iberis and Aubrietia (Plate 61)

There are situations where bedding out is admissible, even advisable. These are rather formal situations, in parks, or on formal terraces. It is usually carried out with bulbs which are followed by tender bedding plants. But here in Plate 61 we have effective bedding done with hardy perennials, which of course will have to be followed by something else after they have finished blossoming if color is to be maintained in these borders.

The border in the near foreground is planted with Aubrietia, in a good mauve-purple tone, and Iberis (Candytuft). The Iberis is doubtless *I. sempervirens* Little Gem, or some other compact variety, as the ordinary *sempervirens* would sprawl all over the Aubrietia. *Iberis sempervirens* is a delightful plant found "all along the Alps from the Pyrenees to Asia Minor." It is as easy to raise from seed as the Aubrietia and makes low evergreen bushes of shining dark leaves, bearing in April and May innumerable heads, more or less dome-shaped, of gleaming white flowers. It is one of the purest white flowers in the garden; and it is as hardy as iron and asks no special treatment, and so is a boon to the bedder, the rock gardener, the border gardener, and whoever. After it has flowered it is well to cut it over, removing the seed heads; but if you do not do this you will be rewarded by a great number of gratuitous babies springing up about the parent plant. The cutting over simply keeps it in its compact and tidy form.

All the forms of *Iberis sempervirens* make fine wall plants, hanging against the wall face in graceful festoons. Along the front of a border they maintain their seemly green show to the shame of many a plant that loses countenance and figure after it has brought forth flowers. A border edged with Iberis kept clipped always appears trim and seemly.

꿈 *Clematis montana* (Anemone-Flowered Clematis) (Plate 62)

Though one of the most beautiful of all climbers the Clematis is rarely grown in American gardens. There are reasons for this, perhaps; it has been difficult to get on its own roots, or its necessities are not understood. When they are, surely our gardens will be garlanded with this graceful and floriferous climber. Mr. Joel Spingarn, the most successful grower and protagonist of the Clematis on this side of the Atlantic, writes:

Though subject to setbacks north of Long Island, this Himalayan species, with its even lovelier varieties, seems quite vigorous when planted on the north side of a low wall; it flourishes in my own garden ninety miles north of New York City with a moderate amount of protection and often with none.

This lovely climber, that bears flowers much like those of the Japanese Anemone in shape and size, flowers in May with the Tulips. A wall draped with the beautiful variety *rubens*, which is a delicate pink in color, behind a mass of Tulips is a sight not to be forgotten. The type is white and less vigorous than *rubens*, and *montana undulata*, white flushed with pink; *montana Wilsoni* has white flowers larger than the type and blooming a month or more later; and there are still others.

These beautiful plants have long been grown in the gardens of Europe, but our perfidious embargo on the introduction of plants from abroad makes it extremely difficult for us to obtain them. But *C. montana rubens* and the type are obtainable here. The flowers are borne in graceful garlands, and whether the vine is grown on a wall or allowed to climb the branches of an old Apple tree, whence its flowery trails reach from branch to branch, it creates a scene of unbelievable beauty.

In planting Clematis there is probably no doubt that the lower part of the plant should be shaded from the sun, the upper part allowed to have all possible light. If possible, obtain plants that are on their own roots, as grafted plants are more liable to disease. Seed of *Clematis montana* and of *montana rubens* is available and easily raised. In this way own root plants will be assured.

The Clematis will thrive in almost any nourishing and well cultivated soil, but there is no doubt that in this country at least, where so much of our soil is acid, a little lime mixed with the soil around the plants is a favor they esteem. Any one who has seen Clematis growing in England on what they call "the chalk" cannot but have noticed their superb luxuriance. The Clematis clings to whatever is near by its leaves, and clings so neat and tight that once these leaves have formed their wirelike ties, cutting asunder alone will release them; and that is not recommended during the growing season.

Corylopsis pauciflora (Plate 63)

Corylopsis belongs to the family of Witch-Hazels, and its members are not seen in gardens as often as they deserve to be. Its home country is Japan and it flowers in March and April. The bushes grow something over three feet, are flat-topped and twiggy, and when they flower they do it with a generosity that warms our own hearts. The blossoms are borne on the naked twigs and hang down in pairs like little inverted Primroses. "The pale green flower buds push their way through membraneous bracts and open into five-petalled primrose-yellow flowers, each with five deeper yellow anthers." The flowers have also the delicate fragrance of Primroses, which adds to their attraction.

Because of their early flowering, a sheltered situation is best for them, against a wall or hedge, and a soil compounded of sand and peat. They may

[*68*]

be planted about with low Heaths if liked, and the association of pale purple and primrose is most pleasing.

After the flowers are gone the Hazel-like leaves appear, and the shrub takes its place in the summer greenery. It is at all times a neat and well shaped shrub, an ornament wherever seen.

There are some twelve other varieties known, all native to eastern Asia and the Himalaya. *C. spicata* is obtainable in this country, as well as the foregoing.

❦ *Malus Kaido* (Plate 64)

There are so many beautiful Crab-apples with which to beautify the garden that it is difficult to choose among them. They are for the most part small trees that do not shade the beds and borders too heavily, so that they may be used right in the garden proper as well as in the shrubbery or as specimens on the lawn. They bloom with the most abundant generosity, becoming veritable pink bouquets during their flowering season. Most of them have a sort of crooked grace that is appealing, and, flowering as they do when Tulips and many other lovely flowers bloom, their uses are manifold and various.

Malus Kaido is a hybrid between *M. spectabilis* and *M. pumila*, or some other nearly related species. It may be *M. Ringo. M. spectabilis* comes from China and Japan.

❦ *Rhododendron Arendsii* (Azalea) (Plate 65)

This is but one of the vast number of hybrid Rhododendrons available for garden use. It is a particularly lovely one, named for Georg Arends, and is of the Azalea type.

The most entrancing pictures may be made in gardens by means of the

[*69*]

free use of these lovely shrubs. But in planting them certain points must be borne in mind. Preparation of the soil before planting and cultivation at frequent intervals after planting are of the utmost importance. All Rhododendrons have a definite and unfailing dislike to lime, and in districts where lime is present, even though beds are carefully prepared, small success will be had. The soil they like is a light, sandy loam with an admixture of peat. Peat is their favorite article of diet. Give them plenty, and you will have no cause for complaint; you will have plants as handsome and flowerful as badly grown plants can be unsightly. Before planting, dig the soil at least eighteen inches deep, and set the young plants firmly, but not too deeply, as they are surface-rooting. Thereafter they must not suffer from want of water, and in dry weather should be watered copiously. "Soil that is permanently moist but sweet and properly drained is the most suitable, and although both groups [Rhododendrons and Azaleas] are often grown in full sun, they are assisted by a little shade during the hottest part of the day, the flowers lasting longer under such conditions." In the autumn a loose mulch of leaves over the roots will keep them safe over the winter, and when spring comes this blanket must be left in place, not forked in, and will gradually add to the nourishment the plants want, and at the same time keep the ground about them moist.

Rhododendrons and Azaleas are lovely massed against evergreens, where their vibrant colors are thrown into relief, or clustered in thickets in light woods, or "difficult" corners.

⚜ *Rhododendron obtusum Kaempferi* (Torch Azalea) (Plate 66)

From the botanical standpoint of today no difference is admitted between Rhododendrons and Azaleas, though at one time, not so long ago, the two genera were separate. And in gardens they are still separate indi-

[70]

viduals, despite the botanists, for their superficial distinctions are very marked, so marked that they should not be planted adjacent to one another, though they both like the same conditions of soil and aspect. There is at bottom a difference in the number of stamens between the two types, which, however, is not always to be counted upon. The most generally distinguishing character from the gardeners' standpoint is that the flowers generally known as Azaleas are leaf-losing in the autumn while the Rhododendrons proper are evergreen. This distinction is also not infallible, but it serves well enough. The flowers of Azaleas are in the main more lightly made, more butterfly-like than those of Rhododendrons, particularly of the hybrid kinds.

Rhododendron Kaempferi, the Torch Azalea, is named for a "Dutch merchant-adventurer, who in 1690 introduced various Japanese plants." It is one of the most beautiful and striking of its kind, as well as one of the most useful. It was, according to Mr. Claude Bowers, "first introduced to western gardens by Professor C. S. Sargent who brought seeds from Japan to the Arnold Arboretum in 1892 and it is undoubtedly one of the most valuable foreign plants ever cultivated in New England."

It grows slowly to a height of about six feet but flowers freely when quite small. The color of these flowers is not easily described. If such a hue as pinkish orange can be imagined, that is it. It is like a flame, and shows up superbly in light woodland or against evergreen trees. Nor is it a fighting color. I have seen it surrounded by *Phlox divaricata,* with charming effect, with white Trilliums crowding about it, and in the rock garden with orange-colored Geums and many-hued forms of *Phlox subulata* near it and the picture was entirely harmonious. In the neighborhood of New York the plants hold their leaves until late in the winter; perhaps in more southern climates they may keep them still longer. They are in full flower about the middle of May in New York. It is said that among seedlings there is considerable variation—some are more pink, some more orange or scarlet —but that no hint of blue ever mars the flowers, even when fading. The flowers are commonly borne in clusters of two and three; they are shallow and like brilliant butterflies in shape, having little depth. *Kaempferi* is quickly burned or faded by direct sunlight, and so a position in partial shade is the best for it. It asks for the usual mixture of peat and sand, with the peat predominating.

❦ *Rhododendron praecox* (Plate 67)

This Rhododendron is a hybrid between *R. ciliatum*, an evergreen species from Sikkim and the Himalayas and *R. dauricum*, a sub-evergreen from Dauria and Manchuria. It is one of the earliest Rhododendrons to flower, and as such is of great value in the garden. It makes a bush of fair height which in April, or earlier in mild localities, is covered by rose-pink flowers that have a tinge of blue in their composition. They are funnel-shaped and borne with great prodigality.

Because of its eagerness to burst into flower this Rhododendron should be protected from frosts that will spoil its flowers. Perhaps an eastern aspect is the best for it with protection from north winds in the form of evergreens or a house wall. It is a lovely thing.

❦ Rhododendrons, Various Types (Plate 68)

For massing in various situations in the garden, particularly in the angles of walls or against evergreens few shrubs offer such variety and amazing beauty. Some shade and a soil deeply dug and compounded of sand and peat is necessary to them all——no lime as you value their lives.

From the many species an almost countless number of varieties have

[72]

Plate 62. *Clematis montana* (ANEMONE-FLOWERED CLEMATIS)

Plate 63. *Corylopsis pauciflora*

Plate 64. *Malus Kaido*

Plate 65. *Rhododendron Arendsii* (AZALEA)

Plate 66. *Rhododendron obtusum, Kaempferi* (TORCH AZALEA)

Plate 67. *Rhododendron praecox*

Plate 68. RHODODENDRON, VARIOUS TYPES

Plate 69. *Rhododendron obtusum, Hinodegiri* (AZALEA)

Plate 70. RHODODENDRON KOSTER'S BRILLIANT RED (AZALEA)

Plate 71. *Rhododendron Maxwellii* (AZALEA) WITH SPRING FLOWERS

Plate 72. BROOM AND SPRING FLOWERS IN DRY WALL

Plate 73. WEIGELA HYBRIDS, ABEL CARRIÈRE AND DESBOISII

been developed. The species come from Europe, North America, the Arctic, northeastern Asia, Japan (in great numbers), all over China, Tibet, the Himalayan region, southern Asia, Malaya, and tropical islands, and range in altitude from sea level up to twelve thousand feet or higher. The colors cover every hue save blue, and include many off tones and tints not found in other flowers. The flowers themselves are borne in large panicles and are of generous size.

North America alone is rich in species; those best known in the Azalea type are *canadense, nudiflorum, viscosum, arborescens, calendulaceum, Vaseyi*. Among the Rhododendron type, from which many others have been developed, are *maximum, carolinianum, catawbiense*. On the Pacific coast *R. albiflorum* and *R. californicum* are fairly common.

If Rhododendrons have a fault it is that in winter they droop their leaves in apparent dejection. They are poor winter company, despite their abiding green. But *R. carolinianum* and its white variety have not this drawback. Their leaves are rather small, and they face the cold without flinching.

ꆛ *Rhododendron obtusum Hinodegiri* (Azalea) (Plate 69)

Though this Rhododendron, which is of the Azalea type, is a low bush, seldom growing higher than three feet and oftener much less, it may well be an embarrassment to the gardener with a sensitive eye for color. The bushes form a mass of close-woven twigs, and the twigs are beset all over with the most brilliant flowers imaginable, not red, not cherry, not pink. To give a name to this amazing color is impossible. Also it is impossible to give it a companion that will get along with it, or nearly so. It is low enough to grow in the rock garden, but when it bursts into triumphant bloom all else within the same vision scope is put out of countenance. Best keep it with white surrounding blooms, or better still with a green background where it can blaze away alone. It flowers in mid-May.

Azalea Hinodegiri is what is termed a Kurume Azalea, of which the earlier described *A. Kaempferi* is also one. A correspondent writes to a British horticultural paper:

It seems incredible that after more than three-quarters of a century of intercourse with Japan the occidental nations should not have known before Mr. Wilson's journeys in that country all about this beautiful race of garden plants which has been developed to perfection by the flower-loving Japanese. This is, however, the case in regard to the Kurume Azaleas.

These plants were found by Mr. E. H. Wilson in a garden at Kurume, a town on Kyushu, the southern island of Japan, in 1918. *A. Hinodegiri* was the first, I believe, to enter the country. It is not considered hardy very far north but is ironclad in the neighborhood of New York. The Kurume Azaleas offer the most exquisite range of colors possible to imagine.

☗ Rhododendron Koster's Brilliant Red (Azalea) (Plate 70)

Azalea Koster's Brilliant Red is a hybrid of *Azalea mollis*, and as may be seen is a most brilliant and floriferous variety. *Azalea mollis*, or *Rhododendron molle*, is a Chinese species found on "open hillsides among coarse grasses and shrubs and in thin pine woods." It has become the parent with other species of a vast number of varieties, embracing almost every color of the rainbow, save blue, and often blotched and spotted and flushed with contrasting hues. The *mollis* Azaleas are not considered of great hardiness, but they do well in the neighborhood of New York City, where the climate is not especially ingratiating. Koster's Brilliant Red is difficult to place because of its vibrant color.

[74]

⚜ *Rhododendron Maxwellii* (Azalea) with Spring Flowers (Plate 71)

Rhododendron Maxwellii is a variety of *R. pulchrum*, a kind found in China and Japan, but unknown in the wild. Its hue is described as carmine-red, and it appears to be a brilliant and floriferous plant. Thus the gardener who planned the scene in Plate 71 handled his fiery material cleverly. He placed it against the soft-toned harmonizing wall, where it could blaze to its heart's content and be offensive to none and the flowers seen with it, especially those in the foreground are for the most part white or of very pale colors. Those who make use of the brilliant hybrid Azaleas are not always so considerate of the persons who are offended by such an uncontrolled display of color.

⚜ Broom and Spring Flowers in Dry Wall (Plate 72)

The dry wall is here shown as an extremely happy home for alpines, particularly those that like to fall in curtains over the wall face. But even the great-leaved Bergenia, with its wads of fat pink blooms, is at home there. And the upright walls take up far less space than would a rambling construction of hills and valleys. Thus a dry wall enables the owner of a small garden to grow a vast number of plants that he would not otherwise have space for.

The Broom planted at the top of the wall is shown particularly well grown and well placed.

Some good plants for walls are Aubrietias, *Campanula pusilla, C. muralis, C. gargantica* and others, *Arabis albida fl.-pl., Saponaria ocymoides,* both pink and white, Pinks of all kinds (Dianthus), *Alyssum saxatile,* Armerias, Cerastiums, Helianthemums, *Gypsophila cerastioides,* and *G.*

[75]

repens, Hypericums of creeping habit, Globularias, dwarf Geraniums and Erodiums, *Veronica rupestris*, Thymes, the choicer Sedums and Sempervivums, *Silene maritima*, *Phlox subulata* vars., Alpine Poppies, *Linum perenne* and *L. alpinum*. All these for a sunny wall.

⚜ Weigela hybrids (Plate 73)

Weigela, or Diervilla, as it is sometimes called, is one of those shrubs that might be called conscientious. It does its duty often under adverse conditions, giving a wealth of bloom in the early days of June in return for a good deal of neglect. Given good culture, a rich soil, full sunshine, it simply surpasses itself. One does not see how another tubular bloom could find a place on the wandlike branches. In shade it is apt to become a bit leggy, but it still flowers. After it has finished flowering, pruning it back a little will often cause it to go on blossoming now and then throughout the summer and fall.

The long branches are lovely for cutting, and there are now a great many fine hybrids, the flowers from the pure white of *candida* through pale pink to deep rose, carmine, and dark red.

In "The Book of Shrubs" Mr. Hottes quotes P. C. Halligan on the discovery of the Weigela:

In the garden of an old mandarin on one of the most beautiful islands of the world, the Island of Chusan, off the coast of Northern China, the common pink Weigela of our gardens was first found. There, in 1843, the eyes of an English plant explorer, Robert Fortune, first fell upon it, loaded with its tubular rose-colored flowers, the pride of the old mandarin and the admiration of the adventurous discoverer. Declaring it to be one of the most beautiful shrubs of Northern China, Robert Fortune sent specimens back to England where it was enthusiastically received and named to honor the German botanist Weigel.

[76]

Discounting the beauty and profusion of its flowers, one is aware that its foliage is somewhat coarse; and when out of bloom it is not especially ornamental, though in no wise really unattractive. In any case it needs space to develop its true grace, and in very cold climates it appreciates a sheltered situation. Some fine varieties are Vestale, early and creamy white; Abel, rose-carmine with primrose throat; Desbois, small crimson flowers; Dame Blanche, blush; Le Printemps, flesh-colored and free; Othello, maroon; Eva Rathke, crimson, dwarf, and much liked; Gracieux, salmon and pale buff, early.

✿ Trees in Young Leaf by the Waterside (Plate 74)

A lake is the eye of the landscape, wrote Thoreau, and how often we see in this eye reflected and enhanced the beauty that surrounds us! The reflection is more beautiful than the reality because every twig and branch, every flower has the sky, perhaps filled with fleecy clouds, as a background.

For every oak and birch, too, growing on the hilltop, as well as for those elms and willows, there is a graceful, ethereal, and ideal tree making down from the roots, and sometimes Nature in high tides brings its mirror to its foot and makes it visible. Anxious Nature sometimes reflects from pools and puddles the objects which our groveling senses may fail to see relieved against the sky, with the pure ether for background.

In planting watersides it is well to keep the pleasure of reflections in mind. Trees should be chosen that have naturally graceful and beautiful branches, and a habit of growth that reaches out over the water. In the spring when the leaves are delicate and young, and the twigs clearly seen, these reflections, or reproductions, in their green frame are the most lovely. But something more is needed than mere trees, and sky and water. As the man of Walden said, "It is only a reflecting mind that sees reflections."

[77]

❧ May Scene with *Phlox subulata* and Bergenia among Birches (Plate 75)

White Birches make a charming setting for almost any flowers. Here in Plate 75 is a peaceful mid-spring scene. The leaves on the drooping branches of the Birches are still young and tender; there are some patches of dark evergreens for contrast; a little path winds away into the distance. In the foreground flaunt the soft rose-colored blossoms of the Bergenia, often known as the large-leaved Saxifrage, a sturdy shining plant with fat heads of bloom down close among the leaves, and masses of the little ramping Creeping Phlox, *P. subulata*. Such a picture might be reproduced anywhere, and being hardy would care for itself; and the revolving seasons would bring it back again each year for the pleasure of our eyes. When the plants are out of bloom it will still be sightly, for the Bergenia retains its glossy surfaces and neatly clumped habit, and the Phlox becomes a furzy mound. Later the Birch trees turn softly yellow and drop gold pieces down among the flowers.

❧ *Ramondia pyrenaica* (Plate 76)

Ramondia pyrenaica is what the catalogues call a gem for the rock garden, but it is a gem that only responds to special conditions. It is a shade-loving plant that grows naturally on the cool side of cliffs in the Pyrenees. It makes a perfectly flat rosette of rounded, rough, and wrinkled, dark green leaves which hug the rock-face, and out of which in May or June spring stems four or five inches long each bearing two or more flowers shaped a good deal like the flowers of a Mullein, five-lobed, and with a bright orange thrust of anthers in the midst of its pure lilac-blue inch and a half of circumference. Long ago old Parkinson ranked it among the Pri-

[78]

mulas; but its texture is more solid, and there are more technical reasons why it is not a Primula. It is somewhat variable in beauty, some specimens being finer in color and form than others; but it is always an intriguing plant and one that every rock gardener wants to grow.

To grow it successfully in a rock garden one must have a north-facing vertical crevice, and it must suffer no lack of moisture at the root. If nature does not attend to this matter of a sufficiency of root moisture, the can or the hose may be called into use frequently in dry weather. It is not enough simply to plant it in its shaded crevice and leave it. It must be pampered a little. The soil behind the crevice may be a mixture of loam, leaf-mold, and sand made porous with broken stone—and there must be plenty of it, for the roots want to run far back in the cool interior of the rock work. Thus situated, the curious corrugated rosettes will increase in number, making wider and wider plates against the rock-face, and give more and more lovely flowers. If this happens you may divide your clumps to increase your stock. Otherwise, and if you have infinite patience and no mean skill, you may raise them from seed; but this is a long slow business and one not to be undertaken lightly. It is said that there are both white and pink forms; but neither can touch the lilac one in the matter of attractiveness, and they are very scarce.

This little plant, as one of the oldest rock plants in cultivation, deserves especial remark. One does not associate rock gardens with the days of Parkinson, and one wonders how he grew them.

There are numerous other species of Ramondia that the curious may seek out if they are so minded. *R. Nathaliae* is thought by some to be far superior to *pyrenaica*.

✲ *Oxalis adenophylla* (Plate 77)

This beautiful Wood Sorrel of the Chilean Andes is as yet very little known in this country. It is said to have been first collected by the late H. J. Elwes, and it is much grown abroad. There seems to be little difficulty about growing it, and it fits a nook in the rock garden in a way to rejoice the heart. It grows from a brownish corm not unlike that of a Cyclamen; from this in May springs a mass of delicate and lovely gray leaves out of which towards the first of June emerge furled buds, pale in color but pink at the tips. These open in full sunshine to the trumpet-shaped blossoms characteristic of the race. They are about an inch across and of the most appealing pinkish lilac hue, paling to white in the throat. The plant is generous in its blossoming and makes a distinguished exhibition in the rock garden. The blossoms are delicately veined with deeper color which concentrates in the striking reddish eye.

It is quite hardy in the neighborhood of New York, and if given a situation in partial shade and a soil made up of sandy loam and leaf-soil, with a little grit added, it should give no trouble at all. The situation should not be wholly shaded, for it takes the sun to open wide the lovely blossoms. If happy, the tufts widen year by year and grow more prodigal of their blossoms. It is one of the most valuable introductions for the rock garden made (in this country) in recent years. It is suitable for the smallest rock garden, for it does not ramp and scramble, but remains neat and tufty throughout its life.

Oxalis enneaphylla, of the Falkland Islands, is as fine and should be its companion in rock gardens where choice things are cherished. *O. Bowiei*, a South African, is also amazingly hardy, standing out in the neighborhood of New York without more than the usual light covering of leaves or salt hay given the rock garden. Its leaves, that are fleshy and a bright lettuce-

[*80*]

Plate 74. TREES IN YOUNG LEAF BY THE WATERSIDE

Plate 75. MAY SCENE WITH *Phlox subulata* AND BERGENIA AMONG BIRCHES

Plate 76. *Ramondia pyrenaica*

Plate 77. *Oxalis adenophylla*

Plate 78. *Onosma tauricum* (GOLDEN DROP) IN ROCK WORK

Plate 79. *Allium narcissiflorum* WITH *Genista dalmatica*

Plate 80. *Amanita muscaria*

green, are divided into three leaflets. The bright pure pink flowers are borne in loose panicles in the late summer and onwards until hard frost. Give this variety a sheltered corner. It is a beauty.

⚜ *Onosma tauricum* (Golden Drop) (Plate 78)

Here is another rock plant of most unusual charm. In our climate it is not so easy to grow because it hates the humidity of summer and the freeze and thaw of winter. Given steady cold in the latter season, it is quite contented. It is what Mr. Farrer calls "Southern and Levantine" in its habitat, which means it lives in southeastern Europe.

It grows from a woody root from which spring innumerable gray-green leaves about three inches long and rather narrow, which form themselves into a veritable bush. In the early summer appear stems six to eight inches long carrying branching heads of buds that unfurl into long soft yellow blooms, real golden drops, pinched at the mouth and of a most indubitable beauty. More than beauty, they have a delicious scent which causes one to bend lovingly above the gold and gray confusion of leaf and flower whenever in their neighborhood.

As has been said, in the climates that prevail in many parts of our country this plant is not easy to keep in health. But one can try, and if one succeeds the reward is greater than many strings of amber. To do one's best for it one gives it the highest and dryest situation in the rock garden, in the fullest eye of the sun, or a wall-face suits it admirably. The soil must be light and absolutely pervious; no lingering moisture must corrode its sensitive roots, and its gray leaves should not touch earth, but should lie upon a good blanket of stone chips. In addition to all these precautions, give it lime in the shape of old mortar rubble if possible, well mixed with the soil. In the plate it is evidently shown growing in a cliff-face, which situation dis-

[*81*]

plays its charms to the best advantage and protects it from standing moisture. There are other Onosmas that the indefatigable plant sleuth may find it worth his while to go after—*albo-rosea, stellulatum,* a few more. They may be raised from seed with care.

✿ *Allium narcissiflorum* with *Genista dalmatica* (Plate 79)

Here in Plate 79 is an effective association for use on a sunny ledge of the rock garden. It is effective chiefly because the two plants are so wholly different in habit that they act as excellent foils for each other. The Allium comes from the limestone Alps of Piedmont. The roots creep about under the earth, and from them emerge masses of strap-shaped leaves out of which spring slender stems not quite as tall as the leaves carrying pendent flowers, six or eight in number, of a "glowing vinous red." Unfortunately they have the onion stench at its worst, and still more unfortunately perhaps this species of Allium has not proved hardy in the neighborhood of New York.

The little Broom, *Genista dalmatica,* on the other hand, is quite hardy and enduring. It is a native of southeastern Europe. It makes a little furzy plate-wide mat of prickly, needlelike foliage only two inches high which curls over a cliff-side in the most engaging manner. In the early summer it is covered with small yellow sweet-smelling Broom flowers and makes a brave if miniature show of itself. It is one of the most attractive shrubs for the rock garden.

Other small brooms which deserve growing are *Genista sagittalis, Cytisus Ardoinii, C. prostrata (procumbens)* and there are numerous others. They are all sun-lovers, like a dry situation, and flower in the early summer. *C. Ardoinii* makes its minute contribution in late April. The Brooms are all easy to raise from seed.

✵ *Amanita muscaria* (Plate 80)

Amanita muscaria is one of the group of Mushrooms—or perhaps one should say in this case, Toadstools—that are known as deadly: Deadly Amanitas. The word comes, according to authority, from a mountain in Asia Minor. Margaret McKenny writes, in "Mushrooms of Field and Wood":

This Mushroom family is one of the first to be mentioned in history; the Roman historian Pliny describes them very clearly. The members of this family are truly aristocratic; they are beautifully formed and colored, some of them showing gorgeous shades of red and yellow.

But they are none the less deadly because of their beauty, "for they carry within them some of the most deadly poisons known to mankind."

The species we have illustrated is known as *muscaria* (from the Latin *musca*, a fly) because in some parts of Europe it is used as a fly poison. A dangerous practice, to be sure. *A. muscaria* is a sinister-looking thing, a large blood-red and yellow cap, covered with horrid white warts tops a fat white stem, the base of which is covered with the shredded remains of the volva. It is said to be found in various localities, in the open, in deep woods, or on the edge of woodland. According to Miss McKenny:

This mushroom has many historical associations. The Emperor Claudius is said to have died from eating it, and it is told that Lucrezia Borgia and Nero both used it to poison cast-off favorites. Lucrezia so loved its vivid orange hue that she had her portrait painted in a robe of that color.

And there is much more of a like unfortunate nature. It is certainly no plant to be encouraged in innocent gardens.

⬛ *Primula burmanica* (Plate 81)

Lovely Primulas are perfectly bewildering in their numbers. Though most Primulas in cultivation come from Europe, and others are found chiefly in the northern hemisphere, the genus wanders as far south as the Straits of Magellan. Some are whole-heartedly easy in the garden, others as whole-heartedly difficult. Few lack charm.

Primula burmanica (illustrated in Plate 81) was found by Kingdon Ward in one of his journeys to Upper Burma at an altitude of about eight thousand feet. It belongs to what is known as the Candelabra section; that is, the flowers on short stalks are borne in whorls one above another, ending in an umbel.

To the gardener with a dampish situation to fill, these Candelabra Primulas are a delight, for they are easy to grow, hardy, showy, come readily from seed; but they do require moisture. A good retentive loam suits them well, and a situation that is in partial shade. They are perfect for stream and pondside planting, and they may be grown in the rock garden or near it if you have a sufficient amount of space to give these robust plants. I have seen them thriving under an old Apple tree adjacent to a rock garden, where they appeared to be a part of the rocky scene, but where they in reality preëmpted none of the area that should be devoted to the smaller alpines.

Primula burmanica, despite its towering height of more than two feet, is a neat plant. The tuft of leaves is much like that of the common Primrose, but the stem rises straight and tall, encircled by its flowery whorls set rather close together so that the effect is very rich and splendid. The flowers are rosy, each with a yellow eye, and the calyx with its long pointed lobes is a distinctive feature. This species is rather new to cultivation, but seeds of it are offered in European catalogues; and if sown in late November or early December in a cold frame it will germinate freely in the spring. A number of the Candelabra Primulas are biennial or short-lived, but *P. burmanica* is a true perennial and as such should be prized. It is said that it will stand more sun than many of its kind—another point in its favor.

✠ Primulas, Candelabra Types of Various Kinds (Plate 82)

In Plate 82 is shown a group of the various types of Candelabra Primulas. From the gardener's point of view they are of utmost importance. They have infinite variety of color, and they are extremely hardy, asking only a retentive, somewhat moist soil to make them grow into great hearty clumps from which issue the tall straight stems with their whorls of gay flowers. They are Asiatic in origin. "All the species of the Candelabra section are plants of the moist meadows that occur so often on the edge of forests or among Bamboo from 7,000 to 12,000 feet in the Himalayas, the mountains of Upper Burma, and in Yunnan." They are easy to acquire, for seed is available of a number of the species as well as of very fine hybrids and it germinates readily if fresh, and great numbers of these striking plants may be had at small trouble and smaller cost. They may be grown in hundreds with fine effect in damp places, by stream or pondside, and when established seed themselves freely. Large clumps may also be pulled to pieces after flowering and set where they are wanted. Some of the finest are *P. anisodora*, one of Mr. Forrest's finds in Yunnan—a beautiful dark plum-purple in color, twelve to sixteen inches in height, and more or less biennial in duration; *Beesiana*, found by Mr. Forrest also in Yunnan—a variable plant often producing flowers that are undeniably magenta, but usually a good tone; *Bulleyana*, still another Forrest find in the wilds of Yunnan—a striking plant with flowers of a reddish orange tone; *Cockburniana*, introduced by E. H. Wilson from western Szechuan—this has less height than some of the others but makes up for the lack in the brilliant tone of its flame-colored flowers (with me it is frankly a biennial but occasionally self-sows on a modest scale); *helodoxa* from Yunnan, tall with pure yellow flowers; *japonica,* rather old in gardens, another variable species, sometimes magenta but producing strains with ruby-colored flowers as well as white ones with a pink eye, and sometimes white flowers stained with crimson that are not so pretty (a good ruby or white strain is to be treasured; if it self-sows it crosses easily with others, and so, to keep the strains pure, the blossoms should be cut off before they form seed). *P. pulverulenta* was found by Mr. Wilson in China near the Tibet border. It is very robust and tall and hardy, but its color falls short of being a good crimson. There are, however, two strains of it that are very lovely: the Bartley strain, having beautiful tones of rose and pink; and Mrs. Berkeley, the exquisite pale pink flower with a saffron eye.

All these Primulas cross very easily, so that it is not surprising that there are now on the market many hybrids and named strains. Asthore has coppery flowers; Ailin Aroon, flowers of a high scarlet; Red Hugh is fiery red, and Lissadel Hybrid has enchanting flowers in a wide range of soft vermilion tones. And there are many more. They come into bloom in late May and June, when most of the Primulas have gone over.

☙ *Tulipa Sprengeri* (Plate 83)

Tulipa Sprengeri is the latest of all the Tulips to flower, and as such it has a place of importance in the garden. It is neither as large nor as showy as some that come before it, but it has a very definite distinction. It is one of the species Tulips and grows wild in Armenia. The stem is about ten inches high, and the many erect leaves are a rich olive-green. The flower is neat and rather narrow in outline, with pointed petals, buff on the exterior and of a curious low tone of red on the interior, which is shown when the sun urges it to open wide. For all its red and yellow coloring it is a conservative Tulip in appearance, not flaunting. It flowers at the same time as the earlier Bearded Irises and makes a very handsome and rich ensemble with some of the warm purple varieties. It is one of the Tulip species that remain long in the garden, a good stayer, though it does not increase save very slowly. It seems not to mind crowding and grows well among other plants, which is not true of many of the species. Any who are interested in the species Tulips will want to grow it. It makes fine clumps in the rock garden, planted high on the hills, or it may be used in the borders. But it should never be brought into competition with the large-flowered hybrids, which put it out of countenance. Few if any of these, however, linger so late in the spring.

T. Sprengeri is nice for cutting, if you have enough of it, and its narrow pointed buds add much to the grace of the bouquet. In some gardens it is said to sow itself, but this is lucky ground. I have not known it to do so.

☙ *Aesculus octandra* (Yellow, Sweet, Big Buckeye) (Plate 84)

The Big Buckeye is an American tree found growing on the slopes of the Alleghenies, from western Pennsylvania south into Georgia and Alabama and wandering westward to Iowa and Texas. It is a very handsome tree, tall and imposing, with leaves composed of five "slenderly elliptical leaflets." It has showy yellowish tubelike flowers in long erect racemes in spring, and in the autumn the nuts, characteristic of the Horse Chestnuts, are smooth and shining. They are not fit for human food, but it is said that cattle munch them contentedly.

"Aesculus" is the ancient name for an Oak "or mast-bearing tree." There are about twenty-five species scattered over North America, south-

[*87*]

eastern Europe, and eastern Asia to India. It is the Horse Chestnut of eastern Asia that is most often planted for ornament in this country, especially in parks and along the streets of large cities. "It is a hardy immigrant, springing up spontaneously in some sections of our Eastern States."

The name "Buckeye," it is suggested, comes from the likeness of the brown nut marked with white to the eye of a deer. The name Horse Chestnut, according to Julia Ellen Rogers, whom I have quoted above, is employed to indicate that the fruit, which resembles the familiar edible Chestnut, is unfit for human consumption. "These nuts lie untouched by squirrels through the most trying of winters. They are intensely rank and bitter. The mission of the trees is therefore purely ornamental."

Ulex europaeus (Furze, Whin, Gorse) (Plate 85)

Any one who has seen an English common alight with blossoming Gorse bushes will understand their value as garden plants. Unfortunately it is only south of Philadelphia, or near the sea, that they will endure our bitter climate. It comes readily from seed, but the seedlings do not endure when planted out; even in Britain, where it is so plentiful, it is unknown in the cold Highlands of Scotland.

The prickly bushes grow from three to six feet tall, and the yellow pea-shaped blossoms make their appearance at all times of the growing season. There is a proverb to the effect, "When the gorse is out of flower, kissing is out of season."

The stems are dark green, and the pretty yellow flowers borne in great abundance lie along them like blobs of light. In England the Gorse flowers even in the winter. It appears to be a tough and hardy shrub but too much heat and too much cold, both of which it is bound to meet with in this country, are detrimental to it. It flourishes more certainly by the sea, in

[*88*]

Plate 81. *Primula burmanica*

Plate 82. PRIMULAS, CANDELABRA TYPES

Plate 83. *Tulipa Sprengeri,* THE LATEST TULIP TO BLOOM

Plate 84. *Aesculus octandra* (SWEET BUCKEYE)

Plate 85. *Ulex europaeus* (FURZE, WHIN, GORSE)

Plate 86. TROLLIUS HYBRIDS (GLOBE-FLOWERS) SHOWING THEIR
DELIGHTFUL COLOR TONES

Plate 87. SYRINGA (LILAC) PRESIDENT GRÉVY

Plate 88. SYRINGA (LILAC) RUHN VON HORSTENSTEIN

Plate 89. DOUBLE AND SINGLE TULIPS IN A JUG

Plate 90. EARLY SPRING FLOWERS ARRANGED IN POTTERY JAR

Plate 91. SPRING FLOWERS FROM WOOD AND BORDER IN JAR

Plate 92. A CARELESS ARRANGEMENT OF SPRING FLOWERS

protected places, than inland. The story is often told that when Linnæus first saw the Gorse in flower in England he fell upon his knees and gave thanks for such radiant beauty. In Europe it grows as far south as Provence; one sees it glimmering in thickets along French rivers, but in the north of Europe it is known only as a greenhouse plant. Anne Pratt writes:

> The Furze-bush is sometimes planted for hedges; and the poor in the neighborhood of a common frequently use it for fuel. In places where coals are very expensive and peat rare, it has even been cultivated for that purpose. It gives a good degree of heat while burning.

Like so many yellow-flowered plants, because of the old doctrine of signatures, it was esteemed in rural neighborhoods as a cure for jaundice.

In the autumn the many seed-pods open with a crackling sound.

> Moors where hares abound,
> While throbbing Furzes heart-struck burst their pods,
> Scattering ripe seeds amidst the moss around . . .

It is one of the few pea-shaped flowers that are known to produce a double form, and this is a most resplendent sight when in full flower. There is a dwarf variety, *Ulex nanus*, that begins to flower later in the year (about July) than the common Furze; but, though I have tried them all, they will not remain with me.

The group in Plate 85, by the waterside, is particularly well placed. It is splendid for clothing dry banks where it is hardy. It is not particular as to soil.

⚜ Trollius hybrids (Globe-Flowers) (Plate 86)

The Globe-Flowers are hardy erect perennials stout enough to require no support. They are useful in various parts of the garden, in beds and borders, by pond or streamside, where they are quite at home, or even in large rock gardens on the lower levels where the soil is not too dry. There are numerous species belonging to the Himalaya, Siberia, the Caucasus, China, Turkestan, Europe, and one American species, a pretty little early-flowering plant with creamy single blooms, *Trollius laxus*.

T. europaeus bears pale yellow globe-flowers in late May. There are now many hybrids of this species that cover a wide gamut of charming hues. In the plate (86) are to be seen Lemon Queen, with large round flowers, a strong and hardy grower; Goldinelle, a darker tone of yellow; Goliath, softly reddish, and finally we have the almost vermilion color of *japonica fl.-pl.* There are also Golden Wave, with giant orange-hued flowers; Etna, also orange-hued but not so large, very free-flowering; and Excelsior, orange in color and vigorous in habit.

Trollius Ledebouri, and its variety Golden Queen, are rather new introductions to American gardeners and are distinctive as well as being considerably later flowering.

The Globe-Flowers belong to the Buttercup family, and like all the Ranunculaceae are slow and difficult to raise from seed.

❦ Syringa President Grévy (Plate 87)

No Lilac grows naturally throughout the length and breadth of the American continent. But the plants came hither almost with the earliest settlers and took to the new country with ardent approval. Today by many a yawning cellar hole, in desolate forest clearings, or along lonely roadsides, the Lilac bushes keep faith with the ideal of a home and the desire for beauty. Pressed upon by the rough woodland shrubbery, given no care, seen by none, they wave their scented plumes unfailingly when May comes round. Their sweetness must be their own reward. When they

[*90*]

are in flower their fragrance seems to fill the world and make it a better place to live in.

According to Mr. Hottes, "They are believed to have reached Europe in 1597 by way of Constantinople and Vienna. Until recent years it was believed that the Lilac was a native of Persia, but it is found in the mountains of Bulgaria."

We are told, by the late Professor Sargent of the Arnold Arboretum, that the improvement of the Lilac is of fairly recent date—

from 1843 when a nurseryman of Liége in Belgium raised a plant with small double flowers. . . . It was this plant that Victor Lemoine chose as the first plant in his initial attempt to improve the garden Lilacs, fertilizing it with the best Lilacs of the day and with *Syringa oblata*, which was found by fortune in a Shanghai garden.

This was the beginning; the end is not yet, but the world has been filled with waving, scented plumes to the delight of all who have eyes to see and the faculty to enjoy fragrance.

The Lemoine hybrid President Grévy (Plate 87) is a very lovely variety. Lilacs are difficult to classify as to color because they change as they age, but the nearest to this one that can be arrived to is a delicate pinkish lilac with a faint bluish cast. It is a double variety, and its trusses are very full and handsome.

Syringa Ruhm von Horstenstein (Plate 88)

There are now so many hybrid Lilacs on the market that to choose among them is difficult, especially as there is a good deal of similarity among them. There are more single varieties, happily, than double, for these are more graceful and lovely than the more congested double varieties. The variety illustrated is a handsome single-flowered kind of a rich reddish purple.

Any one making a collection of "French Lilacs," as they are called, should visit them in Highland Park, Rochester, New York, or in the Arnold Arboretum, Boston, and see them in their glory. At these two parks are magnificent collections, and with pad and pencil one can leisurely choose the varieties that are the most pleasing, ordering them later.

The countries which have chiefly contributed to the improvement of the Lilac, until it is certainly the finest shrub in the world, are France, Belgium, Holland, and Germany.

No shrub in our gardens is more amenable to culture than the Lilac. It prefers an open location, free to sun and air. The soil should be deeply dug, and good for a long way down, slightly moist and well enriched, always well drained—this for the best results. Humus and lime mixed with the soil, it appreciates. "A light application of nitrate of soda early in the spring will be of temporary benefit, but it is not desirable as a regular thing. The nitrate, if applied late in the season, forces a growth which may not have time to ripen before winter comes."

The best time to plant Lilacs is early spring or late fall, when the leaves have fallen away. The gardener will choose a small plant in the nursery—that is, one about two feet tall—rather than the gangling five-footer which may attract him with the hope of quicker results in flowers. The hole into which the new plant is put should be spacious, and the soil well broken up at the bottom. In pruning Lilacs it is well to remember that none is better than too much. Remove old heavy canes entirely, cut out dead wood, and snip off the blossoms after they have faded. That is usually enough. In the early spring a generous amount of bone meal and wood ashes may be spaded in about the plants. These are counsels of perfection; if you cannot follow them, you will still have Lilacs of a beauty and sweetness that will enchant you. The colors run from snowiest white through cream to blush and quite deep pink, and on to reddish maroon; then there are those that have a decided bluish cast, and these are lovely. A fine collection of Lilacs is a proud and joyous possession; one good bush is food for the soul.

SPRING FLOWER ARRANGEMENTS

✠ Double and Single Tulips in a Jug (Plate 89)

In Plate 89 we have a gathering of May Tulips of many kinds and types rather closely crowded into a pottery jug. There are numerous double varieties, some Cottages with their vaselike shape—these are chiefly the yellow ones—some cup-shaped Darwins and Breeders. Fewer in the jug or some contrasting foliage or flowers, such as Apple blossoms, Lilacs, or Kolkwitzia, would have brought about a more pleasing effect. Nor are the double and single kinds particularly happy in each other's company.

✠ Early Spring Flowers Arranged in Pottery Jar (Plate 90)

Here in Plate 90 is a delightful arrangement of early spring flowers. It is unaffected and simple, and what could be prettier! We find, after studying the little bouquet, Snowdrops, Snowflakes, Hellebores, Crocuses, Anemones, Primroses, Hepaticas, Lungwort, some sprigs of Heather (*Calluna vulgaris*), and a few bits of early foliage. A low bowl holds them and embodies the very spirit of the young year in a small space.

✠ Spring Flowers from Wood and Border in Jar (Plate 91)

In Plate 91 we have an unstudied arrangement of slightly later-flowering blossoms than in Plate 90. They make a harmonious assemblage despite

[*93*]

their differences of form and color. There are Grape Hyacinths, Arabis, Violets, branches of Japanese Quince, Bellworts with their long pale bells, Barrenwort (Epimedium) with its pale yellow flowers and delicate foliage, Cyclamen, Lungwort, Golden Alyssum, and the red and green foliage of some foliage plant.

⚘ A Careless Arrangement of Anemones, Primroses, and Other Spring Flowers (Plate 92)

It is delightful to bring the early spring flowers indoors, for often the winds are too sharp to permit our enjoying them where they grow. In Plate 92 is a low, white rectangular bowl in which have been carelessly assembled the fruits of a quick turn around the garden. There are the little early-flowering *Scilla bifolia*, Anemones both blue and white, as well as the scarlet *Anemone fulgens*, the gold and purple flowers of *Iris reticulata*, Forget-me-nots, Muscari, and blue Primroses. The color scheme is mainly blue and white, and the touch of scarlet is just what is needed to give it life.

SUMMER

THE GARDEN IN SUMMER

SPRING is tense, exciting, but often withholding, sometimes even lean and stingy. It is a time of expectancy, of unrest. One peers about constantly anticipating something. "Expectation whirls me round" might be quoted of this season that is as maddening as it is lovely.

But when the days lengthen and the sun lies long on hill and field and garden, there is relaxation, realization. Leaves have gained size; colors, strength; grass is fully green and pied with small flowers; brooks flow more quietly, young birds are born, seeds sprout with assurance for frosts are over and done with, bees go about their business early and noisily. Overhead the sky is meekly blue. Before us lies June. Close the library door, get out smock and sunbonnet. "There can be no business in life more pressing than to wait in the still, green world, and to absorb the young summer with every breath."

Perhaps no month of the year is so wholly satisfying to the gardener as June. It offers a multitude of lovely flowers—Roses, Peonies, Iris—these three are enough for any one. "Enter, then, the rose-garden," wrote Dean Hole, "when the first sunshine sparkles in the dew, and enjoy with thankful happiness one of the loveliest scenes on earth." In June weeds have not got their full impetus, nor heat its full force. June is spring with its sharpness gone, its uncertainty become certainty, and it lacks the lavishness and the discomforts of full summer. "A gentle wind is in the heavy trees." To be out of doors from dawn and well into the dark is a delight. Who would not prolong the days of June? There is still so little to regret, so much to

[97]

hope for, so much to enjoy. Scents fill the air—from the flowers already mentioned, and from the dangling Locust tassels, from the ivory-strung Mock Orange bushes, from ribbons of snowy Pinks, from Lupines, Garden Heliotrope, Day Lily, Sweet William, Fraxinella and many more. June scents are rarely heavy or, as the old books had it, stuffing. They are light and pleasing, often delicately spicy.

When July comes in, summer, it may be said, gets down to business. There may be extreme heat, sultry nights, angry thunderstorms. Annual flowers take the garden and bring it unusual sparkle and variety. The sturdy Zinnia, the warm-hued Calendula, the pungent Marigold, Sweet Peas, Stocks, Snapdragons, Sweet Alyssum, Petunias, Verbenas, Nasturtiums make the summer colony, while the old settlers, the tall spires of Delphiniums, the early Phloxes, like Miss Lingard, numerous Lilies, many Campanulas, Hollyhocks, like village maidens in their Sunday clothes, the Mallows, watch the gay doings of the temporary inhabitants with some condescension.

Some of the starch and zip has gone out of ourselves and to relax beneath a heavily leafed tree seems the pleasantest occupation in the world. But there is little righteous rest for the gardener in July. Weeding must be carried on inexorably if he would keep ahead of these speedy outlaws; dead blossoms must be removed from the plants in order that the borders remain fresh and seemly; staking must be looked to with care, for it takes only one smashing storm to spoil the contours of a whole garden, and, once they are down, it is difficult to raise the stalks of tall plants or untangle the matted stems and flowers of low-growing things. Better stake early and thoroughly and avoid a ruined garden. At this season of the year, too, when days are long and hot, watering must be done. July is often a drought-ridden month, and the cool nights of August and September have not yet come to the relief of the suffering plants. The best time to water is when

[*98*]

the sun has begun to go down behind the horizon. And do not *sprinkle*—this does more harm than good. If you do not enjoy standing and holding the hose, letting your thoughts run out of the nozzle and spray in all directions, invest in one of the many sprinkling devices now on the market. Many of them will cover an area of fifty feet and more. Let it remain in one place until the ground is soaked well down beneath the surface. An hour is usually not too long. Then move it to cover another area. The fragrance of thankfulness that arises from the thirsty earth will be your reward for effort. No, you must not choose July as a month of relaxation if you are a gardener.

Perhaps with the arrival of August you may draw a few long breaths; you may have the weeds discouraged, you should have the staking done. There will still be wilted blooms to be removed and probably some watering—but watering is never really a task. In the garden the tall Phloxes hold glorious sway, and their warm scent fills both house and the outdoor world. If we have not been careful the August garden may show a monotonous predominance of the Daisy type of plant, members of the Compositae. They are innumerable, and most of them are so easy to grow that we turn to them lazily sure that they will thrive with little effort on our part.

But there are a number of things to be considered if we would have an attractive garden in August—coolness for one. If there is water in the garden—a little stream, a pool of any size, perhaps with a flying jet of water, you will be thankful for it in the weeks of warm, long days. Nothing more certainly brings a sense of refreshment than the sound of falling water; next are the wide green of Lily pads and fragrant Lilies lying upon quiet water that reflects the tumbling clouds against their blue background. The use of many white flowers is pleasant in the August garden—white Tobacco, Phlox, Petunias, Plantain Lilies, Cosmos, the flat white of Zinnias, Boltonia, white Stocks and Snapdragons, white Gladiolus. It is easy enough to fill the late summer garden with flowers of hot hues and coarse growth, but it takes a little casting about and careful selection to bring about a sense of repose and coolness. Beds of Heliotrope, Rose Geranium, and Lemon Verbena help, the cooler-colored Phloxes, seats under the trees, comfortable arbors, shielded by twining Honeysuckles, Blue Moonflowers, and the like.

In August, added to the scents of the garden are those of the countryside, of blossoming Clover, of new-cut hay, of ripening fruit; and the harvest sounds, the song of the mowing machine, the drone of crickets, have taken the place of the bird songs of the earlier year. The days are perceptibly shorter, the nights cooler, and opal mists creep thinly over the land. Summer is almost gone.

✠ *Astilbe Arendsii* (Plate 93)

A magnificent new race of hybrid plants has been created by the crossing of the old *Spiraea japonica, S. Thunbergii, S. sinensis*, and others with *Astilbe Davidii*, and probably with others of this hardy race. They are strong-growing perennials with 2–3 ternately compound leaves, having beautifully cut leaflets, and bearing in early June and July superb plumes of small flowers ranging in color from pure white through cream to pale pink and salmon to richest carmine. These plumes are often a foot and a half in length, and when massed make a splendid display.

The plants are easy to grow if they are given a rich soil with plenty of moisture. Dry situations are inimical to their best development. Waterside situations are happy for them, and they grow well under the same conditions as suit the Japanese Iris; also they are the most becoming companions for these regal flowers, the spreading Iris blooms and the long plumelike panicles of the Astilbes complementing each other to perfection.

[*100*]

There are many named *Arendsii* hybrids to choose from, some of the best of which are the following: America, pale pink, 2 ½ feet, July; Avalanche, pure white, three feet, July; Betsy Cuperus, white and pink, three feet, flowering late, July–August; Gerbe d'Argent, pure white, 2 ½ feet, July; Gloria, deep pink, 2 feet, July–August; Granat, deep crimson, 2 feet, July–August; Irene Rottsieper, salmon-pink, 2 feet, June–July; Juno, fine violet-rose, June, 3 feet; Marguerite van Reechteren, rose-red fringed panicles, very tall, nearly four feet, August; Professor van der Wielen, fully four feet, pure white, flowering in July; Pyramidal, white, 2–3 feet, July; Rose Pearl, blush-pink, 2 ½ feet, July–August; Salland, rich carmine, 3 feet, August; Vesta, mauve-pink, 3 feet, July–August; Queen Alexandra, pure soft pink, 2 ½ feet, June–July; Peach Blossom, pale pink, July, 2 ½ feet.

❦ A Border of Astilbes Against a Green Background (Plate 94)

In Plate 94 we see the hybrid Astilbes massed in a more or less formal planting. The green background and edging help to show up their glowing color. Later in the season the other plants in the border doubtless take their place in making a display.

If one starts with a few Astilbe plants it is easy to increase the stock until such a massing as the one here shown is accomplished. Not only are they easy to grow, but they are easily propagated by division of the roots or the removal of rooted offsets. A few plants will furnish almost any number of rooted bits. The operation of division may be carried out at almost any season, but the best time is perhaps when the foliage has died down in the autumn. Wherever they are planted, if naturally dampish conditions do not prevail water must be given artificially without stint for the best results.

[*101*]

✠ *Hemerocallis aurantiaca major* with Bearded Iris (Plate 95)

Bearded Iris and the yellow Day Lilies belong naturally together. They like the same sorts of situations and look exceedingly well in each other's company. The Hemerocallis or Day Lilies belong to the Lily family, and the name comes from the Greek *hemera*, a day, and *kallos*, beauty, in reference to the fact that each flower remains in beauty for a day only. They grow from short rhizomes with numerous fleshy roots, and they are extremely hardy and enduring. They grow well in ordinary borders, but prefer a soil that is not bone-dry; and they are ideal waterside subjects. They are readily propagated by division.

The plant shown in Plate 95 is a fine Japanese species, growing from two to three feet tall, with handsome tufts of bright green foliage and wide Apricot-colored flowers. It is a great improvement on the type, which has orange-red flowers. It blooms in June and, unlike many of its kind, is without scent. It is said that this species came from Japan "as a tiny stray seedling in a batch of water Iris" and proved at once "a find." The blossoms are almost six inches across, and their Apricot color is tinted on the outer petals with brown. The leaves are handsome, an inch across and strongly ribbed.

Today, collecting Day Lilies is a major and very rewarding garden sport. Besides the many species there are now innumerable hybrids, for accomplished horticulturists on both sides of the water are giving their attention to the creation of new and improved varieties. They are to be had with flower stalks from a few inches in height to, in some cases, nearly six feet. In color they cover the whole scale from primrose to full yellow, to orange and the tawny fulvous tones. They can be had in bloom, one kind or another, from May until August. Dr. A. B. Stout of the New York Botanical Garden, one of the foremost growers, says of them: "They

[*102*]

thrive in an ordinary flower garden without special care or attention. Garden weeds cannot crowd them—cannot compete with their compact and sturdy habits of growth. The fleshy roots of Daylilies withstand and defy ordinary periods of drought. The home gardener may take a vacation in summer without fear that his choice Daylilies will suffer for want of care. No garden plant is more reliable, more self-sufficient."

⚏ Iris, Hemerocallis, and Japanese Maples Bordering a Rectangular Pool (Plate 96)

Along the sides of this narrow canal-like pool is an early June planting that is very effective (Plate 96). Here are massed the early-flowering Day Lilies with Bearded Iris, the latter in pale yellow, light blue, and pale pink tones. Towards the upper end may be seen a plantation of Globe Flowers (Trollius), and there are a Japanese Maple and a few plumes of Astilbe. Among the many Hemerocallis (Day Lilies) that flower early enough to companion the Bearded Iris are the following: *citrina*, 3 feet, pale yellow; *Dumortierii*, 18–24 inches, orange-yellow; *flava*, the old Lemon Lily and one of the sweetest-scented, 3 feet; *luteola*, 4 feet, golden yellow; *minor*, the earliest and one of the dwarfest, 12–18 inches, soft yellow; Apricot, 2 feet, pure orange; Gold Dust, 2 feet, a lovely yellow; Orangeman, 3 feet, early June; and *Middendorffii*, early, 2 feet, orange-yellow. The trend in the creation of new Day Lilies is towards later flowering, larger blooms on taller stems, and variety in hue. Some lean towards pink, but it is still a far cry to a genuinely pink Day Lily. Dr. Stout is developing some very dwarf kinds, only a few inches tall, that will be of the utmost use in the rock garden. He has also done much to improve the harshness of the fulvous tones. He also has his chariot hitched to the star of a pure white Hemerocallis.

[*103*]

Both Irises and Day Lilies make a good permanent planting because their foliage remains sightly and in good condition throughout the season—many plants, when their blossoms fail, seem to lose ambition and more or less go to pieces, but these two with their narrow, fresh green leaves are sightly until after hard frosts. Thus they keep their sections of the borders looking well kept and neat.

✿ *Iris sibirica superba* (Plate 97)

Iris sibirica, the type, was introduced to gardens from central and southern Europe and Siberia about 1596; so it is an old inhabitant of gardens and one of the most commonly grown. It is distinguished in its best forms by a hollow stem three feet tall and more that rises high above the narrow foliage and bears several flowers that have the light appearance of butterflies. These flowers are smaller than those of the Bearded Irises, but their floriferousness creates a fine effect. A number of plants set near together present a solid sheet of color. They are ideal waterside plants and indeed require a rich, deep, and dampish soil for their best development. If there are low places in the garden, a plantation of Siberian Irises will thrive there. But they must not be set beneath trees; they require plenty of sunshine, as well as moisture.

This type of Iris is easily raised from seed, and those who embark upon this interesting operation may expect some happy surprises among the seedlings, which if well treated will flower the second year. While the color is usually some tone of blue marked with white, there is infinite variety on this theme, some with taller stems, with more flowers, with a greater proportion of white, or with the blue of a deeper and richer tone. Hybridists have been at work on this versatile Iris, and there are now many varieties to be had. Among the better known are *superba* (illustrated)

[*104*]

with large violet-blue flowers and handsome foliage, a splendid kind for waterside planting; Blue King, deep blue-purple; Distinction, violet; George Wallace, soft blue with much white veining; Lady Godiva, white with lavender markings; Perry Blue, a superb light blue; Snow Queen, flowers pure white and produced in great numbers; Emperor, large flowers of deep violet-blue. And there are many newer kinds: Butterfly, Skylark, Kingfisher Blue, and others.

To increase our stock of these Beardless Irises the roots may be freely divided, the best time for this operation being in late August or early September. It may also be done in early spring, but this will result in a lack of bloom for that season.

Unless it is desired to increase the stock, plants that are doing well may be left to themselves. Mrs. C. S. McKinney, in her book "Iris in the Little Garden," says she has kept plants in "fine vigor and within bounds for ten years by taking pieces off from the sides and filling the holes with rich compost." She also uses bone meal and tankage—"a valuable nitrogenous fertilizer"—to feed these hungry plants.

Some of the varieties now known as *I. sibirica* hybrids are in reality the offspring of a closely allied species, *I. orientalis*, which is perhaps the true Siberian Iris.

The season of blossoming of these Irises is late May and early June. They should not be planted near the large-flowered Beardless group as they suffer in comparison; or, rather, in the presence of these great-blossomed varieties their smaller butterfly flowers are less appreciated.

☞ Lovely Color Forms of *Papaver orientale* (Oriental Poppy) (Plate 98)

The old Oriental Poppy, a plant introduced from Armenia about 1714, has been of late years on the black list in gardens because of its flaming scarlet color. In *Curtis' Botanical Magazine*, Volume II, is a colored drawing of it and the following account: "Though a native of the East, as its name imports, it bears the severity of our climate without injury, flowers in May and as its blossoms are extremely shewy, it gives great brilliancy to the flower-garden or plantation; prefers a dry soil."

Later this "great brilliancy," that intrigued our gardening forbears, brought it into disrepute. A scarlet flower was only less terrible than a scarlet sin; in fact, it was regarded as just that in a nicely color-schemed garden. But it was such a hardy and valuable plant, growing and blossoming vigorously with almost no care, that something had to be done about it. Today there are a vast number of them in the most delicate and lovely colors that need offend no one. A few of these to choose from are the following: Ethel Swete, brilliant cherry-pink with black markings; Mahony, maroon, shaded crimson; Mrs. Perry, lovely salmon-pink; Mrs. Stobart, soft old rose; Perry White, gleaming white with maroon blotches at the base of the petals; Princess Victoria Louise, delicate salmon-pink; Rose Beauty, clear rose-pink; Salmon Queen; Wunderkind, brilliant carmine-pink; Mrs. John Harkness, orange-apricot; and Queen Alexandra, soft rose.

The Oriental Poppies grow from two to three feet tall; their leaves are somewhat coarse and hairy, their stems strong and also hairy. The flowers are so large and heavy that save in sheltered locations it is the part of wisdom to tie the stems to light slender stakes. After flowering and maturing their great crowned seed-pods, the plants die away, but revive again with the autumn rains. While a plant is taking its well earned rest, a *Gypsophila paniculata* Bristol Fairy may be set near it, and the cloudy masses of this plant will fill the blank space for a time. The plants like full sunshine, though they will flower in partial shade, in a good soil.

These Oriental Poppies do not come true from seed—that is, they are

[*106*]

not to be counted upon—and so it is best, if we are very sensitive to color, to see a collection in flower in some near-by nursery and pick them out then and there. The plants increase rapidly into good-sized clumps, and these may be divided to increase the stock of some especially liked hue, or they may be propagated from root cuttings.

❀ Paeonia Mme. Louis Henry (Plate 99)

In the neighborhood of New York the first of June usually brings a burst of Peonies—that is, of what we commonly call the Chinese varieties, most of which are descendants of *P. albiflora* or its variety *sinensis*, still found growing wild, it is said, in northeastern Asia. "When Chinese Peonies were first brought to Europe, about 1800, there were more than a hundred distinct varieties already existing in Chinese gardens."

These superb flowers immediately became popular in European gardens and were soon brought to America, where they settled down as to the manner born. It is difficult to think of any faults possessed by these plants. They are as hardy as iron, will live for years, outlasting whole families, indeed, without special attention, are beautiful, and many of them have a delicious fragrance. There are today literally thousands of varieties to be had in every tone of pink and scarlet, rose and maroon, as well as pure white, often flecked with red. There are no pure yellows among the Chinese Peonies, though some incline in that direction, and no pure blues. *P. lutea* is a Chinese species with bright yellow flowers, and in Primavère and Laura Dessert, the center of the flower is primrose-colored, and Couronne d'Or is tinged with it. Many Chinese Peonies have a delightful opalescent effect, among these the semi-double Marie Jacquin and the truly double Solange. The forms the flowers of the different kinds take are many and lovely; some are single with a brush of golden stamens at

[*107*]

the heart; some, semi-double; some, fully double; and there are numerous additional types, the Japanese, the Anemone-flowered, the Crown, the Bomb, the semi-rose, and the Challenger. Any representative Peony catalogue offers untold riches to the seeker.

As is the case with many plants that will survive with little attention, results will be doubled with fair or good cultivation and care. In the first place, buy your plants of a reputable dealer and prepare your bed or border thoroughly beforehand. The soil should be on the heavy side (but not clayey) and fairly rich; also it should be well drained. Wood ashes, lime, humus, and well rotted manure may all be used to put the soil in prime condition. Sand and coal ashes may be added when clay predominates. The plants will do well in either full sun or partial shade, and protection from driving winds, in the shape of a fence, wall, or hedge is an advantage. Fall planting is far more satisfactory than spring planting. I have planted Peonies as late as December, when the holes had to be dug with a pick, and they throve. But this is not desirable. September and October are perhaps the best planting months. As a well grown plant has a wide spread, the plants should be set at least three feet apart. Do not set the plants too deep in the soil. Two inches down is sufficient. To keep the young plants from being disturbed during the winter freezing and thawing, a light mulch of leaves or salt hay should be spread over them. In after years, when the plants have become established, this is not needed.

When one has the intention of making a collection of Peonies, it is well to visit a nursery specializing in these plants and there make the selection. To read a Peony catalogue plunges one into confusion and indecision.

❦ *Potentilla nepalensis*, Miss Willmott (Plate 100)

This is a beautiful and free-flowering dwarf variety suited for use at the front of sunny borders or in fairly spacious rock gardens. The type comes from Nepal, but Miss Willmott's variety or *Willmottiae*, is a great improvement over it. It grows about a foot high, and the blossoms are a lovely salmon-rose color with darker centers. Unless the weather is very hot and dry, they will continue to appear all summer. In any case, with the late summer and autumn rains the plants will revive and begin to flower again. As is the case with all the race, the leaves are much like those of a strawberry. There are many other Potentillas worth growing, the largest number having yellow flowers.

❦ *Geranium platypetalum* (Plate 101)

Geranium platypetalum is sometimes regarded as a form of the Caucasian *G. ibericum*, an improved form. It is a splendid border plant, beautiful throughout the season and having but one fault. It crowds its flowering into too short a period—into, as a matter of fact, about ten days early in June. Before it flowers, it makes a beautiful rounding mass of handsome downy leaves. After its brief flowering, if the withered blooms and seed pods are cut off it again assumes this pleasant contour. In the autumn the leaves are tinged with rich red.

The flowers, so copiously borne, are a warm blue-purple in tone with the usual crimson veining common to so many Geraniums. They are of no use for cutting, but in the border they make a quite resplendent effect. The plants grow about eighteen inches high and do not need staking; but they should be set near the front of the border, so that the rounded mass of leaves can curve outwards to the ground and the pleasing outline will

[*109*]

not be destroyed by the inroads of plants in front of it. This Geranium likes and responds to rich soil and sunshine, though it does not care for damp situations. A plant may be left for years without division; it will not spread out of bounds but merely grow more opulent year by year.

The border Geraniums are not nearly so often grown as they should be in this country. Among the first-class kinds are *G. sanguineum album*, which makes great rounded masses of small leaves that in early June are almost hidden beneath a cloak of paper-thin white flowers; *G. Endressi*, with raspberry-pink blossoms; *G. pratense*, the Meadow Geranium or Cranesbill, which comes with blue, pale blue, or pure white flowers (it grows two or three feet tall, has the usual handsome leaves, is a fine subject either for borders or for massing at the edge of woodlands, and does not mind a bit of shade). *G. grandiflorum*, from the Himalaya regions, is perhaps the bluest of all, and not as tall as some; *G. Wallichianum* is a sprawling plant that flowers all through the late summer and autumn, and as its leaves begin to turn red the combination made by blue flowers and reddening leaves is a delightful one. The variety Buxton's is the best and bluest. It also is a Himalayan plant. These Geraniums are easy to raise from seed, so none need go without them.

⚜ *Iris Xiphium* (Spanish Iris) (Plate 102)

The Spanish Iris has been called the poor man's Orchid, because of its lovely range of colors and its exquisite lightly modeled form. It flowers rather late and is valuable in prolonging the Iris season. In some localities it seems not to be absolutely hardy; this tenderness seems not to be accounted for by the behavior of the thermometer but is more a matter of a sufficiency of snow, which protects the young growth that these Irises make in the autumn.

[*110*]

They love sunshine and a warm protected location out of the neighborhood of heavily pressing perennials which would lean upon them and distort their slender grace. The Spanish Iris is an old flower in gardens, for it was grown by the ancient herbalist Gerard (1633); of late years it has been a chief concern of florists, who have multiplied its numbers and extended its scale of colors. The foliage is slender, and the flower stem rising far above it carries two or three blossoms that have the fluttering aspect of butterflies. These plants grow from true bulbs and should be set out in September or early October. The wise gardener will grow a collection in the cutting garden, for no flowers are more delightful for this purpose. They last well in water.

There are many varieties, the colors embracing most tones of true blue, yellow, lavender, pure white, bronze, and some delightful combinations of these hues. A selection would include the following: Cajanus, canary-yellow with orange touches on the falls; Belle Chinoise, pure yellow and early; Flora, cream and pale blue; Excelsior, violet and French gray; Golden Wonder, a rich color and delicately crimped petals; Golden Lion, lemon-yellow, with deeper-toned falls, a tall and sturdy grower; King of Blues, very fine deep blue and a strong plant; King of Whites, purest white with an orange touch on the falls; Philomela, blue with white falls; Hercules, bronze with orange blotch; Thunderbolt, a very large bronze-colored flower.

❦ A Handsome Form of Bearded Iris (Plate 103)

The tall Bearded Iris is perhaps one of the six most important plants grown in our gardens today, the others being Narcissus, Tulip, Delphinium, tall Phlox, and Chrysanthemum. A modern catalogue of Irises presents a confusing problem, for their name is legion, and still they come,

[*111*]

year after year their numbers being added to. New varieties are easily raised, and the enthusiasm of Iris raisers seems never to wane.

It is easy, however, to have too many in the garden, for they take up considerable space, spreading generously. The tiny root purchased today for a fat price will in a few years have become the great-great-grandfather of many. So it is wise to buy carefully, visiting a good Iris collection and choosing those that please us most from the flowering specimens in the field. The great trouble is that nearly all are beautiful. One may, however, have a particular color scheme in mind that will help one to make a selection—pink, blue, maroon, purple, yellow, brown and fawn, gray or pure white, and combinations of these colors *ad infinitum*. The modern Pogon, or Bearded Iris, tends to grow larger of flower, taller of stem, and sometimes these tall-stemmed flowers do not make as fine, close masses of color in the garden as do some of the dwarfer forms, such as the old Mrs. Alan Gray or the dainty and charming Bluet. The modern wonders may reach to the amazing height of well over fifty inches; the stems will be three- to four-branched; the flowers, perfect in symmetry and of firm texture. As spectacles they are astonishing; as garden flowers they are a little overpowering.

Their culture offers few difficulties; one finds bold clumps of "escaped" Bearded Irises flourishing by the dusty wayside. But better culture of course brings better results. What they prefer is abundant sunshine, a rich soil deeply dug and with plenty of lime (devoid of manure, however), and generous watering while the buds are forming if the weather is dry. The best time to plant or to transplant is soon after they have flowered. Cut the plants back a little, and after they are set out do not give them a great deal of water until they are settled in.

When it comes to a choice of kinds I name here a dozen, not the newest, not the most expensive, not the largest, and embracing a wide

Plate 93. *Astilbe Arendsii*

Plate 94. A BORDER OF ASTILBES AGAINST A GREEN BACKGROUND

Plate 95. *Hemerocallis aurantiaca* (DAY LILY) WITH BEARDED IRIS

Plate 96. IRIS, HEMEROCALLIS AND JAPANESE MAPLE PLANTED ABOUT A NARROW RECTANGULAR POOL

Plate 97. *Iris sibirica superba*

Plate 98. LOVELY COLOR FORMS OF *Papaver orientale* (ORIENTAL POPPY)

Plate 99. PAEONIA MME. LOUIS HENRY

color range: Alta California, 48 inches, deep yellow with bronze on the falls; Baldur as illustrated (Plate 103); Black Wings, 40 inches, intense blackish blue and sweet-scented; Mary Geddes, 36 inches, a lovely blend of pink and reddish tones; Mary Senn, 42 inches, rosy-pink and brown, fragrant; Pink Satin, 46 inches, one of the best "pink" Irises; Sierra Blue, 50 inches, exquisite tone of soft blue; Shah Jehan, an amazing blend of buff and gray and plum-red; Modoc, velvety blackish purple, 36 inches; Mary Barnett, 42 inches, lovely light blue and fragrant; Easter Morn, 48 inches, pure white; Dauntless, 40 inches, rich reddish tone.

Iris Kaempferi (I. laevigata Kaempferi) (Japanese Iris) (Plate 104)

Japanese Irises are among the wonders of the flower world. The astonishing ingenuity and skill of the Japanese hybridists have gone to the perfecting of this their beloved flower. So beautiful are they in color, in blends of color, in shape, and so amazing in size that words are inadequate to describe them. Their flowering closes the Iris season, early in July. Some of the flowers are single, some double, and the colors embrace most of the spectrum.

For culture they require a deep rich, well cultivated soil and all the water that we can give them. They are noble plants for growing by lake or stream where the roots can go down to water, but they may be grown successfully in dryer locations if the ground is kept stirred so as to form a dry mulch, and water is given them freely, especially when the buds are forming. They may be planted in April and May, or in September and October.

The plants are tall and lend themselves to what might be termed "scenic displays." No Japanese garden is complete without masses of them, and they are effective with a background of Japanese Maples. Also,

[*113*]

if they are grown by the waterside, Astilbes in harmonizing colors are perfect with them. Masses of white Japanese Irises against blue Delphiniums constitute a lovely association, and the blue and purple varieties are attractive associated with the yellow-flowered Meadow Rue, *Thalictrum glaucum*. They bloom at the same time, and the gray foliage of the Meadow Rue is a fine background for the wide flat flowers.

Japanese Irises do not like the encroachments of other plants; they should be grown well away from the heartier perennials, their royal aloofness respected.

⚘ Varieties of *Pyrethrum roseum* (Painted Daisies) (Plate 105)

Among the most effective and useful plants for the late spring and early summer borders are the Painted Daisies. The name describes them very well. The flowers are Daisy-like in form, and the colors run from white through pale pink to deep crimson and maroon. Some are single and some are double. The foliage is a clump of feathery leaves, out of which the flowers arise on long stems and in great profusion. The plants are absolutely hardy, and they are certain doers in any sunny border where the soil is reasonably rich and well drained. If the situation is sheltered and there is certain moisture during the summer, so much the better. But they are not demanding in these matters. These amiable plants will give a fair degree of satisfaction even in partially shaded situations and where the soil is on the poor side. But good culture and a rich soil are well repaid by the great number of blossoms and the lush foliage. It should be borne in mind, however, that while these plants are very accommodating they dislike above all things a heavy clay soil, and such should be improved by the addition of sand, coal ashes, strawy manure, or even gravel. In borders they are most effective when placed in groups of three or five rather than as single specimens, with a space of at least twelve inches between plants. The flowers seem to possess all the virtues inherent in a good cut flower— a generous length of stem, long life in water, and a wide scale of charming hues. The double flowers last longer when cut than the single, but they are less graceful when seen in the garden.

Pyrethrums are raised from seed with the greatest ease, but they are not to be counted upon to come true to color. The best plan is to buy a few plants of the preferred colors and increase them by division. The plants quickly grow into thrifty clumps, and these may easily be pulled apart in spring to make any number of new plants. In fact, division every three years is a necessity if the quality and quantity of the blooms is to be kept up to standard.

Some persons stake their Pyrethrums, tying each stem to a slender stake or winding strands of raffia between stakes placed around the plants. In very exposed situations perhaps this is a necessity, but it is an unfortunate one as they are not among the plants that may be well and inconspicuously staked. It is better, it seems to me, to take the chance of having the blossoms battered down by storms than to spoil the grace of the plants by the intrusion of stiff stakes. Among the plants that flower with Pyrethrums are the little Chinese Delphiniums, Irises, Pinks and Violas, and Columbines.

Anchusa italica, Dropmore Variety (Italian Bugloss) (Plate 106)

This blue-flowered plant was introduced from the Mediterranean region about 1810. There have been times in its short history when it threatened to supplant the Delphinium in the hearts of gardeners. It was as purely blue and it was so much easier to please. But florists have now placed the Delphinimum upon a firm pedestal, while the pretty Anchusa

[*115*]

has remained comparatively unimproved. For all its wealth of blue flowers in the early summer days, it has to be admitted that its foliage is coarse and hairy and the whole plant as well suited to the wild garden as to the borders. There have been a few "improved" forms introduced—Dropmore, Opal, Pride of Dover, Morning Glory, Lissadel Variety—all good sturdy plants growing from three feet to, in the case of Morning Glory, nearly six feet, and varying somewhat in their tone of pure blueness.

In some soils they prove to be biennial, but often they continue from year to year and contribute an easily attained beauty to the borders. They require to be staked in some inconspicuous manner, perhaps with stout brush that the stems may lean against or with slender stakes. Interplanted with certain other plants, they are charming. The old Garden Heliotrope, *Valeriana officinalis*, with its pinkish gray heads of fragrant bloom is lovely with the Anchusas, as are the salmon-colored form of *Lychnis chalcedonica;* Sweet Rocket, *Hesperis matronalis alba;* numerous Day Lilies (Hemerocallis); Oriental Poppies, all colors; Sweet Williams, and Pinks.

Rose Hofgaertner Kalb (Plate 107)

This lovely and glowing Rose is said to be a cross between Rose Souv. de Mme. Eugène Verdier and Gruss an Teplitz. It is a good bushy variety, vigorous and upstanding. The flowers are a fine carmine-rose in color, tinted with yellow, and they are "large, well-shaped, double, full and moderately fragrant." It is very floriferous and blooms intermittently throughout the season. Although it is usually classed as a Hybrid Tea, J. Horace McFarland in his book "Roses of the World in Color" classes it as a China, saying, "Another really good China Rose . . . properly to be classed with Hermosa and similar persistent blooming types, this rose brings some of the virtues of Gruss an Teplitz into its fine carmine-rose blooms tinted with transparent yellow." He goes on to say that this variety has never been boomed or exploited but deserves greater prominence.

The China Roses all have a certain delicacy of texture and modeling, and their continuous flowering right up to hard frost is a most ingratiating quality. And they begin to flower very early in June. They are delightful for bedding. Gruss an Teplitz blooms in open clusters, and this pleasant habit is inherited by Hofgaertner Kalb.

⚑ Rose Lady Forteviot (Plate 108)

A Hybrid Tea Rose of exceptional beauty, Lady Forteviot is one of those varieties whose color is difficult to describe. It lies somewhere between gold and apricot of a deep tone. It has large buds that open out into "large, double high-centered flowers, very lasting and extremely fragrant, borne several together on a long strong stem." The foliage is luxuriant, a fine bronze-green in tone, and its shining surfaces seem to be proof against disease. The habit of the bush is vigorous, and it grows no more than two and one-half feet tall. It blooms constantly throughout the summer and is exceptionally hardy. This fine Rose won the Gold Medal of the N.R.S. in 1927 and an Award of Merit from the R.H.S. in 1928.

⚑ Rose Dame Edith Helen (Plate 109)

This remarkable Rose, upon its introduction in 1926 by A. Dickson and Sons, sprang into immediate and almost world-wide popularity. It made a genuine sensation in the world of Roses and won the Clay Cup for that year and the Gold Cup for the best Rose of the year, as well as many gold medals and awards of merit and testimonials from various sources.

And it deserved them all. Though it made its bow more than ten years ago, it is still one of the most popular of Roses. The flowers are extremely large, cupped and fully double. They are borne singly on long stems, which makes them fine for cutting. The color is a full warm pure pink, and the flowers are long-lasting in water or on the bush. They have the lovely fragrance that we know as the "old Rose scent." The foliage is rather small but of good substance and disease-resistant. The growth of the bush is vigorous.

Its chief flowering time is in June but occasionally thereafter a lovely flower may be given, especially as the days grow shorter and the nights cooler. Dr. McFarland says of it, "This Rose should probably be in the Hybrid Perpetual class, though the flowers do sometimes recur, and when they come each flower is an event."

❦ Rose Le Rêve (Plate 110)

Rose Le Rêve was introduced by the French firm Pernet-Ducher in 1923. G. A. Stevens in "Climbing Roses" says of it: "Beyond doubt this is the finest clear, unfading yellow climbing rose which will grow in the northern states. The large, clear yellow buds and blooms are produced in bewildering profusion very early in the season. Plant is moderately vigorous, reaching twelve to fifteen feet. Foliage is beautiful but very susceptible to disease, and the plant is usually bare from midsummer on. In spite of its disreputable appearance at that season, it is worth particular care because of its great beauty in springtime."

This Hybrid Tea Rose is said to be a cross between Mme. Eugène Verdier and Persian Yellow. The flowers are described by Dr. McFarland as pure sunflower-yellow, borne several together on a long stem, and very fragrant. It is a profuse bloomer in June.

One of its forbears, the Persian Yellow, is a very old Rose in gardens.

[*118*]

It was introduced from Persia in 1837 by Sir H. Willock. It makes a beautiful free-growing bush of considerable height and vigor, or climbing where conditions of climate suit it sometimes to the upper stories of old houses. The flowers are bright yellow and full and freely produced. It is a better Rose than the old Harison's Yellow, for the flowers have a charming way of following along the cane and so making of it a sort of flowery wand. The foliage is faintly and pleasantly scented, but the flowers are better held away from a sensitive nose. Its formal name is *Rosa foetida persiana.*

☙ Rose Hiawatha (Plate 111)

This is a climbing Rose of American birth, introduced by M. H. Walsh in 1904. It is one of the finest of the *Wichuraiana* Roses, though not new. The flowers are single and borne in great open clusters, deep carmine in color with white centers. It is a vigorous, strong-growing variety, flowering late, and a well grown plant is a brilliant sight on a shining June day. The brush of golden anthers in the center seems to make the whole flower glow. It is a very handy variety with strong, disease-resistant foliage, abundant, shining, and of much substance. It may be made to climb or to trail over stumps or rough banks, and it is lovely trained against a garden wall with spires of pale blue Delphiniums using it as a background. It is a Wichuraiana hybrid. The true *Wichuraiana* Rose is a native of Korea. It is a creeper rather than a climber, and the foliage is nearly evergreen. When introduced into America about the middle of the nineteenth century, it was immediately recognized as something unusual, its tough, almost evergreen foliage making it an ideal ground cover. The flowers of the type are creamy white and borne in profusion.

According to Mr. Stevens ("Climbing Roses") the first hybrids were produced at Newport, Rhode Island, by M. H. Horvath, not later than 1896. "Four were originated, two of which came from pollen of the old Polyantha, . . . and the other two from the China rose, Agrippina." The French later became interested in producing Roses of the *Wichuraiana* type, and today there are a vast number to choose from, most of them cluster-flowered but some like Dr. Van Fleet with very large flowers on long stems; but always there are the sturdy character, the strong shining foliage and the rampant growth. "The trailing habit has been largely overcome, but these roses are never as stiff as Multifloras and lack the coarseness of that type." Some charming *Wichuraiana* hybrids are the following: Albéric Barbier, creamy white with yellow centers, small sprays, fragrant; Alida Lovett, large shell-pink flowers shaded pale yellow, extra strong-growing; American Pillar, brilliant crimson-pink with large white center and conspicuous golden stamens; Breeze Hill, large flat double flowers, white tinted with yellow, rose, and apricot, in clusters, late-flowering; Mary Wallace, bright pink, semi-double; Aviateur Bleriot, coppery orange in the bud, opening white, needs protection; Bloomfield Courage, extremely vigorous and astoundingly floriferous, "enormous, loose clusters of small, single, blackish crimson flowers with quilled petals, followed by a fine display of scarlet hips in autumn"; Emily Gray, semi-double, pale primrose flowers, needs protection in winter; Evangeline, pale pink small flowers in large clusters, delicious perfume; Gardenia, one of the earliest *Wichuraiana* hybrids, very vigorous, fine foliage, flowers pale yellow in the bud but opening white; Ile de France, enormous clusters of warm pink, semi-double flowers, slow to fade; Jacotte, large, coppery blooms, and hardier than most yellow climbers, very fine foliage; Mary Lovett, large beautifully modeled white flowers borne profusely in mid-summer and with an occasional bouquet offered in the autumn, lovely; Newport Fairy, flowers in large cluster, pale pink, lovely and vigorous;

[*120*]

Plate 100. *Potentilla nepalensis*, MISS WILLMOTT

Plate 101. *Geranium platypetalum*

Plate 102. *Iris Xiphium* (SPANISH IRIS)

Plate 103. A HANDSOME FORM OF BEARDED IRIS

Plate 104. *Iris Kaempferi (I. laevigata Kaempferi)* (JAPANESE IRIS)

Plate 105. VARIETIES OF *Pyrethrum roseum* (PAINTED DAISIES)

Plate 106. *Anchusa italica*, DROPMORE VARIETY (ITALIAN BUGLOSS)

Plate 107. ROSE HOFGAERTNER KALB, HYBRID TEA

Plate 108. ROSE LADY FORTEVIOT, HYBRID TEA

Plate 109. ROSE DAME EDITH HELEN, HYBRID TEA

Plate 110. ROSE LE RÊVE, CLIMBING HYBRID TEA

Plate III. ROSE HIAWATHA, CLIMBING OR TRAILING ROSE OF RAMBLER TYPE

Paradise, large clusters of single white flowers with notched petals, very vigorous and fine; Paul's Scarlet Climber, a magnificent rose of moderate vigor, bearing a conflagration of vivid scarlet flowers, rather large; ("At present it is the most popular red climbing rose"); Purity, one of the finest white flowered climbers of the large-flowered type; Royal Scarlet Hybrid, one of the most effective of the scarlet *Wichuraianas;* Silver Moon, an exquisite rose, large, almost single, creamy white, the plant extraordinarily vigorous, suffers in severe climates.

⚜ Rose General MacArthur (Plate 112)

This has long been considered one of the best bedding Roses, and few surpass it in its endurance of hot weather. The flower is of medium size, and though counted a red rose is not of the flaming type. The color has been called "Tyrian rose," and it has the delicious fragrance so often carried by red Roses. The bush is a moderate grower, 18–20 inches tall, and it blooms, off and on, throughout the season. A thoroughly reliable member of the Hybrid Tea class. It is a great favorite in England though originated by the E. G. Hill Company in America, in 1905.

⚜ Rose Duchess of Sutherland (Plate 113)

This beautiful Rose is sometimes classed as a Hybrid Tea and sometimes, because of its habit and type of foliage, as a Hybrid Perpetual. Its growth is strong, and its chief time of bloom is in late May and June. Its buds especially are exquisite. These are long and pointed; the flowers open fully double, and high-centered, the color a soft rose-pink with flushes of yellow at the base of the petals. It has a delicate fragrance that will fill a warm room. It is not as free a bloomer as many Hybrid Teas, but what flowers there are, are very lovely.

[*121*]

⚘ *Rosa glauca rubiginosa Dingleri* (Plate 114)

This rose seems to have originated in the botanical garden at Nymphenburg; just what is its origin, is not very clear. *Rosa rubiginosa (R. Eglanteria)* is the Sweetbrier, of small pink flowers and deliciously fragrant foliage, beloved everywhere, and gone wild in New England pastures, where it has escaped from prim gardens. *R. glauca* is a species related to the Dog Rose, *R. canina*, of Europe, the commonest wild Rose in England, found everywhere about the countryside, "its deep pink or delicate blush-coloured young roses and buds gleaming among the bright sprays of leaflets, and shedding on green lane and sunny bank, or shady wood, their sweet rose-like odour." The root of this rose was supposed of old to cure the bite of a mad dog—hence the name *canina*. But it is also the Canker Bloom of Shakespeare, who wrote of it the well known lines,

> The rose looks fair, but fairer we it deem
> For that sweet odour, which doth in it live.

The Rose in Plate 114 may be a hybrid between the Dog Rose and the Sweetbrier. In appearance it partakes of the good qualities of both. It is closely leafed and apparently very free-flowering. It would doubtless make a delightful free-growing bush in some half-wild part of the grounds, or in the shrubbery. Whether it inherits the scented leaves of its Sweetbrier parent is not made clear.

⚘ Rose Minnehaha (Plate 115)

This Hybrid *Wichuraiana* Rose is merely a variation on the older Dorothy Perkins. It is a cross between *R. Wichuraiana* and the old Hybrid Perpetual Paul Neyron. The flowers are borne in large close bunches.

[*122*]

They are small and very double, though a little larger and a little lighter in color than the famous Dorothy. Its fragrance is faint but distinctly sweet. "The foliage is small, glossy, dark green, disease resistant." The plants grow to a height of about twenty feet and are fiercely armed with thorns.

In the bud stage this Rose is especially appealing; the buds are like little round bright pink balls. As the flowers age, they turn to a paler tint. It is one of the most reliable of the *Wichuraiana* hybrids, though not new. It was introduced by M. H. Walsh in 1905. An American Rose with an American name.

☙ Rose Tausendschön with White Petunias (Plate 116)

Rose Tausendschön belongs to the same group of Roses as the old and omnipresent Crimson Rambler. It is what is known as a Multiflora Hybrid. "The roses commonly called Multiflora Ramblers," says Mr. Stevens ("Climbing Roses"), "make a highly complex, badly misunderstood group. To the casual student, *Rosa multiflora* does not seem to be the name of a species so much as a designation applied to numerous more or less closely related forms of climbing roses from China, Korea, and Japan." Crimson Rambler was introduced into England from Japan in, or about, 1890. It is a vigorous climber, but the pace with which it scrambled all over the world, painting gardens with its almost virulent hue, has never been exceeded by any other plant. It was an epidemic that only recently has shown signs of dying out.

Many *multiflora* hybrids have since been introduced. They are less interesting both in foliage and in flowers than the hybrid *Wichuraianas;* the canes are heavy and strong, and the plants of great hardiness. "They have a slight tendency toward everblooming, and occasional flowers may be produced on almost any Multiflora hybrid at any time. They also tend to produce thornless varieties, of which Tausendschön is, perhaps, the best example." (G. A. Stevens in "Climbing Roses")

Like all the *multiflora* hybrids, Tausendschön blooms in huge bunches of fairly small flowers that are practically scentless. When this Rose appeared in 1906 it made an immediate sensation, with just reason. It was unbelievably floriferous. The great bunches of soft pink flowers with large white centers, double and cup-shaped, literally cover the plant like an enveloping mantle. To the gardener its thornlessness made it a boon, for it was easily and painlessly handled, and its great bouquets of pink and white flowers made it charming for house decoration.

Some other worth-while *multiflora* hybrids are the following: Blush Rambler, pale pink, semi-double flowers in huge bunches. Dr. Reymond, fairly large pure white double flowers tinged with green and produced in "pyramidal corymbs." Electra, an old sort with yellowish buds, opening into creamy white flowers, very freely produced and faintly fragrant. Strong grower. Frau Lina Strassheim bears long-lasting flame-salmon flowers in generous bunches. Ghislaine de Feligonde, "loveliest of all Multifloras," bears apricot-yellow buds in profusion opening to creamy flowers with coppery lights; it flowers, off and on, throughout the season; the canes are almost thornless, and it is hardier than most yellow-flowered climbers. Lyon Rambler, at a little distance, has the appearance of a great flame; the flowers are borne in great trusses on strong canes. Mrs. F. W. Flight, clusters of medium-sized double flowers of a fine pink tone; not vigorous but makes a good pillar Rose. Tea Rambler, pretty, pink and fragrant, the buds coppery in tone, the plant healthy and a rampant grower. The Wallflower, enormous clusters of bright red semi-double flowers; very striking if you like a red-flowered climber.

The *multiflora* hybrids have had a tendency to run to purplish tones. Veilchenblau is one of these doubtful blessings that we, it seems to me, can well do without.

[*124*]

In Plate 116 a window box full of white Petunias is placed above the cloud of pink and white Rose Tausendschön. It is an attractive arrangement. The Petunias would, of course, have to be started indoors or under glass, but they would flower freely throughout the season.

⚜ Roses Dorothy Perkins and Excelsa (Plate 117)

This old *Wichuraiana* hybrid Dorothy Perkins, has enjoyed a popularity only less than that of Crimson Rambler but with a good deal more reason. It is still holding its own against all others of its type, a rose of real beauty and unusual grace. It is very hardy and vigorous, climbing high; and, though the foliage in some seasons is subject to mildew, this does not detract from the splendor of the display it makes when in flower. The flowers, after the manner of its kind, are borne in great bunches; they are small, very double with a ruffled effect, of a pure pink color, and pleasantly fragrant. One of its good points is that it flowers late, after most of the climbing roses have had their day. Its parents are *R. Wichuraiana* and Mme. Gabriel Luizet, a Hybrid Tea, from which it doubtless inherits its fragrance and its habit of occasional later flowers. Dorothy Perkins has produced numerous sports, among which White Dorothy is perhaps the best known. It is a good white-flowered climbing Rose of extraordinary vigor.

Excelsa is a hybrid *Wichuraiana* that has attempted with indifferent success to take the place of Crimson Rambler; the foliage is subject to mildew, and it is not a really first-class Rose. Mr. Stevens recommends Bonfire and Fernand Rabier in its place.

Training climbing Roses on iron arches, especially as accents in a Rose garden, is a charming way to grow them. The canes may be twined about the arches as they grow, thus enabling them to stay in place, even when weighted down with bloom.

🔣 *Moltkia petraea* with White Rose and Dwarf Chamaecyparis (Plate 118)

The dominant note in this rock garden scene is the little double white-flowered Rose Perle von Britz. Below it and hanging over a rock is a mass of *Moltkia petraea (Lithospermum petraeum)*. "It might be hazarded that this plant," says Mr. Farrer, "is commoner in gardens than at home, where it is of the most rare occurrence, in the Alps of Greece (as on the face of Oeta looking eternally down upon Thermopylae)." Considerably rarer than in England is it in this country, and perhaps it is of doubtful hardiness. It belongs to the Borage tribe and makes a small slow-growing bushy plant a foot or more high, woody with narrow, thick dull green leaves and profusely borne heads of blue flowers, which one would expect from its family affiliations. "It should have," says Clarence Elliott, "a fully sunny position in light well-drained loam, and looks most effective when planted on a rocky slope, where it may develop among small choice neighbors, undwarfed by coarse or rowdy rampers. . . . It is one of the choicest of all dwarf blue-flowered rock shrubs."

Its habit and charms are well shown in the plate, and it is plain that it is being protected from the neighboring "rowdy rampers," if the Rose and the dwarf Chamaecyparis can be so designated.

Chamaecyparis obtusa nana with its lovely flat plains of overlapping dark foliage will one day grow into a fairly tall bush, and the little Moltkia will have to go elsewhere for that spacious peace which it fancies. There are numerous dwarf forms of *C. obtusa*, including *pygmaea, compacta, nana densa, nana gracilis,* the gold-leaved *nana aurea, ericoides, nana prostrata, tetragona,* and *tetragona minima,* the last named "a minute, dense cushion of light green foliage, sixteen-year-old plants being only a few inches high by about half as many across." Needless to say, all of these are "gems" for the rock garden.

[*126*]

ꙮ *Campanula Medium* (Canterbury Bell) (Plate 119)

The Canterbury Bell has rung its chimes these many Junes in gardens. It is a plant of southern Europe, but one that the florists have taken in hand and molded to their fancy. It is a biennial plant, which means that if a stock of it is to be kept in the garden it must be raised from seed every year, for it is not, like the Foxglove (another famous biennial), a ready self-sower. It is an old favorite, and when first introduced, about 1597, was cultivated chiefly as a pot plant. The flowers are numerous and large and bell-shaped, and are disposed in long racemes on a central stem something over two feet high. It is the only Campanula known to me that produces pure pink flowers; besides these it may bring forth purple, lavender, or pure white bells which may be single or double (the doubles are frightfully stodgy) and there is one monstrous variety known as *C. calycanthema.* This is the famed Cup and Saucer Canterbury Bell, which has been greatly admired. "The enlarged Calyx is colored like the corolla, the latter placed on the former as on a saucer, giving the appearance of a double inflorescence, about three inches across." Who wants a stalk of cups and saucers in his garden!

The ordinary single Canterbury Bell is a lovely thing. It flowers about the same time as do Foxgloves; grown in masses of one color or of all the colors together, when it looks like a pattern of old chintz, its effect is delightful. If the central stem gets damaged the plant will send out branches and form a little bush; and if the bells are removed as soon as they begin to fade a second crop will be the reward.

Canterbury Bells are easily raised from seed sown out of doors about midsummer, or in flats somewhat earlier. Prick them out in pots when large enough to handle, and place these in a cold frame, plunged up to the rims in the earth. Cover the sash in winter with mats, and transplant the little plants to the outdoor garden as soon as mild weather arrives the following spring. If they remain out of doors over the winter, it is well to draw a blanket of salt hay or hard leaves about the plants, leaving the crowns uncovered. This avoids the winter rotting to which they are subject in mild winters. You may also get a head start and larger plants by sowing your seed in frames or in flats indoors in February.

⚘ Clematis Jackmani (Jackman's Clematis) (Plate 120)

Clematis Jackmani is one of the first introduced of the large-flowered hybrid Clematis, as well as one of the most easily grown. It is thought to have originated in the famous nurseries of George Jackman and Son, at Woking in 1862. It has been pointed out that there is a Japanese plant that bears a close resemblance to the Jackman variety; nevertheless, the plant bears the name of Jackman, and it was from his nursery that it was distributed to the world.

The plant is amazingly free in growth and very hardy, growing to a moderate height. The flowers attract more by their profusion and regal color than by their great circumference. In early July it is literally covered with a garment of rich purple flowers, reddish towards the center and with a bunch of pale green stamens in the middle. The texture of the flowers is velvety, and each sepal has a ribbed bar down the center. These lovely blooms are about five inches across.

Clematis Jackmani may be grown on poles at the back of the borders with a foreground of Madonna Lilies, or trained over a trellis or arbor, or allowed to scramble over a fence or stump. Often the large-flowered hybrids are encouraged into the branches of fruit trees, where they do very well and in no way interfere with their hosts. Like other Clematis, they like to have their roots in the shade and their heads out in the sun. Thus it is important to have some shadowing growths about the base of

[128]

Plate 112. ROSE GENERAL MACARTHUR, HYBRID TEA

Plate 113. ROSE DUCHESS OF SUTHERLAND, PERPETUAL-FLOWERING HYBRID TEA

Plate 114. *Rosa glauca*

Plate 115. ROSE MINNEHAHA, HYBRID WICHURAIANA

Plate 116. ROSE TAUSENDSCHÖN, CLIMBER, WITH WHITE PETUNIAS

Plate 117. ROSES DOROTHY PERKINS AND EXCELSA

the plants. The soil they prefer is one that is deeply dug and composed of rich loam and humus; if it is on the heavy side, a quantity of sand may be added. In parts of the country where the soil is acid some lime in the shape of old mortar rubble should be dug into the mixture; indeed this is an appreciated consideration anywhere.

Clematis Jackmani is lovely for cutting and, if a bit of the woody stem is taken with the branch, will last well in water, trailing down from a high shelf with the utmost grace, displaying its wide flowers and lovely foliage to advantage.

Other large-flowered hybrids to be recommended are the following: Duchess of Edinburgh, double white; Gipsy Queen, dark violet; *Henryi*, enormous creamy white flowers, almost continuously in bloom—one of the most striking of all the hybrids; *Lawsoniana*, bright rosy purple marked with darker veins; *lilacina floribunda*, pale gray-lilac, conspicuously veined; Madame Edouard André, velvety mauve-carmine; Madame Baron Veillard, rose-lilac; Miss Bateman, white with chocolate center; Nellie Moser, light mauve with a red bar through the center of each sepal; Ramona, light lavender-blue flowers; Sir Garnet Wolseley, bronzy-blue with a plum-purple bar through each sepal; Ville de Lyon, bright carmine-crimson flowers.

(This list was recommended by Joel Spingarn in the *Bulletin of the Garden Club of America*, November, 1932.)

❦ *Thymus serpyllum splendens* with *Campanula pusilla* and Pinks in a Rock Garden (Plate 121)

A gay scene such as is depicted in Plate 121 is easily enough accomplished in any sunny bit of well built rock garden. The plants crowd but do not interfere with one another. The time is late June or early July.

[*129*]

The Thyme used is *Thymus serpyllum splendens,* one of the most richly colored of the Thymes, and the flowers are borne in such profusion as to quite hide the neat foliage. *Campanula pusilla,* sometimes called Fairy Thimbles, is one of the prettiest of its race, and is indispensable and easy. It goes under various names including *Bellardi, caespitosa,* and *cochlearifolia.* It is a common plant in European mountains, where it rambles freely in the shingly ground, making sheets of little blue or white bells. In the rock garden it loves a sunny situation, particularly on a slope, and it makes an ideal plant for a wall or crevice between steps. There are various forms of it, all lovely. Miranda is a dwarf form discovered by the late Reginald Farrer, dwarf only in stature for its bells are as big as any of the others; it is a soft pastel shade of blue; Miss Willmott is perhaps the finest of the *pusillas,* with a better and more definite color and a more sturdy growth; then there is the white form *alba,* one known as *lilacina,* and probably others. *C. pusilla* is a rambling, mat-making plant and seldom grows more than a few inches tall. It carries its bells on erect, branched, slender stems that allow them to tremble with every passing breeze. *C. pusilla* is easily raised from seed, and, once we have a stock, the plants may be endlessly divided.

There are many Pinks (Dianthus) in flower at this season to join with the Thyme and the little Campanula in making a gay festival.

⁂ *Thymus serpyllum coccineus* and Artemisia (Plate 122)

It would be entirely possible to plant a whole rock garden with the different species and varieties of Thyme. They are close-growing, creeping, and mat-making plants for the most part and weave into one another with the most delightful effect. Of *Thymus serpyllum* alone there are a great number of color forms. There is the lovely white form, *albus;* there is a pretty pink-flowered kind called Annie Hall; there is the crimson *coccineus* of the plate, very showy and handsome; there is *lanuginosus*, with soft densely hairy mats of whitish foliage; there is *splendens* shown in the preceding plate; and there are among others the tiny *minus* described as "a mere film of sweet-scented greenery." And these are only a few of the available kinds of Thymes. They all have the delightful quality of aromatic foliage which adds immensely to the pleasure we derive from them, and when they are out of flower they spread a neat and seemly gray or green coverlet over earth and stones.

With the Thyme in Plate 122 are some clumps of velvety gray-leaved Artemisia, and on the left some stalks of Gladiolus. The latter are distinctly out of place in a rock garden and are a false note in an otherwise pleasant scene.

☸ *Coreopsis grandiflora* (Plate 123)

This is probably one of the showiest and most easily grown of all hardy border plants. If its golden-yellow flowers are a bit harsh in tone, it makes up for this fault in the profusion of its flowering. Indeed, if prevented from going to seed by the removal of the spent flowers, it will bloom right through the season until frost—not, of course, with its initial prodigality but furnishing a few long-stemmed blooms for cutting. The plants grow about 2½ feet tall. The flowers are Daisy-like in form with notched petals; the center is a deeper tone of yellow than the petals, the leaves are narrow, sometimes three- to five-parted, and of little importance in the general effect. It is a splendid cut flower and one that may be easily raised from seed or propagated by division. A rough bank planted with this Tickseed presents a glowing spectacle, and as it self-sows freely very little replacement will be required if plants for one reason or another die out. It may also be grown in the borders among other perennials, but if it is to remain erect a few bits of brush should be inserted among the plants to support them. On no account should they be tied stiffly to stakes. The spreading brush allows them to keep their naturally graceful pose.

There is a form of it with semi-double flowers called Perry's variety. This grows somewhat less tall and makes a more solid show in the borders. *Coreopsis grandiflora* may be called the best long-season yellow flower. It will grow in any soil but likes ample watering during the heat of midsummer. It is a native plant found growing wild from Georgia to New Mexico.

Plants in bloom with it are the early tall Bearded Iris, *florentina*, with its gray-white flowers, and others; Columbines; *Centaurea montana*, with whose blue flowers it makes a nice show; Foxgloves; the early Meadow Rue; Day Lilies; Oriental Poppies; *Lychnis chalcedonica*; Garden Heliotrope (*Valeriana officinalis*); *Anchusa italica*; the old Sweet Rocket (*Hesperis matronalis*), and many more. It has no lack of companions.

⚜ *Coreopsis verticillata* with Phlox Firebrand (Plate 124)

In Plate 124 is shown a scene that would seem too highly colored in the eyes of most persons. The green background and the white summer house serve to tone it down somewhat, yet most of us would not choose these two strong-colored flowers as companions.

Coreopsis verticillata (*C. tenuifolia*), the Threadleaf Coreopsis or Tickseed, like all the race, is a native plant. This one is a hardy perennial that may be found growing wild from Maryland westward to Arkansas and Nebraska. Its habit is slender, the plants growing to a height of two to three feet. The leaves are in whorls "ternately divided into thread-like segments," giving the plants a light and feathery appearance. The bright

[*132*]

yellow flowers are about two inches across and have a yellow center of a darker tone than the ray flowers. Combined with lavender, blue, or white flowers of its season, it is a valuable border plant.

Phlox Firebrand is one of the newer Phloxes and one of the most brilliant. Its hue may be described as vermilion-scarlet, the eye of an even deeper tone. The trusses are enormous, and the plant makes a brilliant display. It is a strong and sturdy grower and does not fade in the sun as do so many of the scarlet varieties. If the individual flowers are cut off before seed is formed, this variety blooms almost throughout the season.

In front of the phlox carpeting the slope is *Thymus serpyllum*, which has ceased to bloom. It provides a pleasant foreground for this brilliant association.

꙲ *Lilium umbellatum* (Western Orangecup Lily) (Plate 125)

Most of the varieties offered under this name, says Dr. Bailey, belong under *L. dauricum* or *L. elegans*. Helen M. Fox, in "Garden Cinderellas," says, "The upright umbellatums (subspecies davuricum) are the first to open and bring a burst of scarlet and orange as the early Iris are fading away." It blooms in June, bearing large umbellate heads of flowers in various tones of orange, yellow, and red, on stems about two and one-half feet high, sometimes less. It has a large bulb that is stem-rooting, which means that it should be planted deeply in the soil—at least four inches over all.

Varieties of *L. umbellatum* are the following: Apricot, a charming color well described by the name. The flowers are borne in large heads and should for their best interest be planted in a cool, partially shaded situation. *Grandiflorum* is easy and very free-flowering, the color a fine orange-red. Mahogany, "the deepest color yet raised, comparatively small

[*133*]

in stature with heads of fine broad petaled flowers, deep glowing crimson-lake, deepening to a rich mahogany hue as the flowers pass over." Orange King, a magnificent Lily with extra large heads of glowing orange flowers with purplish spots on the interior. Prince of Wales is more golden in color, but tinged with orange and with a few dark spots on the interior. It is one of the earliest of the *umbellatum* group to flower. Splendens is a tall variety with flowers of an orange hue so brilliant as to be almost vermilion but shading to a coppery tone. It is one of the most striking of the group.

❦ Delphiniums (Plates 126, 127, 128)

Perhaps it may be said that today the Delphinium is the most popular of hardy perennials; there can be little doubt that it is the most beautiful. Not only is it in the public eye, but it engages the public mind. There are books written about it, innumerable articles, societies formed to promote its culture and welfare. Many accomplished horticulturists devote their lives to its improvement. "The modern Delphinium owes its origin to the fusion of the qualities possessed by numerous species existing scattered widely over the surface of the earth. From the woods and prairies of North America, the sun-baked plains and sierras of California, the high tableland of Tibet, the Swiss Alps, the dry and rocky lands bordering the Mediterranean, the forests of Central Europe, they have come to merge their individual charms into one glorious whole." This quotation is from "Delphiniums: Their History and Culture," by George A. Phillips.

Before embarking upon a description of the beautiful hybrids I would urge Delphinium lovers to grow some of the wild species, native or foreign. They will be a revelation and a surprise. There will, of course, be disappointment at their small flowers, short spikes, dull colors (excepting California's two red-flowered species, *D. nudicaule* and *D. cardinale*);

[*134*]

but only by knowing some of these can we measure the great advance made in the culture of these flowers. For centuries the Delphinium has been cultivated in gardens (Parkinson mentions several kinds popular in his day), but only in recent times has this flower reached the heights, literally speaking, that it now measures. The modern Delphinium is a thing to marvel at. As the years have passed, its form—that is, the form popular at the time—has undergone considerable change. "Light as a loop of Larkspur" has not for many years described the spike of the Delphinium. The type in vogue forty years ago was a stumpy spike, with closely packed blossoms; in twenty years the spike had considerably elongated, and the blossoms were set less closely together. The present-day favorite is still longer—tapering to a delicate point and with many subsidiary branches. The flower spike itself may be several feet long, the plant more than seven feet tall. In the seventeenth century double flowers were introduced, and these are still grown. The old Bee Larkspur of our grandmother's gardens, *D. elatum,* is said to have had much to do with adding stature to the plants. Not a great deal of progress in the improvement of the Delphinium was made until 1859, when James Kelway, founder of the present firm of that name, showed a number that were a great advance over any that had heretofore been grown. This firm has continued its interest in Delphiniums and is responsible for many of the lovely new varieties.

The individual flowers that compose the spike show an enormous variety of shape and form—they may be double, semi-double, single, what is termed Ranunculus-flowered, Clematis-flowered, and so on. And the colors vary from pure white to pale and deep sky-blue, porcelain-blue, cornflower-blue, gentian-blue, ultramarine, violet-blue, plum-purple, pansy-violet, royal purple, lavender, mauve, lilac—all these in self colors; and besides there are the vast number of varieties that are shot or shaded, banded or suffused with other colors, often with pink. Indeed, these iridescent effects have become more and more popular. No longer is the Delphinium a *blue* flower primarily. It may have almost any color scheme. And as there are yellow wild species—*D. Zalil*, from Afghanistan, for one—we may soon be standing in wonderment before spires of yellow-flowered Delphiniums.

With its improvement, the culture of the Delphinium has become a more complicated process. Good well-flowered spikes follow careful and understanding cultivation. The best time to plant Delphiniums is thought to be in the spring, though some success may attend early autumn planting, while the roots are still actively in growth. "On no account," says Mr. Phillips, "should roots be disturbed while in a dormant state, for they will not begin activity until spring and more often than not will perish during the cold winter weather." In this state also they are fair game for slugs and snails, which devour the roots voraciously. The best soil is a rich deep loam, sufficiently well drained to hold no stagnant water, and yet not so porous as to lose all moisture in summer during dry spells. The very tall spikes are easily broken or injured by high winds, and so some protection in the shape of walls, fences, hedges, or windbreaks of evergreens is advisable. Full exposure to the sun is important, so that a southern or south-western aspect is the best. The soil should be trenched to a depth of some eighteen inches, and the bottom soil broken up below this. Into the lower section of the trench must be spaded a liberal amount of strawy farmyard manure. A warning has been issued against that which has been polluted with wood shavings or moss litter. If the ground is prepared the autumn before planting, it will be in prime condition in the spring. Delphiniums like plenty of lime, and if it is suspected that the soil is deficient in this necessary ingredient it must be supplied. In any case a top dressing of good slaked lime is a consideration that is appreciated by these plants. "Three to

Plate 118. *Moltkia petraea (Lithospermum petraeum)* WITH WHITE
ROSE AND DWARF CHAMAECYPARIS IN ROCK GARDEN

Plate 123. *Coreopsis grandiflora* (LARGE-FLOWERED TICKSEED)

Plate 124. *Coreopsis verticillata* WITH PHLOX FIREBRAND

Plate 125. *Lilium umbellatum* (WESTERN ORANGECUP LILY)

Plate 126. A GROUP OF DELPHINIUM HYBRIDS

Plate 127. DELPHINIUM MOEGENSTRAHL (LARKSPUR)

Plate 128. DELPHINIUM BERGH IMMEL

Plate 129. AN EFFECTIVE USE OF *Sedum reflexum* IN THE ROCK GARDEN

Plate 130. *Kirengeshoma palmata*, A MEMBER OF THE ORDER SAXIFRAGACEAE

four ounces to the square yard, taking care to distribute it as proportionately as possible" is recommended. Set the tall-growing varieties two feet apart. Less than that will be sufficient for the lower-growing *Belladonna* varieties. After planting, the soil should be kept stirred about the plants and never allowed to bake as it so often does in our hot dry summers. Unless the plants are grown for exhibition, all the strong shoots may be allowed to develop; thus we get the lovely massed color effects that are so valuable in the borders. Application of liquid manure or a dressing of farmyard manure at least once while the stalks are growing is advisable; and when the plants reach a height of about three feet stout stakes or bamboo canes should be driven into the earth to a considerable depth, and the stalks lightly tied to them with raffia. Several tyings may be necessary as the plants grow taller. The low-growing *Belladonna* types will often manage without staking, but even with them a little stout brush thrust in among the growths will be of advantage. When the main spike has begun to wither it may be removed so as to throw the strength of the plant into the development of the lesser branches. There has been a good deal of controversy over the good and bad effects of cutting down the Delphinium stalks after the flowering is over. I believe it has now been decided that to cut the plants a foot from the ground does no harm and, moreover, permits them to make the generous gesture of a second flowering in the late summer or autumn.

Delphiniums are readily raised from seed, but seedlings are not to be counted upon to be true to name. If named varieties are to be increased, it must be by careful division with a sharp knife in early spring when the plants have grown a few inches high.

Some plants to grow with Delphiniums are the following: *Thalictrum glaucum*, with its silvery foliage and puffs of yellow bloom; Japanese Irises; *Lilium candidum* and *L. croceum*; *Campanula latifolia macrantha*

[*137*]

with its large purple bells. Delphinium plants are lovely also against walls or arbors covered with pink or white climbing Roses. The long spires of Delphiniums are perfect for cutting and are especially lovely in deep white pottery containers.

Delphiniums are heir to numerous diseases and pests. They are subject to mildew, crown rot, the latter "characterised by yellowing of the lower leaves, wilting of the plants and a black rot of the crown's roots." For control of diseases and pests it is best to turn to a good book on Delphinium culture, or to appeal to a friendly grower.

❧ An Effective Use of *Sedum reflexum* (Plate 129)

Sedum reflexum is a variable plant and belongs to what is called the *rupestre* group. In common with many of its relatives it has a creeping stem, forming a loose evergreen mat. The flowering stems rise to a height of nearly six inches; they are crowded with narrow glaucous leaves. The tip of the stem recurves and bears a small drooping head of yellow flowers. It is quite hardy and is a native of many parts of Europe.

It is often found naturalized on old walls both in this country and in Europe. Its rather alarming spreading power makes this really pretty plant a danger in rock gardens, where it is prone to occupy space required for its betters. Where it may be given a wall-face, it shows to great advantage, and there may spread about without doing harm to choicer plants; or it may be planted on rocky banks among the tougher rock plants that are able to withstand and even repulse the pressure of its advance.

There is a curious form of it called *S. reflexum cristatum*, in which the shoots are fasciate, or compressed, so as to give a congested appearance, the flattened stems often being two inches broad. "In this condition it never flowers, but normal shoots are frequently produced, and these flower

[*138*]

freely if allowed to develop." I have not found the *cristatum* variety a troublesome spreader; nor is it beautiful, simply curious.

The introducer of Sedums into his rock garden should find out something about their habits. Many are conscienceless spreaders and invade the mats of choicer plants to their ultimate destruction. On the other hand there are numerous really choice Sedums that may be included in any collection of rock plants without danger.

🏵 *Kirengeshoma palmata* (Plate 130)

This rather curious-looking plant comes from Japan. The clumsy name derives from Japanese words meaning yellow. It is hardy in England but not reliably so here in the colder parts of the country. It is said to grow at an elevation of some 5,000 feet in Japan, on Mt. Ishizuchi. It grows about two feet high, is upright, the stems slender and glabrous. The leaves are large and papery, and somewhat hairy on both sides. The lobes of the leaves are lightly toothed. The leaves are overtopped by the flowers, which grow in three-flowered sprays, on short peduncles, nodding, and of a soft yellow color. They are bell-shaped and over an inch and a half long, wide at the mouth and slightly recurving.

K. palmata prefers partially shaded places and is recommended for rock gardens, but it seems overtall for this region. It is propagated by division and is a member of the order Saxifragaceae.

🏵 *Hibiscus rosa-sinensis* (Rose of China, Chinese Hibiscus) (Plate 131)

The Rose of China is a beautiful native of the East Indies, China, and elsewhere. It is widely grown in tropical countries, one of the most characteristic plants of these regions, and has long been a popular greenhouse

the fairly experienced gardener with some chance of success. The rock garden is of course the place for all three of them, and here it is easy to manufacture the conditions that they require.

⚑ *Lilium auratum* (The Gold-Banded Lily) (Plate 133)

The Gold-Banded Lily of Japan is one of the splendors of the Lily family. And by and large it probably causes as much heartburning as any of them. In 1862, when this Lily was first exhibited by Francis Parkman at the Massachusetts Horticultural Society, it caused a furore. And there was good reason for the excitement. Here was an enormous creamy-white Lily, bowl-shaped and with rippled margins, the segments turning back at the tip, and gleaming down the center of each a golden band "terminating in a glistening green nectar furrow. They exhale a strong Oriental fragrance languorous at night but too strong in the daytime or in the house for most of us" (Helen M. Fox in "Garden Cinderellas"). The stem perhaps was from six to eight feet high. Naturally, to see it was to want to possess it. And sales of the bulbs mounted accordingly.

But unfortunately this beauty is not easy to keep in the garden. It is subject to a disease, though according to Mr. Wilson he never saw a diseased bulb in the wild. This trouble is something that civilization has brought upon it.

The bulbs are large and have great masses of stem roots, and so deep planting—at least eight or ten inches—is indicated. As the wild bulbs are found growing eight to ten inches down in poor soil in perfect drainage amongst low shrubs, Mrs. Fox says in cultivation "it should be grown in poor, sandy soil in a sunny situation with a low growth about the base of its stems." It is a very hardy Lily and may be grown far north, but when the dread disease attacks it, it soon dies out, though we may have been thrilled at the size of our *auratums* for several years. They bloom in July and August, and one of the finest plantings I ever saw was in Massachusetts where the great Lilies rose out of a mass of annual Gypsophila and seemed to float above it. A good place to grow it is in a Rhododendron or Azalea bed. Authorities do not agree about the conditions under which it best thrives. One that I have before me says it favors "a cool, thin woodland where it is damp at the roots. Not a woodland plant in the sense that it grows in the thick of the forests, but it flourishes on the fringes of the woods, in glades and clearings, always among vegetation, which while screening the lower part of the stem and keeping the ground cool leaves the sun free to play on the blooms. Given the necessary conditions of shelter (for exposure to cold winds invites disease) and of half shade, it can be grown in well prepared holes in other soils." This authority recommends the holes being filled with a mixture of peat and sharp sand, or sandy loam, leaf mold, and rubbish-heap burnings with some well rotted manure. The situation should be well drained.

There are several kinds of *auratum* Lilies now on the market. A comprehensive catalogue will give a list.

Rudbeckia speciosa (Showy Coneflower) Massed Near Garden Pool (Plate 134)

As the summer days grow longer the colors of the flowers seem to grow warmer in tone. Here beside this round garden pool, on the surface of which float the wide pads and the charming flowers of white Water Lilies, is massed that good hardy plant *Rudbeckia speciosa*, the Showy Coneflower. It is well placed, for whether or not some water seeps through the stones about the pool the Rudbeckia looks better by water. If it gets no moisture from the pool, it must be artificially watered in dry weather, or it droops and withers prematurely. To grow in, it likes a rich compost. Given this and plenty of water, it has a long season of flowering, sending up its orange-yellow "daisies" from July well into the autumn, good to look at and good to pick. If it cannot have moisture, it is best grown in a partially shaded spot. The plant grows about two feet high, is very hardy, and may be increased by division very easily.

Plate 134 shows a pleasant if very informal garden scene. A mat of Pinks, now gone out of bloom, lies upon the stone curbing, a few Forget-me-nots linger. A Weeping Willow and several evergreens, including a Blue Spruce, form a background for a clump of tall *Senecio clivorum*, with its large heart-shaped leaves and much-branched heads of wide orange-yellow flowers held well above them. This is also a plant naturally at home by the waterside, and not otherwise particular as to soil. It is from China and flowers in July and August, a bold plant of easy culture. This giant Groundsel is now, I believe, called *Ligularia clivorum*, instead of Senecio. It is too coarse for most situations, but by the waterside, its great flower heads and greater leaves reflected in the placid surface of the water, it is well placed and very effective.

❀ *Thalictrum dipterocarpum* (Yunnan Meadow Rue) (Plate 135)

The Meadow Rues are among the plants that lend lightness and grace to the borders. The foliage of all of them is conspicuously lovely, and when the flowers, which take the form of puffs of bloom, are over, the foliage remains as a distinct ornament. They are not very widely grown in this country, and this is the more strange when the ease of their culture is taken into consideration. About fifty species are known, but only a few of these are offered in catalogues. Some are native plants and may be seen waving their delicate flower-heads in meadows above the summer grasses.

[*144*]

Plate 131. *Hibiscus rosa-sinensis* (ROSE OF CHINA, CHINESE HIBISCUS)

Plate 132. *Gentiana Freyniana* TUMBLING OVER STONE EDGING

Plate 133. *Lilium auratum* (THE GOLD-BANDED LILY)

Plate 134. *Rudbeckia speciosa* (SHOWY CONEFLOWER) MASSED NEAR
GARDEN POOL

Plate 135. *Thalictrum dipterocarpum* (YUNNAN MEADOWRUE)

The Garden in Color

To make a collection of Meadow Rues, or Thalictrums, is a worthy enterprise for any one, for there are kinds suitable for almost every situation, even for the rock garden.

Thalictrum dipterocarpum is the only one that offers any difficulty to the grower. It is a magnificent plant when well grown, but it is seldom seen doing its best. The plant was introduced by the late E. H. Wilson from high altitudes in western China. In his "Aristocrats of the Garden" he calls attention to the fact that the Meadow Rues are not regarded as showy garden plants, "yet the new *T. dipterocarpum* is one of the loveliest herbs imaginable. It grows from eight to ten feet tall and the flower stems are very much branched and bear relatively large lavender-purple flowers in great quantity." These flowers are enlivened by bunches of yellow anthers, which add to their fluffy appearance. The foliage is exceptionally beautiful even for this race, the leaves being broader than is usual and much divided.

It is too bad that this lovely species is not often seen in a flourishing condition. The nursery stock we are able to procure is usually not in prime health, and it cannot just be put into any border and expected to thrive. Drainage, I believe, is a first requisite; in heavy waterlogged soils it dies off during the winter, and I have known it to go off in spells of humid heat in summer. The soil to give it is a deeply dug loam, enriched with farmyard manure, and it seems to like lime. I have never seen it succeed in an acid soil or even in one that might be called neutral. And though it wants drainage, it also suffers in spells of dry weather and must be faithfully watered every few days. It seems to be a plant of contradictions, for though it comes from a cold climate in this country, north of Philadelphia, it needs protection—a covering of evergreen boughs, of salt hay or hard-wood leaves. Its place is at the back of sunny borders, and it is safest to plant it in the spring. Success with it means genuine delight in its gray foliage, its heads of rosy-lavender flowers with their masses of sulphur-colored anthers. It brings to the lush and rather coarse assemblage of the August garden a note of refinement and elegance for which we are grateful. There is a white variety offered by some nurseries.

❦ *Nelumbium Nelumbo* (East Indian Lotus) (Plate 136)

This strong-growing water plant is commonly known as the Egyptian Lotus, though it is said to have originated in India. Its beauty is very much out of the ordinary. From the long, jointed rootstocks spring the great leaves, grayish from the waxlike substance that covers them. These leaves are immense, often more than two feet in diameter, and are carried on tall stems from three to five or six feet above the water. Higher still rise the flower stems carrying the magnificent flowers. They begin to bloom towards the end of June and continue to flower until mid-August. The flowers open three days in succession, the first day not fully but on the second and third widely enough to display the mass of golden stamens. They remain open only a few hours, and on the third day the petals begin to fall. The plant was regarded as sacred by the Hindus, but when it was introduced into Egypt the Egyptians made use of the immense seed-pods as a food. These seed-pods are almost as decorative as any part of the plant, being flattish with the top perforated with holes like a giant's pepper shaker. Flowers and pods are often seen on the plants at the same time. The flowers, both double and single, come in numerous colors, pure white, deep rose-color, carmine. Perhaps, of all the fine qualities possessed by this plant, none is more appreciated than its delicious fragrance.

This Lotus, it is said, was introduced to America by E. D. Sturtevant of Bordentown, New Jersey, about 1876. "A year or two later he set out one plant in the open which grew so luxuriantly that in eight years a space of three quarters of an acre was covered with a mass of flowers and foliage."

[*146*]

It is hardy in the open near New York and in Massachusetts. The best time to plant it is in the spring, and care should be taken not to break the long roots. The Lotus may be set directly in the mud of ponds, lakes, or even ditches or in boxes submerged in a pond or pool, and in any case should not be disturbed over the winter. They will be quite safe unless ice forms to the bottom of the pool. "If this should happen the boxes should be removed to a cellar where there will be no danger of them being frozen."

The Lotus is obviously no plant for a very small pool. It requires soil and good food in generous quantities for its best development. "Nelumbiums throw out roots a distance of fifteen feet in a single season, with leaves at every joint, generally about eighteen inches apart. In "The Book of Water Gardening" Peter Bisset gives complete directions for growing these lovely and desirable flowers under a variety of conditions.

⚑ Water-Lilies (Nymphaea) in Garden Pool (Plate 137)

Perhaps no adjunct of the garden gives more pleasure than a pool in which are grown the many lovely varieties of Nymphaea. The pads in themselves are attractive against the blue of the water, and there is today a vast number of different kinds of Lilies in many colors—white, all shades of pink from blush to carmine, rich reddish violet, pale and deep blue, pinkish lavender, apricot, yellow, garnet, dark orange, and so on.

The blue and pure purple varieties are tender kinds from tropical lands and will not stand out over our winters in the North. But there is a great number of hardy kinds that need no other care than division of the roots and replanting (if they are in tubs in the pools) every two years. Wet or dry, the Water-Lilies flourish, and I know of nothing more refreshing on a hot summer day than a shining wind-ruffled pool bearing on its surface the wide cool leaves and the lovely fragrant flowers of the Nymphaeas. In

[*147*]

the vicinity of New York they begin to flower in June and continue to send up buds and blooms throughout the season.

They may be planted in the soil at the bottom of a pond. The method of planting is to press the roots down into the mud and hold them in place by means of forked sticks or by placing a stone upon them until they have taken hold. A much easier way, and one that is usually practiced in pools, is to plant the roots in tubs or boxes and sink these in the water. Butter tubs or half-barrels may be used, or boxes of any sort, provided they are large enough to hold sufficient soil. The soil should be rich, good loam and manure with a little sand and gravel. It is important to keep the pool as full as possible in order to avoid having to let in a great amount of fresh water to fill it. This is apt to check the growth of the Lilies, especially of the sensitive tropical kinds.

The roots of the hardy varieties need not be disturbed on the approach of winter "if a sufficient depth of water can be maintained above the crowns so that they will not be actually frozen." In the case of concrete pools that are apt to crack during the winter it is wise to put several logs of wood into the water to take up the expansion. This has been practiced here for many years without disaster. In some cases the water may be drawn off from the pool entirely and the pool filled with leaves or straw well covering the Lily tubs. This also has been found successful. But it is more trouble.

A catalogue from a reliable grower of Water-Lilies will offer untold riches. Many of the finest kinds spring from our own native Pond- or Water-Lily, *Nymphaea odorata.* Some of the best of these are *odorata Luciana*, Mary Exquisita, W. B. Shaw, and the common white kind. Then a selection of other varieties would be the pale yellow *chromatella*, *Marliacea albida*, Loosé, Rose Arey, *lucida*, Radiance, Comanche, and William Falconer.

[*148*]

Some of the tropical kinds bloom only at night and loose their delicious fragrance to the evening garden, making it a place of real enchantment.

The tender or tropical Lilies must wait for planting until settled mild weather has come. The hardy kinds may be set out in April if desired. After a hard frost the tubs containing the tender varieties must be removed from the pool or pond and brought indoors and placed in a cool cellar; when this is done it must be seen to that they do not suffer for want of water during the winter. The soil must be kept damp.

❦ *Agapanthus umbellatus* (African Lily, Blue Lily of the Nile) (Plate 138)

This fine plant, now properly known as *Agapanthus africanus*, belongs to a small genus of half-hardy plants from South Africa. In "South African Plants for American Gardens" Sarah V. Coombs says, "Great masses of them growing in their native land are a beautiful sight." In this country they are known chiefly as tub or large pot plants, ornaments of terraces, porches, pool-curbs, and like situations. The plant is an evergreen with masses of strap-shaped leaves nearly two feet long, from among which arise the stems two to three feet tall bearing umbels of light lavender-blue tubular flowers throughout the summer and autumn months. These great bunches of bloom are frequently ten inches or more in diameter. There are numerous varieties, including a white-flowered kind, *Leichtlini*, a deeper blue than the type; a double-flowered kind; and several dwarfs, the best being *Mooreanus*, with rather small flowers but a nice compact habit and a fine deep blue color.

The varieties of *A. africanus* are sometimes planted directly in the earth beside ponds or pools and look particularly appropriate and at home in such situations, producing fine masses of color.

Any good loamy soil suits it, and it is grateful for plenty of well rotted manure. When grown in pots its cultivation is simplicity itself. "Leave it in its pot or tub," says Mrs. Coombs, "without disturbing it just as long as possible till it threatens to burst the container . . . After blooming it should have the long rest or drying which South African bulbs need. . . . Put the pots or tubs in the cellar during the winter; dig in a little fresh earth and fertilizer in the spring." This is all simple enough for such a rich reward. One point is important, however: they should be given plenty of water while in growth.

❦ *Phlox Drummondii* (Drummond's Phlox) (Plate 139)

This lovely and multicolored annual Phlox is a native of Texas. The word "Phlox" means flame, and to none of the many species is it more appropriate than to this low-growing Texan. From a very modest status as a wild flower it has arisen to the place of one of the most important of summer-flowering annuals. Florists have taken it in hand, and the erstwhile weed from the sandy Texan countryside is now offered in a great many lovely colors. The plant is a semi-erect branching annual, slightly hairy, bearing wide heads of flowers, self-colored or with a white or cream-colored "eye." Some of the colors now offered are white, deep purple, deep rose with a darker eye and white throat (this is called Brilliant), pale pink or flesh-colored, chamois-rose (a lovely tint), cinnabar-red, scarlet, a delicate tone of buff-yellow, light rose with white eye, vivid crimson, and deep violet with white eye.

Phlox Drummondii makes lovely beds that flower all summer, or it may be used as an underplanting for Roses, or an edging for herbaceous borders. Seed is best sown under glass in frames or flats, and the young plants set in place when settled warm weather has arrived.

[*150*]

In order to get bushy plants that will cover the ground well the leading shoot should be pinched off when the plants are quite small. It should be given well drained soil in full sun and the addition to the soil of some lime. It will not thrive in the shade, but it requires to be faithfully watered in dry weather.

Phlox Drummondii was named for Professor Drummond, a keen botanist. He it was who found the plants in Texas and sent the seed to Europe. Though he died soon afterwards it is nice to feel that his name lives on in these gay and useful annual plants.

Many-Colored Phlox with Annual Sunflowers (Plate 140)

The story of the rise of the tall Summer Phlox, *P. paniculata*, a poor-colored weed that wanders over our eastern states from Pennsylvania to Florida and Louisiana, flowering in summer, to its present place as the glory of the summer garden is only one more romance that had its inception in the quiet workshops of hybridists. Lemoine in France and Pfitzer in Germany worked part of the magic. And there are now growers in America, England, Holland who yearly add to the Phlox wealth that is ours for the taking. A vision of no common order it must have taken to see in the gypsy plant with its magentaish flowers and poor figure the possibility that is the present-day Phlox, superb in form and glamorous in its range of colors. There are many species of Phlox, but the hybrids of *P. paniculata* form the largest and most important group among them.

They begin to flower late in July and continue until September; and for the best results they should be planted in a sunny open situation, though they will flower in partial shade. The soil should be carefully prepared for them; a clay loam is considered the best, rich in manure and well drained, but these cheerful plants will make some sort of show in almost any kind of soil. Every four or five years the clumps should be dug up and divided, in early spring or late fall, allowing about three stems to the division. They require room for their development—room and air; and so they should not be planted too close together and other plants should not be allowed to crowd them. Two feet apart is not too generous an allowance of space for them. The wise gardener will not let them go to seed, for seedling Phloxes quickly rise up all over the place, crowding the original plants, and are seldom of any value, reverting immediately to their original old clothes and careless carriage. Also, if the spent blooms are picked off, the plants will continue to flower for a longer period.

Not many pests attack this sturdy plant. Mildew in some seasons is troublesome, and for this a dusting of powdered sulphur, or a number of dustings, is the best remedy. Keep an eye on the plants after the end of June, and, should either this trouble or the Phlox plant bug make its appearance, deal with it quickly. For the latter pest the remedy recommended is spraying the plants with Black Leaf-40, 1-500, with an ounce of soap.

The modern Phlox has heads made up of a great number of florets, and the plants range in height from twelve to forty inches. But some of the older kinds also make magnificent masses of color in the garden. There are now so many different kinds on the market that it is difficult to make a choice. Visit a nursery where there is a fine collection of Phlox, and pick out the colors and types you prefer while they are in bloom. There are no blues or yellows among them, but every shade of pink, rose, scarlet, salmon, red, maroon, amaranth, lavender, and almost pure purple, as well as pure white, some with a contrasting eye, others with suffusions of harmonizing colors. The shape of the individual floret may be round and wheel-like, slightly cupped, or starry; and there are early and mid-season and late

Plate 136. *Nelumbium Nelumbo (Nelumbo nucifera)* (EAST INDIAN LOTUS)

Plate 137. WATER-LILIES (NYMPHAEA) IN GARDEN POOL

Plate 138. *Agapanthus umbellatus* (BLUE LILY OF THE NILE)

Plate 139. *Phlox Drummondii* (DRUMMOND'S PHLOX)

Plate 140. MANY-COLORED PHLOX WITH ANNUAL SUNFLOWER (*Helianthus annuus*)

Plate 141. *Salvia splendens*, FIREBALL

Plate 142. A PATH BANDED WITH *Salvia splendens* AND SWEET ALYSSUM IN MAUVE AND WHITE

Plate 143. FRENCH MARIGOLDS WITH *Verbena venosa*

Plate 144. AN ATTRACTIVE ARRANGEMENT FOR A CUTTING GARDEN WITH TRELLIS AND DIPPING WELL

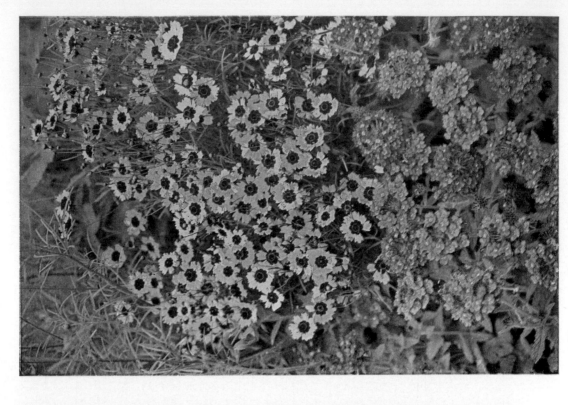

Plate 145. *Coreopsis tinctoria* (CALLIOPSIS) AND
Verbena venosa

Plate 146. *Helianthus annuus* VAR. *globosus*
(DOUBLE ANNUAL SUNFLOWER)

Plate 147. *Coreopsis radiata* (CALLIOPSIS)

Plate 148. *Tagetes patula* (FORMS OF FRENCH MARIGOLD)

Plate 149. PETUNIAS, SNAPDRAGONS, CANDYTUFT AND *Verbena venosa*

Plate 150. *Nemesia grandiflora*, SUTTON'S VARIETY (*N. strumosa*)

blooming varieties. Do not let the plants suffer for want of water in dry weather; on the other hand, do not water-log the soil.

Few flowers are more effective in the garden, but it may be said that you can easily have, and if you become a Phlox fan you surely will have, too many in the garden. Their wheel-like regularity produces a monotonous effect, and plants of other forms should be grown with them. Suggested are Lilies, Hostas, Globe Thistles, Eryngiums, *Veronica virginica*, *V. longifolia subsessilis*, *Salvia uliginosa* and *S. azurea*, the August flowering Aconites, *Clematis Davidiana*, Limoniums, Verbascum Miss Willmott, and the gray foliage of Nepeta, *Elymus arenarius*, Rue, and Santolina. It is also a good plan to depart from the pink and scarlet scale occasionally by introducing some of the purple and lavender varieties. Magenta is still rife among the Phlox tribe but is being gradually eliminated.

Seen growing among the Phloxes in Plate 140 are the great heads of the annual Sunflower, *Helianthus annuus*. This is a cottage garden, and so such an association is permissible; ordinarily the Sunflowers would be better left out, or planted in another part of the garden.

Salvia splendens, Fireball (Plate 141)

When I see a bed of *Salvia splendens*, that unfortunate association of a red rag and a bull always comes to mind. It has its uses; it pleases some eyes. But, though red is a glorious and courageous and a stimulating color, the hue of *Salvia splendens* is somehow cheap, and the foliage is of a cheap quality. This plant was introduced from Brazil about 1822—as a greenhouse plant. But it was soon found that it could be grown outside and that it made an admirable bedder. It raced around the world like a bonfire gone mad until all the lands were alight with its glare. It is not now as popular as it was in the last century. Good taste has more or less prevailed.

There are now numerous improved varieties of it, among them Fireball, of Plate 141, and Harbinger, another scarlet form, and Pride of Zurich, which may be had in bloom very early. And besides these the revolt against its terrible brilliance is shown in the introduction of such varieties as Parma Violet, a variety with purple flowers of rather a dead tone, and of Salmon Beauty, almost as brilliant in its special hue as the red ones, though distinctly salmon-colored. There is also Rosy Gem, with bright rose flowers.

"These splendid bedding plants," says a catalogue, "are easily raised from seed. They germinate readily if sown in heat in January, February or March, and should be planted out in June."

A Path Banded by *Salvia splendens* and Sweet Alyssum (Plate 142)

If in any situation the Scarlet Sage could be made tolerable to the sensitive eye, it would be in such a situation as is shown in Plate 142. Here a broad path is bordered by a wide planting of lavender and white Sweet Alyssum. They are the ordinary *Alyssum maritimum* and the variety known as Lilac Queen. Just behind is a strip of Scarlet Sage, the rawness of its tone softened by the foaming Alyssums. The rest of the picture is composed in ameliorating greens—dwarf fruit trees, vegetables and, beyond, larger trees.

The Scarlet Sage is best started indoors and planted out when warm weather arrives. The Alyssums may be sown where they are to flower and should bloom all the summer through.

French Marigolds with *Verbena venosa* (Plate 143)

French Marigolds and *Verbena venosa* make a long season display. There are any number of kinds of French Marigolds that may be used, some tall and some dwarf. Of the tall ones two good varieties are Josephine, with dark velvety petals edged with gold, and Royal Scott, a showy kind striped with gold and maroon. Among the dwarfer kinds, these chiefly used for edging and bedding, are: Fire Cross, orange suffused with red; Golden Ball, a double flower of pure golden orange; Legion of Honor (Little Brownie), yellow edged with brown, single, a common and desirable variety; Lemon Ball, all lemon-yellow and very double, and Robert Beist, a pretty brown double flower. The taller French varieties may grow more than two feet tall but have smaller flowers than the African varieties. They are fine for picking. Seeds may be sown in place where they are to flower after settled weather has arrived, or may be started in flats under glass and planted out when they are large enough to handle and the weather is warm. A little time is gained by following this method.

Verbena venosa (V. rigida) is a valuable bedding plant from Brazil, Argentina, and thereabouts. It is sometimes used in rock gardens, where it makes billowy masses of leaves and flowers that last throughout the season. The flowers are borne in dense racemes and are of a pleasing purplish color. It is not hardy over the winter in the neighborhood of New York City but frequently springs spontaneously from self-sown seeds. These seedlings may be moved to any situation where they are needed to fill a vacancy. Or seeds may be started under glass and will flower the first year.

Verbena venosa also makes a very nice wall plant, especially planted at the top and allowed to tumble down the wall-face. It blooms until after the first killing frosts.

❦ Cutting Garden with Trellis and Dipping Well (Plate 144)

An attractively planned and planted cutting garden is a desirable adjunct to any garden. It enables the main plantings to be left undisturbed, golden-yellow in color, and in shape more like a huge Chrysanthemum than a Sunflower. It grows four to five feet high. Double Sunray is even larger in flower than the above, pure yellow in the ball-like center surrounded by a ring of quilled petals. This is very tall, sometimes reaching a height of six feet. Indian Moon is not so tall, growing from three to four feet high, with large deep golden moon-shaped flowers borne in abundance.

These tall large-flowered plants may be grown at the back of borders, among other annual or perennial plants, but they appear at their best in a setting of another kind. A planting of them alone against a high stone wall or fence or hedge is most effective. In such a situation they do not dwarf the other plants but display their full magnificence without competition.

They grow rapidly from seed planted where they are to flower.

☙ *Coreopsis radiata* (Calliopsis) (Plate 147)

This is an odd and showy variety of annual Coreopsis, or Calliopsis. The petals are narrow and very pointed about the dark center. The color is red and yellow. It is probably the variety known as Tiger Star, that grows only ten inches high and so makes rather nice edgings and is amusing for cutting. It is especially appropriate for use in bowls of Mexican pottery.

There are numerous kinds of annual Coreopsis besides *C. tinctoria*, already described in Plate 145. The Sultan has large flowers of a warm maroon hue, and grows something under two and one-half feet tall; Golden Wave is rich pure yellow with a chestnut center. It is a dwarf, ten inches in height, and so is good for edgings, as is Golden Ray, only nine inches tall, having rich maroon flowers edged with gold and twisted. Crimson King is another low-growing kind of a pretty garnet-red color;

[*158*]

marmorata grows taller, two feet, and is done in red and yellow; *nigra speciosa,* with large reddish brown flowers, grows two feet high.

❦ *Tagetes patula* (Forms of French Marigold) (Plate 148)

There are many varieties of French Marigold, both double and single: some are mottled; some are self; others, striped yellow and brown. There are tall and dwarf varieties also, and some of the modern introductions are very compact. As they grow they spread out and produce masses of flowers valued both for cutting and for making a grand show in the garden throughout the summer and autumn. They have been in use in gardens since 1783, when they were introduced from Mexico. The name French Marigold has no significance. Few flowers can vie with these French Marigolds in richness of color towards the close of summer. As the cool nights begin they seem to redouble their efforts, and each individual plant becomes a bouquet in itself, an old-fashioned tight bouquet such as our grandmothers carried. The scent of the foliage of Marigolds is very unpleasant to some persons; it is strong and pungent and has a bitter quality. But the so-called French varieties have a less powerful odor than the common African varieties. Modern Marigolds are being de-scented by the clever hybridists, but these odorless blooms seem to have lost something of their attraction. We may not exactly like the odor; but we are accustomed to it, and we are apt to miss it.

Long ago the old botanist Dodonaeus noticed that if the leaves of the French Marigolds are held up to the light they "appear as if perforated," and he also advanced the opinion that they have some poisonous qualities.

They are best started under glass or in a window and planted out when mild weather is established. They are sun-lovers and do not thrive in shaded places.

✤ Petunias, Snapdragons, Candytuft, and *Verbena venosa* (Plate 149)

Here in Plate 149 is a scene of summer luxuriance that might be reproduced in any garden, large or small. It is a bright mixture of summer annuals that charms by its very carelessness, its apparently unpremeditated gaiety.

The present-day Antirrhinum or Snapdragon is a fine flower. The florists have taken it in hand and changed it from the simple European wild flower it once was to the elegant plant it now is. Its range of colors is almost unbelievable, and it is especially rich in tones of pink to garnet, white through yellow to flame and bronze; often there are two colors in the same flower, coral and amber, deep pink and buff, white and yellow, gold and orange, yellow and lilac, canary and chamois-pink, terra cotta shading to orange, and so on almost *ad libitum*. But no blues or pure purples to date. These are all forms of *A. majus*, the flower one sees clinging to the walls of old ruins in chalk districts of England with the Wallflowers. But these florist-beguiled Snapdragons have large flowers, well filled spikes, and they may be very tall, two and one-half to three feet, or medium-sized, one and one-half feet, or little fellows, Tom Thumbs, under a foot high. These are fine for edging. The medium-sized ones flower longest, and they are the most useful all round. Although Antirrhinums are hardy where they are native, with us in the cold climate of the middle and northern states they will not live over. But they are easily raised from seed, which should be sown under glass in flats in March and pricked out when large enough to handle into small pots. Pinch out the tops to make the plants bushy, and harden off before planting out of doors.

The Petunia is now a lady, but it was not always so. Down in South America it is just a weed, a poor relation of Tobacco. The florists again have been at work and have changed the Petunias so that their nearest

[*160*]

Plate 151. *Gazania splendens*

Plate 152. *Godetia grandiflora* (FAREWELL TO SPRING)

Plate 153. *Lavatera trimestris* (L. rosea)

Plate 154. *Mesembryanthemum pyropaeum (Dorotheanthus gramineus)* (FIG MARIGOLD)

Plate 155. *Senecio elegans nanus fl.-pl.* (DWARF DOUBLE JACOBAEA)

Plate 156. *Salpiglossis variabilis*
(PAINTED TONGUE)

Plate 157. *Senecio elegans fl. pl.*
(DWARF GROUNDSEL OR JACOBAEA)

relation would not know them: dressed them up in frills and furbelows, made them large and gross, little and dainty, single and double, and washed out their magenta hue, replacing it with pure pinks, with velvety dark red, with a very respectable blue, with rich purple, pure white, and now a faint-hearted yellow, and striped and splashed some of them until they look like harlequins in a play.

Petunias are among the most satisfactory of bedding flowers. They bloom all summer, and they bloom with a will. The smaller kinds are perfect for window boxes or large jars on terraces. They should be raised from seeds "by sowing on the surface of a compost of loam, leaf-mold and sand, in well-drained pans in February or March." Toward the end of May or early in June, they may be planted out in the open border. They want a sunny situation and water if the weather is dry. No flowers will give more satisfaction for so little trouble; none will better repay good culture. They are very valuable for cutting, seeming to arrange themselves in the most graceful manner.

Annual Candytuft (Iberis) is important as an edging plant, and there are numerous attractive varieties. It is a hardy annual and may be sown out early where it is to flower. It comes in white, pale lavender, delicate rose, and a deeper rose. The annual varieties of Candytuft are forms of *Iberis coronaria* and of *I. umbellata*. Some grow more than a foot high, others much less.

⚘ *Nemesia grandiflora*, Sutton's Variety *(N. strumosa)* (Plate 150)

Nemesias are native in South Africa, and they are among the plants from that part of the world that thrive in England and do not do well in the eastern United States. They are called "easily grown hardy annuals," and when one sees them running in rainbow scarves along English flower beds and borders one is ready to believe it. You are told to pinch out the leading shoots to make the plants more bushy and compact; you do this, but you still get a straggly, faint-hearted plant. They are best started indoors or under glass in March and transplanted out when weather is settled and mild, or they may be sown out of doors in May. Good fibrous well manured loam with the addition of a little wood ashes is the best for them.

The lovely flowers in Plate 150 are Sutton's creation, forms of *N. strumosa;* they come in white, yellow, pink, carmine, orange, and blood-red. There is a variety called Blue Gem with flowers the color of a Forget-me-not. They are a foot high or under.

✤ *Gazania splendens* (Plate 151)

Gazanias are among the glories of the South African flora. They belong to the Daisy family and take that form. "From every roadside gutter and depression in the veld where moisture has lodged this winter, a riot of glorious gazania blossoms has broken out. It is a unique sight, for the colors range from tangerine-red to orange-crimson and they are borne in a profusion which can only be described as sheets of blossoms." Save for three or four annual species they are half-hardy perennials. *G. longiscapa* is an annual that will bloom from seed if it is sown early. It is offered in many catalogues.

G. splendens is not known in the wild but is supposed to be a hybrid of the half-hardy perennial *G. rigens*, the oldest and best known species. It is an upright plant less than a foot high, the leaves narrow and of a silken texture. The plants spread over the ground and produce their flaming orange and yellow daisies in great profusion. "Each is marked with a black and silver zone at the base of the petals" which adds to the brilliance. Sarah

[*162*]

V. Coombs, whose book "South African Plants for American Gardens" is quoted above, says that **G.** *splendens* is extremely useful for summer bedding in sunny locations, and will flower the first year if the seed is sown early.

The Gazanias are much more popular in Europe than they are in this country. They make magnificent beds, long-flowering and brilliant. The colors are out of the ordinary, not the usual orange, or orange-reds, but a subtle manifestation of these hues, at once soft and vivid, with a sort of sheen or luster; and the black and silver zones at the base of the petals give them distinction. Beds of Gazanias might well take the place of the beds of lurid Scarlet Sage that now desecrate our parks and public gardens, and they would grace the proudest terrace.

❦ *Godetia grandiflora* (Farewell to Spring) (Plate 152)

Godetias are among the annual plants that we owe to California's vast wealth. They grow magnificently in English gardens, where the air is moist and the mercury seldom soars to torrid heights; and we, of the dry eastern coast and the Middle West, seeing them there and encouraged by the misleading advice of writers on California flowers, see no reason why they will not give us the same enthusiastic service. The contrary is the fact. Very few of California's wild children will grow east of the Rocky Mountains with anything like the vim and vigor that they display at home. You can choose your dry hillsides and give them every advantage that is possible within our limitations, but, as a distinguished horticulturist has recently said, "they just don't like the East and show it plainly."

Long lists of Godetia hybrids are found in every English catalogue. They sound alluring. The flowers are bowl-shaped, some double and some single, the heights ranging from a foot to two feet. In color they cover an entrancing scale from pure satiny white through cream-pink, shell-pink, salmon-pink, on to dazzling scarlet, and there are a number that are mauve or lilac in hue, and even maroon. Often the center is paler than the rest of the flower; sometimes there is a narrow white selvedge along the edge; sometimes the petals are heavily blotched with a contrasting color.

They are hardy annuals. If you live in a climate that they will tolerate, sow the seeds indoors or under glass in flats in February, prick them off, and plant them out in May about six inches apart, or sow them out of doors where they are to flower in April, thinning the plants to six inches apart as they come up. Ordinary good garden soil is right for them—but water them in dry weather or give them some sort of cooling mulch such as leaf mold.

⚘ *Lavatera trimestris (L. rosea)* (Plate 153)

The lovely flowers in Plate 153 are also seen better grown in English and Continental gardens than in this country. They belong to the Malvaceae, and the flowers are like enormous Morning Glories. This Lavatera is native to Mediterranean regions.

The plant grows from three to four feet high, very bushy and with large lush leaves. It requires plenty of room for its development, at least two feet between plants; and it also requires sunshine and a soil made rich and nourishing by the addition of well rotted manure or some good commercial fertilizer.

The flowers are usually solitary, borne in the axils of the leaves, and in color may be white, pink, or in the variety Sunset very deep rose. (This variety grows only two feet high.) They look like the most permanent of hardy perennials but are in reality hardy annuals only. Their seed should be sown where it is to flower out of doors in April.

The plants make magnificent beds, as they have a long blossoming

[*164*]

after midsummer, or they may be grown in the borders towards the back with other tall and large-scale subjects. They will need to be staked and should be well watered in dry weather.

⚜ *Mesembryanthemum pyropaeum (Dorotheanthus gramineus)* Livingstone Daisy (Plate 154)

The Livingstone Daisy, known also in South Africa as Buck Bay Vyjie, is more properly a Dorotheanthus than, as labeled, a Mesembryanthemum, though the plants have something of the same general appearance. It is an annual and spreads about over the sandy wastes of South Africa, making the most brilliant patches of color, ranging from ivory-white to crimson of the most penetrating, eye-blinding tone. Magenta is a hated hue by many, but used with care in its associations, among creamy or pale buff flowers, with atmospheric blues and pale lavenders, or with gray foliage plants, it is not so bad. Some varieties of the Dorotheanthus are magenta with a will.

Sarah Coombs, whose knowledge of South African plants must be accepted as authoritative, says: "It grows quickly from seed and is recommended for borders or rockeries. In its own land it starts growth at the end of the rainy season, and like other South African plants, should not be allowed to suffer from lack of water when young. Under dry conditions at first, it is likely to become stunted and never recover. In America there has been trouble sometimes in bringing it into flower. If planted in flats and these flats exposed to the sun *with no water* for a couple of weeks, water being given at the end of this time, the seeds may obtain a ripening which they failed to have when gathered as soon as they were matured."

Mesembryanthemum as a group is an enormous one; the plants have fleshy leaves and may be annual or perennial herbs, mostly growing in desert regions. They belong to the Aizoaceae, and "all but a handful of the nearly one thousand species are South African and all cultivated species come from there, although some of them are naturalized escapes in California." This vast group of plants has been divided into various genera by systematic botanists. Dorotheanthus is one of these new genera.

❦ *Senecio elegans fl.-pl.* (Dwarf Groundsel or Jacobaea) (Plate 155)

This pretty little unassuming annual is a relative of the Giant Groundsel, *Senecio clivorum* (Plate 134), though to the untutored eye there is little family resemblance between them. It has been known and grown in gardens for a long time and was called by ancient botanists "Flos sancti Jacobi," or the Flower of St. James. It is a native of South Africa, where it is called Purple Ragwort, or Wild Cineraria. The double form here represented is known as the American Jacobaea—why "American" is not known. There is a white variety of it that is very pretty. There is also a single pink variety. These Jacobaeas are cousins to our pestiferous Tansy Ragwort, *Senecio vulgaris*, one of Europe's gifts to a too hospitable country.

Beds of *Senecio elegans fl.-pl.* are very pretty. The plants grow about eighteen inches tall and may safely be planted in mixed colors. Seed should be sown one-eighth inch deep out of doors in late April where they are to grow, and thinned to five or six inches apart. Or for earlier bloom they may be sown under glass in the late winter and planted out in May.

❦ *Salpiglossis variabilis* (Painted Tongue) (Plate 156)

Salpiglossis variabilis, or *S. sinuata variabilis*, is one of the most lovely of tender annuals. It was introduced from Chile in 1824. The plants grow two to three feet high and, when massed, make a display that is hardly to be surpassed. The flowers are trumpet-shaped, and appear something like large Petunias, in loose terminal clusters. The leaves are broadly lance-shaped, the margins widely toothed. The whole plant is slightly sticky.

The range of colors of the flowers is amazingly attractive. There are lovely selfs in rose, purple, primrose, crimson, scarlet, and purple-brown, all of them delicately penciled. Then there is a strain all of which are veined with gold, rose and gold, violet and gold, scarlet and gold, and so on. The soft brilliance of the flowers is a delight, and their velvet texture adds to their attraction. Some kinds are veined with black. Indeed, in few flowers are such unusual effects to be found. And they are carried on long erect stems. They are among the few flowers that it is perfectly safe to buy and plant in mixed packets, but a good strain should be secured.

The seeds may be sown in February or March in pans or flats of light soil, and as they are very small only the merest sprinkling of soil over them will suffice. "Transplant when leaves have formed one half inch apart in pots of loam and leaf-mould. In May begin to harden off in cold frame and plant out in June six inches apart in a sunny situation." They may also be grown in the greenhouse and make lovely cut flowers.

They are to be seen particularly well grown in this country in gardens near the sea; there the colors are richer, the plants more floriferous. They make lovely long-season beds, or may be planted towards the back of the borders.

✿ *Senecio elegans fl.-pl. nana* (Dwarf Groundsel or Jacobaea) (Plate 157)

This is simply a dwarf form of the ordinary double Jacobaea. Its height is only about nine inches, so that it may be used where the taller variety is not suitable. Its habit is neat and compact and its colors soft rose or pale purple. Its treatment is the same as for the Jacobaea in Plate 155.

[*167*]

❦ *Zinnia elegans*, varieties of (Youth-and-Old-Age) (Plate 158)

In the very forefront of the great company of annual plants that decorate our summer gardens marches the Zinnia. It is important on many counts. It flowers from the time its comes into bloom until the frost puts its good intentions to rout, and the plants are covered with flowers all the time; its range of colors, heights, sizes, and types is astonishing; the flowers are long-lasting on the plants as well as when cut, and cutting only provokes them to a greater generosity of giving. It has perhaps come a longer distance from weedhood to elegance in a shorter period of time than any other flower.

The Zinnia was originally a not too attractive Mexican weed. This was its state not much more than a hundred years ago. It was introduced to gardens and tolerated there because it flourished with little or no attention. Its rise to fame began in comparatively recent times, and no Hollywood obscurity has with more sensational speed become a headliner than has this crude Mexican gypsy. American hybridists saw in it a world of possibilities, and they bent their attention upon its improvement. Their success has astonished the world and brought to our drought-ridden summer gardens the assurance of bloom and beauty. However subtle the color scheme, there is a Zinnia that will fit into and enhance it. There would be little monotony, indeed, about a whole garden of Zinnias. They may be had from a few inches high to several feet high, as small as dimes and as large as saucers and all sizes between. Their range of hues almost puts the rainbow to shame. There are all the primary colors clearly and cleanly expressed, and then almost every hue, tint, shade, variation that can be imagined save pure blue. In most cases the plants are self-supporting, needing no staking—a quality deeply appreciated by the busy gardener. Very tall plants may occasionally need a single stake, but this is not usual. Ordi-

[*168*]

Plate 158. *Zinnia elegans*, VARIETIES OF (YOUTH-AND-OLD-AGE)

Plate 166. *Begonia crispa*
A HANDSOME FORM OF TUBEROUS BEGONIA

Plate 167. *Lathyrus odoratus*
(SWEET PEA)

Plate 168. GLADIOLUS FRÄULEIN M. WITTELSBACH

Plate 169. GLADIOLUS ATHENE

Plate 170. *Tigridia Pavonia* (MEXICAN TIGER FLOWER OR SHELL FLOWER)

narily they may be left to meet the forces of wind and weather with no artificial assistance.

Zinnias are of the easiest culture. They may be started in flats indoors or in a cold frame, or they may be sown out of doors where they are to flower; but if this course is followed it must be borne in mind that they are southerners, heat-lovers, and will not stand frost, and so they should not be planted out until after danger from this scourge is past. If sown directly in the ground also, the plants should be thinned out in order to have space for free development. How much space is needed will depend on whether one is planting the pygmies, that look like old-fashioned bouquets when in flower and are only a few inches high, or some of the giant Californians that have almost the stature and circumference of shrubs.

The ground they prefer is one that has been deeply dug and well manured, and they should be watered freely in dry weather. They like a fully sunny position and do not thrive best in even partial shade. Very few, if any, pests attack healthy Zinnia plants, but in shaded places the leaves will mildew badly.

Advice to one who does not know Zinnias well would be to secure a catalogue from some firm specializing in them and buy a packet of seed of each kind listed. Use a vegetable garden if necessary for this try-out. The results will be astonishing, a revelation in beauty and of what the art of the hybridist can do.

❧ Pentstemon Southgate Gem (Plate 159)

Few if any Pentstemons are annuals, but many of this large genus are not hardy enough to stand over the winter in cold climates. Southgate Gem is one of these. It is a hybrid of a Mexican species, *P. Hartwegii*, and is much used abroad for bedding purposes, as well as for groups in the

[*169*]

border. It grows about two feet high and blooms all through the summer and autumn—at least in England. The flowers, as may be seen in the plate (159) are tubular and borne in a long raceme. The color is a lovely rose-scarlet. There are numerous others of these large-flowered bedding Pentstemons available. There is *albus,* pure white, and a Scotch Prize Strain, which offers many colors, almost an endless variety, and there are others.

Sow the seed in January or February in flats, and prick off in tiny pots or in other flats or frames when large enough to handle. They may be planted in their permanent situation in the garden in May, in a well dug and generously enriched soil. Cow manure and humus are the best means of improving the soil.

The flowers are not unlike those of a Gloxinia, and the plants throw up successive spikes. From a packet of mixed seed many a beauty may materialize, but if it is desired to perpetuate some special color resort may be had to cuttings of the young shoots, which strike easily.

Brachycome iberidifolia (Swan River Daisy) (Plate 160)

The Swan River Daisy is one of the dainty trivia that make up the rank and file of garden annuals. Its native home is in Australia in the Swan River district. The foliage is light and delicate, the plants branching and about eight or ten inches tall. The flowers are like small Cinerarias, soft blue to purple with a white halo about a black eye. There are also a pure white horticultural form and a pinkish form. One called Little Blue Star is especially neat and compact with delicate blue daisies borne in profusion.

The main use of the Swan River Daisy is for edging flower beds or for filling blank places in the borders. Or it may be planted over the situations that have been vacated by bulbs.

[*170*]

It likes ordinary soil on a warm sunny border. The plants are fragile and easily overthrown by rough winds or rains, so that it is well to insert short bits of brush among them to keep them from being laid low and their appearance spoiled.

The seed may be started in flats of light soil in a hot bed or cold frame in March or April. Or it may be sown directly where it is to grow in the open in late April or early May, and thinned to about six inches apart. A few plants make no show at all; it takes many to make a modest show. For edgings do not plant them in a straight single row; let there be several rows, or stagger the plants so as to make more of an effect. The plants begin to bloom towards the end of June and continue throughout the summer. Not indispensable but pleasant enough to have about, and the colors are so soft and unassertive that they blend with any others, as well as helping to reconcile some of the more aggressive hues to one another.

❧ *Convolvulus tricolor* (Dwarf Morning-Glory) (Plate 161)

It has always been a matter of surprise to me that the Dwarf Morning-Glory is so little grown nowadays. It was once very popular. It is a low-growing plant suitable for edgings of beds and borders. It grows erectly to about a foot in height, branching, and is very leafy. It makes a full bushy growth, and the flowers, like small morning-glories, are borne with the greatest freedom. True, they share the predilection for early closing time with their tall twining sisters, now more properly called Ipomoeas; but they are not nearly so hasty about it, and while they are open they provide a real feast for the eyes; and they are not quite as common as some annuals that are used in garden so freely. The flowers are about two inches across, deep blue with a yellow throat surrounded by white—for this reason are they given the name *tricolor*.

There are also a pink or rose-flowered form and one with pure white flowers, but none are as lovely as the blue ones. Nothing could be easier than their culture. Sow them under glass in February, and plant the seedlings out in May; or sow them out of doors where they are to flower late in April or in early May, planting the seeds about one-eighth inch deep.

The plants are native to southern Europe and love a warm border in full sunshine, and they prefer a rather poor soil. They bloom cheerfully the summer through, and their rounded bushes of pleasant leafage covered with morning-glories which, though individually short-lived, follow one another in quick succession make a delightful display. They are charming for edging paths in simple cottage gardens or in rows in children's gardens. They were once generally known as *Convolvulus minor*.

❦ *Papaver Rhoeas fl.-pl.* (Double Shirley Poppy) (Plate 162)

How the Shirley Poppy came to be is another horticultural romance. It is the tale of the long patience of an obscure flower-loving clergyman of Shirley, England, one of the vast number of modest clerics who have immeasurably added to the world's horticultural riches. The Rev. W. Wilks noticed among the wild Poppies, or Corn Poppies, that fluttered on the outskirts of the vicarage garden, one that deviated slightly from the usual red coloring of this common wild flower which in some localities was called Redweed. This slight difference from its fellows fixed Mr. Wilks's attention, and he marked the plant and later gathered the seed. Then began the many years of seed sowing and patient selection that has resulted in the well known Shirley Poppy, which has by now girdled the globe with its silken blooms.

The flowers are large, quite four inches across, and range in color from pure white through the most enchanting tones of pink, salmon, rose,

[*172*]

scarlet, crimson, often with an edging of pure white. They were at first single-flowered, but recently a double-flowered strain has been introduced, and the color range has been increased by a new strain called Celeste, containing blue shades, something quite new in Poppies. The petals of the Shirley Poppy have the texture of silk and are delicately crinkled. No flowers could be lovelier.

Three mistakes are commonly made in the growing of annual Poppies, which are otherwise of the easiest culture: The seeds are very small and require the barest covering of soil; really to press them into well pulverized soil with a flat board is sufficient. Too deep covering means no results or very poor ones. Too late planting is another common mistake. Even in the cold climate of New York the seed should be sown in March, on a windless day so that the fine seed will not be scattered by the breeze to situations where it is not wanted, if there can be such. The third mistake is almost impossible to avoid—too close sowing. But this is easily remedied by drastic thinning of the seedlings while very young to not less than a foot apart. The plants are graceful if they have space in which to develop, but grown close together they are spindly and unsightly.

Annual Poppies, the Shirleys among them, do not transplant easily. So they should be sown where they are to flower, in sunny borders or beds of good fine soil, not too heavily manured, and where strong-growing plants will not press upon them. They will often sow themselves and reappear year after year, sometimes where we least expect them, in the crevices between stone steps or paths, even in the grass.

It is a mistake to hold that these Poppies are useless for cutting. As a matter of fact they are exquisite for house decoration, but the flowers should be cut just when the buds are beginning to open. They will then expand slowly and remain in a presentable condition for several days.

In mild climates the seed may be sown in the autumn out of doors and will germinate thickly with the first mild days of the spring.

⚜ *Calendula officinalis fl.-pl.*, Ball of Gold (Plate 163)

Calendula officinalis is the old Pot Marigold once deemed important in culinary and medicinal decoctions. Today its uses are wholly ornamental, but it has changed its garb to suit its changed status in the world of flowers. Once it grew in the herb garden, now it has a proud place in the flower garden, and is forced in quantities by florists for the winter trade.

It is easily grown and has several good points to its credit: It is fine for cutting; it flowers all summer and through the autumn; and it will, curiously enough—for it seems a soft and sappy plant—withstand several degrees of frost in the autumn. Zinnias grow black beside it, even the true Marigolds succumb; but the Calendula goes serenely on.

Its seed may be sown in the border as early as the soil can be worked, and the young plants thinned out to at least a foot apart. They will then grow bushy and present themselves as veritable bouquets of bloom. The plants have a nice pungent scent which some do not like, but it is not nearly as strong as that of the true Marigold and has a pleasing, exhilarating quality.

There are now many varieties of Calendulas on the market. The colors range from pale yellow to warm orange, sometimes with a dark center; others tend towards apricot in hue, and a new strain is citron-colored. Many are double-flowered, and there is a new variety called Orange Shaggy, very well described by its name, which is an unsightly and unseemly flower, not fit to consort with such beauties as Apricot, Chrysantha, Golden Beam, Radio, Campfire, that has an almost scarlet sheen, Ball's Orange, Ball's Gold, Ball's Masterpiece, Orange King, and Lemon Queen.

꯭ Gay Plantings of Begonias (Plates 164 and 165)

When we speak of bedding plants, we refer to such plants as are commonly massed together in beds to produce a long-lasting and brilliant effect. Usually one plant of a kind is used in this type of planting, or there may be several in the old manner—*Cineraria maritima*, Ageratum, Geranium, and again Cineraria, Ageratum, Geranium. What is sought is persistent color and precise arrangement in conspicuous places—in parks and public gardens, on formal terraces. But bedding out is not resorted to today nearly as much as it was in years gone by; and where it is employed it has been made less formal, more gracious and graceful.

The Tuberous-rooted Begonias lend themselves ideally to this type of gardening. Begonias are all tender plants in our climate but they make a great show out of doors in summer, or in the winter greenhouse, especially the Tuberous-rooted kinds that have large flowers in brilliant colors. They are derived from various species: from *B. Evansiana*, from China and Japan, said to stand a temperature of zero in Washington, D.C. (leaves are more or less oval, lobed and toothed, and red beneath, flowers flesh-pink); *Lloydii*, a group of hybrids of drooping habit, useful for baskets; *socotrana*, from the island of Socotra (plants about a foot tall and flowers over an inch and a half across of a nice rose-pink color); *tuberhybrida* ("a group name for many hybrid tuberous rooted begonias"), from Peru. The flowers of these hybrids are very large and come in nearly all colors save blue, some single and some double, "some of the forms Camellia-like, others Narcissus-like." An English admirer writes: "The singles are beautiful enough, with their great flowers borne in abundance well above the thick, massive leaves, and with their brilliant and varied colors. But the doubles are even more strikingly handsome. The flowers differ greatly in form. Some are like huge Camellias; others resemble Water Lilies. Some

[*175*]

are of the form of large Hollyhocks; others as massive and rich as Peonies. The range of colors is not complete because we have not yet got blue, but it is very considerable. There are whites as pure as new-fallen snow, yellows of various shades, beautiful blush, and Picotee-edged flowers, delicate pinks, soft rose shades, brilliant salmon and orange hues, glowing scarlets, and deep rich crimsons."

The Tuberous Begonia is not an old flower in gardens; its first usage dates from quite recent times. The species are of little value in themselves; but their offspring are of enormous importance, and more and more hybrids appear with every year that passes. It has to be admitted, however, that they are of less use in this country as bedders than they are abroad. They flag unhappily in our hot dry summers; and, while much can be done to keep them in heart by digging the soil of the beds deeply, by manuring it richly and generously, spreading a layer of manure about nine or ten inches below the surface of the soil, still they suffer. When the cool nights of the late summer and autumn begin, the Begonias revive and spread themselves.

Another thing the gardener can do to earn success: "He can buy his tubers, or take them out of their winter quarters, about the end of March, and place them six inches apart in boxes filled with a compost in which leaf-mould predominates. A situation in a greenhouse, or in a frame (with a covering in cold weather if there is no artificial heat), will suit them, and in the course of a week or two buds will show. Never let the soil get quite dry, and the shoots will push strongly. If kept close to the glass they will be short and sturdy, not long and weak. They should have abundance of air to help to keep them healthy. . . . By the first week in June the plants will be very strong." When the plants are transferred to the open the soil should be kept moist so that they will continue to grow strongly in their

Plate 171. PELARGONIUMS IN POTS USED AS A BORDER TO A TRELLIS

Plate 172. THE SOFT-COLORED LEAVES OF *Coleus Blumei*

Plate 173. FUCHSIA GÖTTINGEN FILLING A NARROW BORDER

Plate 174. FUCHSIA VARS. ANDENKEN AND HEINRICH HENKEL IN BORDER WITH HELIOTROPE

Plate 175. STANDARD FUCHSIAS USED IN BEDS OF BRIGHT-COLORED SUMMER FLOWERS

Plate 176. A BED OF THE MANY-COLORED FORMS OF *Celosia argentea* (COCKSCOMB)

Plate 177. A HANDSOME
YELLOW-FLOWERED CANNA

Plate 178. EFFECTIVE BORDER OF CANNAS IN FORMAL SURROUNDINGS

new quarters. Some growers advise a mulch of short decayed manure as soon as they have begun to grow, and occasional applications of liquid manure thereafter.

In the autumn, when their exuberant beauty begins to fade and the leaves to thin out, it is time to think of their welfare for the winter. They may then be taken up, cleaned of the remnants of leaves and flowers, and the tubers put away in a dry, cool, but frost-proof place until they are wanted again in the spring.

In Plate 164 we have a massing of deep rose-red Begonias, single-flowered, set off by the surrounding rather formal green setting. In Plate 165 we have an informal planting along a path, all colors mixed, with a background of trees and shrubs. They look very well in this informal setting; and, as they bloom the summer through, color and gaiety along this path are assured.

Begonia crispa (Plate 166)

This is an exceptionally beautiful form of Tuberous-rooted Begonia. The flowers are very large and ruffled in the manner of some of the new Petunias, and they are held well above the handsome foliage. Beds of this soft yellow-flowered variety would be lovely and cool-looking on terraces. This same ruffled form comes in many other colors. The treatment is the same as for the other Tuberous Begonias (see under Plates 164–165).

Lathyrus odoratus (Sweet Pea) (Plate 167)

All the world loves the Sweet Pea, the little flower which was first noticed some two hundred years ago by an ardent botanizing monk, Father Francis Cupani, an Italian, in the island of Sicily. The plant,

[*177*]

Lathyrus odoratus, which the monk found was, as we say, then nothing to write home about; but it made its gentle appeal to its discoverer and he started it on its amazing way of conquest in the flower world. "How little he knew the tremendous part which his poor, small-blossomed, purple-petalled flower was to play in the world of gardening!—that in the twentieth century it should be grown in every garden in the United Kingdom, become a favorite flower in the distant states of America, found an industry, and have a society devoted solely to its interests." He did not *know*, but perhaps he had a vision of this simple flower winding its tendrils about the heartstrings of gardeners high and low, rich and poor. It is said that the Sweet Pea first found its way to Britain about the year 1700. "In 1713 Dr. Petiver, in a paper read before the Royal Society, said that the seed was sent to Dr. Uvedale who, in his garden at Enfield, had a number of rare and curious plants from foreign parts." That was the beginning; the end is not in sight. No monument has been raised to the memory of Father Cupani, yet such distinction has been paid to deeds of far lesser consequence. The Sweet Pea has brought delight to countless millions, and though it has been improved immeasurably, garbed in new finery, befrilled and beruffled, endowed with all the colors of the rainbow, it remains intrinsically a simple flower, simple and sweet. Great horticulturists have devoted their lives to its improvement on both sides of the water, but they have not taken from it its unaffected charm and naturalness. We read that in 1842 James Carter, an English seedsman, listed six varieties, and that it was not until 1860 that he offered nine varieties, "among them being a blue-edged one." Then followed the great work of Henry Eckford, in England, who began the work of cross-breeding the Sweet Pea, "and laid the foundation of the wonderful developments which have since taken place in the flower. . . . It may be said with truth that not until 1877 did the Sweet Pea hold out much promise of becoming a power among

[*178*]

garden flowers." It was at this time that Mr. Eckford began to work "persistently, skillfully and methodically" at the improvement of the Sweet Pea. He raised and introduced more than two hundred named varieties. There are now many times that number and part of the work of the Sweet Pea Society is to weed out the too-much-alikes, the less-goods, and to keep the multitude of names down to a manageable number.

So far as culture in the United States is concerned, it has to be admitted that in many sections the Sweet Pea presents almost insurmountable difficulties. It loves cool conditions of soil and atmosphere. Our hot dry summers are highly unfavorable to it. In the northern states and the Pacific Northwest, and by the sea generally, Sweet Peas thrive, but elsewhere there is a struggle to keep them in bloom after the warm days of July begin. The ground for Sweet Peas should be prepared the autumn before planting. It should be deeply dug and well manured, and by the end of February, or early in March, it will have settled firmly in place; in the neighborhood of New York the seed may be sown in March two inches deep and covered with a mixture of sand and light loam. This early planting is an absolute essential to any success in the hot-weather states. Some persons advise digging a trench in this well manured soil and sowing the seed at the bottom, then filling it in as the plants grow, the idea being to secure cool conditions for the roots far below the natural soil level. They are usually planted in rows or double rows with twiggy branches firmly pushed into the ground between them, or a length of chicken wire run for the vines to climb upon. When the plants begin to flower, daily picking of all the flowers is of genuine value in keeping the vines at their work of producing flowers. Let them go to seed, and they soon give up the effort.

A Sweet Pea catalogue gives the best idea of the number and kinds that are to be had, but all are lovely and nearly all have the delicate fragrance that has given them first place among flower lovers both in the garden and in the house, as cut flowers for use in winter. Their culture under glass is comparatively simple, so that all winter long one may enjoy these charming flowers.

❦ Gladiolus (Plates 168, 169)

The Gladiolus belongs to the Iris family, and for many persons it is the flower of flowers. Originally it came from South Africa, where there are more than two hundred species known, with a few in tropical Africa and elsewhere. But the modern Gladiolus bears little resemblance to the slender and modest flowers that gave it birth. It is today a flower of true splendor; there is nothing modest about it, and devoted entirely to its culture and improvement is one of the largest flower societies in the world—the American Gladiolus Society, while several state agricultural colleges are concerning themselves with research work among the "Glads," and the number and enthusiasm of their admirers grow by leaps and bounds.

In "The Garden Dictionary" edited by Norman Taylor, it is written, "The origin and history of gladiolus reach far into the past. As late as A.D. 1000 gladioli were known as sword lilies and about A.D. 200 Dioscorides described several different *corn* lilies, which today we know were gladiolus species." So this flower is no newcomer to gardens though its present-day manifestation would astound those gardeners of ancient times.

The Gladiolus grows from a corm, which is often mistakenly spoken of as a bulb. This corm will not live over the winter in cold climates, but must be dug and stored in a frost-proof place until spring again visits the land. Moreover the corms should not, must not, be put into the ground until settled warm weather has arrived, when they are planted from three to six inches deep, according to the size of the corm. When they are dug up in the autumn it will be found that the old corm has a number of new

[*180*]

ones attached to it; these must be separated from it before the corms go into winter storage. After digging, it is a good plan to let the plants lie out in the sun for a day or two, when the earth is easily rubbed from the corms and the tops removed. "Storage for the corms should be at a temperature of from 35° to 50° in a place neither too damp nor too dry and with ventilation facilities. For the amateur who has but a few corms, a cellar or a place proper for the storage of fruits or root crops is suitable."

There are nowadays early, mid-season, and late-blooming varieties, and this should be kept in mind when choosing varieties for the garden. There are also many types of Gladiolus to be had, from the small decorative kinds to the large-flowered varieties with blooms six or seven inches across, and there are some with small blooms that measure only a half-inch across. In form "the petals may be plain, ruffled, fringed, recurved, needle-point, rosebud, tulip, twilled, elongated, or twisted, with certain varieties having a combination of two or more of these." The color range is immense, embracing almost every tint and tone save pure blue, but including many purples and lavenders and some attractive smoky tones. There are self colors and many that are streaked, blotched, freaked, edged, feathered, and otherwise marked with contrasting or harmonizing colors. A modern list of Gladioli offers a wide choice, and it is a good plan to see a good collection in bloom before ordering, as descriptions are often misleading.

The Gladiolus is subject to an insect pest—called thripes, which has recently given growers a good deal of trouble. "Thripes live in the stored corms and infest new plantings, destroying their beauty." They are very tiny and difficult to detect until the mischief is done. "Corms may be treated while dormant with naphthalene flakes or with warm water." This water treatment consists of "keeping bulbs in water at 110° F for two to three hours."

The Gladiolus is not overparticular as to soil. One writer says that "soil that will grow anything will grow glads." It, however, stands to reason that a good sweet loam will bring the best results, and it is an accepted fact that a heavy wet soil is the worst for them. Good drainage and good culture—that is, keeping the soil constantly stirred—are important factors in growing fine spikes of flowers. They are happiest planted out in the open, in full sun, yet with some protection from high winds in the form of a not too distant wall or fence or house. The corms may be planted from six to twelve inches apart according to the height to which the plant will grow, and tall varieties will need to be staked to keep the heavily burdened stalks from being overthrown by high winds or by their own weight.

Tigridia Pavonia (Mexican Tiger Flower or Shell Flower) (Plate 170)

Tigridia Pavonia is among the many fine bulbous plants sent to us from Mexico. It is there called the Peacock Tiger Flower. The Tigridia belongs to the natural order Iridaceae, and the genus contains a number of species with which we are not here concerned.

The species illustrated has a forked stem, leafy, and from one to two feet high, and the brilliant three-cornered flowers with their bowl-shaped spotted centers are about six inches across. The outer segments are usually self-colored—and may be white, scarlet, violet, yellow, rose, etc. The bulbs are not hardy in the neighborhood of New York but may be planted out in late April or early May three to six inches deep in warm mellow soil, compounded of leaf mold, sandy loam and a little well rotted manure. They like sunshine, being southerners, but they also like plenty of moisture, and so if the rainfall fails they should be artificially watered during the heat of summer.

[*182*]

The individual blossoms are short-lived, but a fresh supply opens daily so that if the bulbs are set in bold clumps they create a unique display. Watering occasionally with liquid manure is said to increase the vigor of the trusses of blossoms and to add brilliancy to the gay flowers.

Besides the flower borders as a place to grow them it is interesting to try a few clumps in the rock garden for summer bloom, especially where a little height is desired. They may also be forced in a greenhouse for winter bloom.

⚜ Pelargoniums in Pots (Plate 171)

Perhaps of all the genera of plants used for indoor or greenhouse decoration none are more universally popular than the various kinds of Pelargoniums. So amiable are they that some of them may be kept in flower nearly all the year round. The Zonal varieties are generally known as Geraniums, and these we see in the cottage window, in fine greenhouses, in parks and gardens, and on the terraces of handsome estates.

These plants were once the most famous of bedding plants; they could be brought to keep up an undimmed show of bright color throughout the season. They are invaluable for use in window boxes, where they flower from midsummer until frost, often combined with Petunias, Sweet Alyssum, and other long-season bloomers.

In Plate 171 we have the Zonal Pelargonium used in a rather novel manner. Large pots of them are placed along the base of a white latticework arbor. Between the pots Petunias grow luxuriantly, and climbers of various sorts decorate the lattice. The foreground is a neatly shown greensward. This simple ensemble means color all summer long, and in the autumn, before frost, the pots of Geraniums may be taken indoors again.

They come in many lovely colors—white, orange-red, blood-red, all tones of pink, scarlet, and crimson, and there are both double- and single-

[*183*]

flowered varieties. They grow well in ordinary garden loam and have the advantage, for those who want a bright show for little expense, of being very cheap to buy. Many may scorn the cheerful old Zonal Geraniums, but it would be hard to find a prettier decoration for a cottage window than a pot of these flowers in healthy bloom.

✠ The Soft-Colored Leaves of *Coleus Blumei* (Plate 172)

The chief value of *Coleus Blumei* lies in the variegated coloring of its leaves. The margins of the leaves are crisped and toothed, and they may display combinations of rose and chocolate, yellow, green and white, brilliant scarlet and yellow, deep crimson and mulberry, pink with white and green markings. This plant, which belongs to the Mint family and comes from Java, was once to be had in a vast number of named varieties. Today they are not so much used. But they had their day of great popularity when no lawn or terrace was innocent of its beds of bright-hued Coleus. Many persons thought they had an advantage over flowers, for they did not go out of bloom, leaving sorry blanks, but kept up a continuous and unblemished show until frost. They were even much used as table decorations. They are still to be found growing before summer hotels and in gardens in the Victorian manner. But more modern gardeners have turned their attention elsewhere.

"The Garden Dictionary" says: "Propagation is easily effected by seeds or cuttings. Seeds sown early in March in a temperature of 60°–65° soon germinate and before long are large enough to pot off singly in small pots. The smallest seedlings are likely to be eventually the best in leaf markings and coloring, the strongest ones being likely to run mostly to green." They may be struck from shoot-cuttings at almost any time of the year, in heat "confined in a close moist atmosphere and shaded from the sun; when they

Plate 179. A GRACEFUL ARRANGEMENT OF TRADESCANTIAS (SPIDERWORTS)
IN A FLAT CONTAINER

Plate 182. BRILLIANT CALENDULAS
IN A WHITE JAR

Plate 183. A BOUQUET OF SUMMER FLOWERS

Plate 184. VARIOUS-HUED GLADIOLI IN A WHITE JAR

Plate 185. AN ARRANGEMENT OF TALL PHLOX

Plate 186. A BLACK BOWL FILLED WITH LATE SUMMER FLOWERS

are rooted they must be potted on in rich loamy soil with some leaf-mould added." If flower buds appear they should at once be pinched out as they are of no consequence and only spoil the neat appearance of the plants. Give the newly rooted plants plenty of light and enough air to keep the shoots from "getting drawn."

Fuchsia Göttingen Filling a Narrow Border (Plate 173)

Fuchsias belong to a large genus of plants nearly all of which are native to tropical America, Mexico, and New Zealand. For many years they have been among the most popular of greenhouse and window plants as well as used largely for bedding purposes out of doors. Their name honors Leonard Fuchs, a German botanist.

They are extraordinarily graceful plants with their masses of pretty eardrop blossoms drooping from every twig. There are a vast number of hybrids of which the above is one, and there is now an American Fuchsia Society interested in furthering the culture of these plants. The natural forms are usually red and purple or sometimes entirely red or wholly crimson, and single. Many of the hybrid varieties have double tubular flowers, and some have a white corolla. E. O. Essig, president of the American Fuchsia Society in an article in *National Horticultural Magazine*, says "the species, *Fuchsia Plumier*, was first discovered in 1703, and the first introduction, *F. coccinea* Aiton, was made into England in 1788." They instantly became immensely popular in England and France as well as in Germany, and "in 1844, Felix Porcher in his 'History and Culture of the Fuchsia' (in French) listed five hundred varieties in commerce. This year marks the peak of the popularity of fuchsias in Europe, but hybridization continued and there were no less than seven hundred varieties in 1890 and about a thousand varieties have been recorded to date, although there are only about one hundred and eighty varieties and species available in commerce at this writing. And with the exception of the *triphylla* hybrids produced in Germany in 1900–1906, practically all of these were created over fifty years ago." *

In California, Fuchsia hedges are a common and lovely ornament of gardens, and there they live out of doors the year round. The species *F. magellanica* is known to live over the winter in the neighborhood of New York City if planted in a sheltered situation in well drained soil and protected by a covering of leaves or salt hay. It blooms all summer and until cut down by the frost and may be trained to a wall or grown at the back of a large rock garden, where it may be allowed to assume its natural habit.

Fuchsias grown out of doors are better off in partially shaded situations. In Plate 173 is demonstrated the fine effect a mass of these flowers is capable of making.

⚑ Fuchsias and Heliotrope in Box-edged Border (Plate 174)

An attractive form of informal bedding is shown in Plate 174. Here in a Box-edged border are growing coral-colored and white Fuchsias and Heliotrope. This combination assures bright color and an attractive color scheme and delicious fragrance from midsummer until frost. The Fuchsias are of the many hybrid varieties, and the Heliotrope is a form with large full-flowered heads.

Heliotropes are bedding plants of great value and beauty; they may be grown as bushes or trained as standards, and they are also flowered in greenhouses and on sun porches. Beds and borders of them, edged with Sweet Alyssum, are lovely and cool-looking during the heat of summer

*National Horticultural Magazine, Jan., 1934.

[*186*]

days. They like heat and a rich soil and, so considered, will many times repay the little trouble that has been expended upon them in abundant bloom and a fragrance that is hardly duplicated by any other flower. There are white varieties of Heliotrope, but nearly all are some tone of lavender, mauve, or rich purple. One of the finest kinds, and the most highly scented, is called Royal Fragrance. The blooms of this are a rich royal purple, and the sweetness is of the best.

Heliotrope belongs to the Borage tribe and is a genus of some two hundred species found in various parts of the tropical world. The species which has given rise to most of the cultivated varieties popular today is *Heliotropium peruvianum*, sometimes called Cherry Pie, because of the supposed resemblance of its fragrance to that of this toothsome pastry. It comes from Peru.

❀ Standard Fuchsias in Beds of Summer Flowers (Plate 175)

Fuchsias are often trained as standards—that is, the plant is restricted to one treelike stem and then at the top allowed to assume a more or less umbrella form. Trained in this manner, they are popular as dot plants in formal beds, and as such they are very graceful and effective. Over beds of Heliotrope or white Petunias they are exceedingly attractive. In the plate (175) they are shown showering their gay tubular blossoms above beds of small-flowered Begonias edged with Ageratum.

Other plants that make good standards are Roses, Wistarias, Flowering Almonds, Lantanas, Chrysanthemums, and Mignonette. Standards are valuable because they give height to beds that would otherwise present a monotonous flatness. They not only are used in formal plantings but are sometimes spaced at regular intervals in herbaceous borders or used as accents at the head of steps or at other points needing emphasis.

[*187*]

✠ A Bed of *Celosia argentea* (Cockscomb) (Plate 176)

Celosias are tender annuals, many of them native in India. Those in the plate are said to be a form of *C. argentea* known as *pyramidalis*. It grows about eighteen inches high and is usually listed in seed catalogues as *Celosia pyramidalis*. The flower heads are rather like plumes and come in soft colors, yellow, purple, crimson, salmon, and so on. A new variety called Flame of Fire has huge plumes of vivid crimson-scarlet.

They are grown in greenhouses but are also rather extensively planted out, furnishing bright undimmed masses of color during the hot-weather weeks. They also last well in water when cut.

Seed should be started under glass at the end of February or early in March. The seedlings should be kept close to the glass and moist, and when large enough to handle transplanted into thumb pots filled with a compost of two parts fibrous loam, one part leaf mold and well rotted cow manure and sand. Again keep them near the glass; and when the flowers show repot into five-inch pots, harden off in a cold frame, and plant out of doors in June, choosing a sunny situation and good soil.

The well known Crested Cockscomb, *Celosia cristata*, "is really an encouraged monstrosity of its original parent, the broad flattened crest being formed by the union of its branches." It is difficult to understand why any one would want to grow it, yet it has had its day of popularity.

The Feathered or Plumb Cockscomb has real beauty and usefulness, especially in parks and public gardens where long-season effects are sought.

✠ A Handsome Yellow-Flowered Canna (Plate 177)

It is difficult to know how the planters of public parks and gardens and of hotel grounds would get along without the flamboyant Cannas. They are not now much used in private gardens, though at one time their vogue was great. They are tuberous-rooted plants with broad, hearty leaves, sometimes green, often colored; the flowers are very showy, borne in erect simple or branched racemes. The natural species are plants of tropical and subtropical America and the East Indies, but these species have been practically lost sight of in the vast number of forms and hybrids that have been developed from them. Famous French nurserymen, in particular, devoted much attention to raising new kinds of Cannas, and Orchid-flowered, Gladiolus-flowered, and similar strains made their appearance. There is today an immense number of named varieties, their colors covering a range of red, scarlet, crimson, yellow, orange, bronze, salmon, watermelon-pink, and so on. The flowers may also be blotched or suffused with other colors and sometimes bronze foliage adds to their colorful effect.

For outdoor planting, Cannas are summer-flowering, and their usefulness comes to an end with the first serious frost. There are tall, medium, and dwarf varieties for use in different situations. The tallest kinds should be planted about two feet apart; the dwarfest, about one foot apart. The soil in which they are grown should be deeply dug, and it is well that it should be thoroughly manured some time previous to planting. If the soil is a good sandy loam, it should suit these plants admirably.

During the summer the only care required is watering in dry weather and weeding. "In order to lengthen the canna season," says "The Garden Dictionary," "it is best to use potted plants instead of planting the root-stocks. The former are cheap and in the markets at the proper time in your locality which is long after all danger of frost is over. The idea is not

[*189*]

merely to dodge a sporadic late frost but to put the plants in soil warm enough to be congenial for a tropical plant—in other words they need summer heat."

❦ An Effective Border of Cannas in Formal Surroundings (Plate 178)

Cannas have come a long way since the old *Canna indica*, popularly known as Indian Reed or Indian Shot, was much in evidence in gardens. This plant was in great demand because of its fine lasting foliage in the days of bedding, for it could be depended upon to keep any spot sightly the summer through. But today this species has been abandoned in favor of the vast number of hybrids that add to the advantage of handsome greenery handsomer flowers. In Plate 178 some of these new Cannas are shown in appropriate surroundings. They border a straight path and are a part of a formal setting—the shorn grass, the Ivy-covered wall with its fine simple balustrade, the clipped trees. In contrast one sees beyond a natural plantation.

Canna indica is an old plant in gardens. It was called Indian Shot "because of the roundness and hardness of the seeds." In the *Botanical Magazine* (Curtis') it is said, "We find it to have existed in our gardens in the time of Gerard [1556]. Parkinson was acquainted with that variety of it which has yellow spotted flowers. . . : Clusius saw it flowering by housesides in Spain and Portugal, and says that the inhabitants there use the seeds for making their rosaries."

And so, though we are inclined to look upon the Canna as a manifestation of the tasteless Victorian era, when expendiency and rule of thumb ousted grace and adventure from gardens, it has, as a matter of fact, a much older history and usefulness. If Cannas are used at all today they should be planted in beds or borders to themselves and not mixed with the

[*190*]

less stable tenantry of the garden. They always appear stiff and out of place in mixed borders. Borders of Cannas may have an edging of some long-flowering plant, and Begonias or Lobelias are commonly used.

SUMMER FLOWER ARRANGEMENTS

⚜ A Graceful Arrangement of Tradescantias in a Flat Container
   (Plate 179)

Tradescantias, or Spiderworts, are not commonly used for indoor flower arrangements, yet their graceful foliage and three-cornered blossoms make them well fitted for this purpose.

All the Spiderworts are native to America. There are about forty species known, and they keep green the memory of the name of John Tradescant, gardener to Charles I of England. The species here shown is *Tradescantia virginica* in three colors, blue, rose, and white. It is a common flower in gardens, where it is apt to sow its seeds rather widely and inconveniently, for the young plants spring up all about, often where they are not wanted. They are also known in various localities as Widow's tears, Snake-grass, Trinity, and occasionally as Spider-lily.

The plants grow from one to nearly three feet tall and begin to flower late in the spring, continuing, off and on, nearly all summer. Almost any situation suits them and any soil, and they are suitable for use in mixed borders, massed at the edge of woodlands or in the rougher parts of the grounds. A border of Spiderworts presents a lovely effect for many weeks of the summer, and they are so inexpensive and so easily increased by division that this is a lovely planting possible to almost every one. It is said that there is a double-flowered form, but I have not found it listed.

[*191*]

The individual blooms are short-lived, but they follow in such quick succession that the plant always has a sufficient number of flowers in evidence. "Flower of a day," it was sometimes called.

Of its introduction Parkinson wrote, "This Spiderwort is of late knowledge, and for it the Christian world is indebted unto that painful, industrious searcher, John Tradescant, who first received it of a friend that brought it out of Virginia, and hath imparted hereof, as of many other things, both to me and others." The common name was first given it because it was supposed to be a cure for the bite of spiders.

✠ A Summer Bouquet of Peonies, Iris, and Meadow Rue (Plate 180)

How easy it is in June to make a charming bouquet! On every hand material of the first quality is to be had. In Plate 180 we have an informal assemblage of pink double Peonies, several kinds of tall bearded Irises with some sprays of white Meadow Rue (Thalictrum) to give lightness to these heavier flowers.

Both for bouquets and in the garden the mission of the Meadow Rues is towards grace and lightness. There are numerous species; the one in the plate is *T. aquilegifolium album*, of which there are also rose and light violet forms. It grows about three and one-half feet high.

✠ Delphinium and White Gladioli in a Happy Combination (Plate 181)

Delphiniums are among the most delightful flowers for cutting. Their long spires of bloom are grace itself and seem to arrange themselves with easy naturalness, while their soft colors blend pleasantly with many other hues.

Flowers often used with Delphiniums both in the garden and for

[*192*]

indoor decoration are *Lilium candidum, L. croceum, Thalictrum glaucum,* Roses (some of the climbing Roses that bear their flowers in great trusses are especially effective with Delphiniums), *Campanula latifolia macrantha,* with purple bells, Thermopsis, with spikes of yellow pea-shaped flowers, Iris Monspur, and seasonable Hemerocallis; but I do not recall seeing the Gladiolus used with them before and the effect is especially pleasing. Almost any of the many colors worn by this versatile flower would be suitable—all the tones of pink, scarlet, yellow, and so on—but the white-flowered variety here shown is particularly lovely used in association with these pale blue Delphiniums.

It is a good plan to grow a row of Delphiniums in the vegetable garden that may be used exclusively for cutting. This enables the gardener to avoid despoiling his borders, and to choose for this purpose the varieties that are best suited for use indoors. For table decoration some lovely kinds are Mrs. Thomson, Fanny Stormonth, Orion; for large receptacles and bold effects such varieties as Millicent Blackmore, Lady Eleanor, Mrs. Townley Parker, and Mauve Perfection might be chosen.

🏵 Brilliant Calendulas in a White Jar (Plate 182)

With little artifice or subtlety Calendulas may be arranged delightfully for indoor decoration. Their colors are rich and harmonious, from pale lemon to richest orange, and they show up well under artificial light. They have sufficient natural foliage to keep the blossoms from massing too closely together, and all that remains for the arranger is the choice of a suitable receptacle. The wide-mouthed white jar shown in Plate 182 is especially good as it allows a sufficient depth of water and permits the flowers to assume a natural uncrowded pose.

The blue background and the orange tablecloth all add to the effec-

[*193*]

tiveness of the picture. Calendulas are also lovely used in rooms of dim coloring, grays, browns, tans, and russets.

✠ A Bouquet of Summer Flowers (Plate 183)

The colors of the garden flowers of high summer rival those on a painter's pallet. Mixed bouquets of these multi-colored flowers have a definite charm in their unstudied gaiety. In Plate 183 we have such an assemblage. There we see double Cornflowers, *Centaurea Cyanus fl.-pl.*, Calendulas in several colors, scarlet Carnations, varieties of annual summer Chrysanthemums in pale yellow, spikes of Snapdragon, and a few other flowers. The plate of cherries near by echoes the hue of the Carnations, but the blue vase at the right might well be left out.

The names of the summer-flowering Chrysanthemums may be found under *C. carinatum;* White Queen and Northern Star have creamy white flowers with dark discs; *C. segetum* Evening Star and *C. s.* Morning Star have large yellow flowers, three to four inches across: bright golden-yellow in the first, yellow shading to primrose in the second. The plants grow about eighteen inches tall. They are hardy annuals and may be sown out of doors where they are to grow in late April, or indoors in March and transplanted when large enough to handle. These annual Chrysanthemums are neglected in this country, though much grown abroad. They have long stems and are fine for cutting.

✠ Various-Hued Gladiolus in a White Jar (Plate 184)

The Gladiolus is among the summer-flowering plants that provide lovely blooms for cutting, and they are now also forced for winter use by florists. The soft tones of the varieties shown in Plate 184 are harmonious

[*194*]

used together—pale yellow, blush, white, a stalk or two of scarlet, and a few purple ones. Their own foliage is the best to use with them. As the lower blossoms fade, they should be picked off. They may thus be made to last in water for many days.

⚑ An Arrangement of Tall Phlox (Plate 185)

The tall summer Phlox is queen of the mid-season garden. They are lovely in the garden and lovely for cutting. Their warm fragrance fills the air indoors and out, being especially marked in the evening.

A jar of mixed varieties has the appearance of a pattern of old chintz. The stalks should be gathered just as the flowers composing the head begin to open; otherwise the flowers soon begin to drop, necessitating a continual tidying up in their neighborhood.

⚑ A Black Bowl Filled with Late Summer Flowers (Plate 186)

To this gay arrangement the late summer garden has contributed richly. In the black bowl, which shows them off to advantage, we have, among others, several kinds of Phlox, a late pale-colored Hemerocallis, Dahlias, Lilies, Gaillardias, some short spikes of Delphiniums (second blossoming), Baby's-breath, purple Coneflowers and some well chosen branches of foliage. For all it is a heterogeneous mixture of colors and forms, the general effect is rich and stimulating and well reflects the lavishness of the season.

AUTUMN

THE GARDEN IN AUTUMN

SEPTEMBER is really a summer month in the garden. If it were not for the golden warning of the harvest moon "swelling like an orange flower-bud" against the background of the dark sky, we might still be in the very midst of August. Flowers are plenty and full of zeal to accomplish their productive ends. The days are perceptibly shorter but not much cooler, though little wispy airs rise out of the garden at nightfall, cool and reviving. Dews fall more heavily, and the Roses, worn and tired by the long heat, take heart and begin to bloom again—more delicately, however, than in June. Their shell-like fragility seems to be the result of having borne much.

In the borders Sunflowers and Marigolds excel themselves, the tall Ironweed, Vernonia, is richest royal purple, the joe-pye, tall also but indecisive in color. Certain new faces have made their appearance among the rioters—Japanese Anemones, the late-flowering Aconites and Salvias, sky-blue Plumbago, Autumn Crocuses and Colchicums, Michaelmas Daisies, Dahlias, and the early Chrysanthemums. Our color sense, strict in the early spring and summer, is blunted. We look upon the jumble of rich hues with a lenient eye. White Tobacco, Mignonette, and Tuberoses (if we have been so wise as to plant these old-fashioned scent purveyors) continue to feed

> With summer spice the humming air.

An occasional red leaf flagging our attention is an omen that is not regarded, a berry here and there is hardly noted. But watch the bees! Early and late they toil; even after sundown they may be found plunging from flower to flower in a frenzy of haste. They heed the warnings if we do not.

The long chair on the cool side of the terrace or beneath the wide-spreading tree still looks inviting. Streams move sluggishly, and so do we. Perhaps this is the time when a gardener may relax and rest! Not, however, if he is going to plant bulbs. Those intriguing packages will now begin to arrive, and there is a peremptory call to wield the trowel and the dibble. Colchicums, Autumn Crocuses, and Sternbergias should be already in the ground; Winter Aconites, Snowdrops, Erythroniums, and Lycoris should go in without a day's delay; Fritillarias, Leucojums, and Puschkinias early in September, and for the best results Narcissi before the month is out. Especially should the highly scented Gardenia-flowered Narcissus find a bed as early as possible. For the rest—Scillas, Grape Hyacinths, Chionodoxas, Camassias, Spring-flowering Crocuses, Brodiaeas, Oriental Hyacinths—any time during September and October will do. Tulips and the lovely western Calochortus, or Butterfly Tulips, should be planted in November.

Then, too, there will be other tasks: More faded blooms to be removed. Phloxes are definitely shabby. Their heads should be cut off before they have time to scatter their hardy seeds hither and yon, putting upon the garden the burden of a horde of undesirable foundlings that will add infinitely to the labor of our weeding in another season. The borders, if we are not careful, begin to lose their figures, so to speak, to look a little frumpish and blowzy. They must be tidied by any means that we can think of. The Dahlia's stakes must be straightened and strengthened, the brittle stalks tied a little higher up, the brush among the showering

[*200*]

Michaelmas daisies thrust more firmly into the earth so that the heavy autumn rains, when they begin, will not beat down the slender heavy-laden branches.

In the air, to be sure, there is that certain something that Hawthorne called "the Septemberish feeling," but this is more of the mind than induced by any outward appearance.

When October comes in, however, Nature begins visibly to relax. She ceases to cling so desperately to youth. In the garden there is a dimming of hues, a gentle fading, despite the kindled fires of the trees and shrubs and the "coral jewelry of the hedge." October is a lovely month; the light is golden, and peace seems to rest upon the misted land. The gardener has done his best and may rest upon such laurels as may have resulted from his efforts. He *may* rest, but if he is wise he will not cease all activity. Autumn weeding saves trouble in the spring; and while he is taking out the real weeds he will also remove such plants as have behaved like weeds, spreading unasked too widely, that have not, in short, garden manners. Especially on the small plot there is no room for such incorrigible tramps. Best be rid of them at once. Cutting down all spent stalks gives the garden a last brief seemliness. And this is not all. As Charles Dudley Warner wrote, "There is a large crop of moral reflections in my garden, which anybody is at liberty to gather who passes this way." November is the prime month to study and analyze this crop. There is only a sparkle of color or a faded breadth here and there to distract us from its contemplation. There have been frosts, but a Rose may still beckon, a Petunia flirt its blemished skirts. Chrysanthemums are jaunty, a small huddle of Autumn Crocuses blows. Many a plant that has been long silenced by summer heat and drought opens a wary eye and offers a flower. Among these will be Primroses, Cowslips, Violets, Pansies, Aubrictias, Japanese Quince, Honeysuckle, Sweet Alyssum, a glowing California Poppy or

[*201*]

two. Such scents as float upon the air seem strange to us. We do not identify them.

There have been high winds, straight drenching rains, a general putting out of fires, blotting out color. Gently but in no uncertain terms, we are made to understand that the time for rest has come, that we must part from much that we have held dear. We go about on fair days saying farewell. But there is always a certain wistful excitement about partings. What will befall before we meet again, before the first Snowdrop hangs out its little shivery bell, before the first robin takes the lawn for his strutting ground? We conjecture, we hope, we plan.

Yes, November is the perfect month for planning in the garden. We see it in its bare bones, so to speak, and we have not yet forgotten where its clothing did not fit or was unsuitable. It is wise to look about and call to mind what a great English gardener once said: "There is an individual character to every plot of land as to every human face in a crowd, and that man is not wise who, to suit preferences for any given style of garden, or with a view to copying a design from another place, will ignore the characteristics of the site at his disposal." If we have sinned in this manner, it is not too late to retrieve our mistakes. That is the beauty of a garden. It is never too late to regrade the land, to change walks and drives, to transplant shrubs and even trees, if they have not grown too large, in short to reconsider and play up to the characteristics that are natural to our own plot. And November is the ideal month for this work. We may change the frame of our picture, or repaint the picture itself. But we should be about it before freezing weather.

"Outside the garden the wet skies harden; the gates are barred on
  The summer side."

⚑ Dahlia King Harold (Plate 187)

Dahlias are among the flowers that florists have taken in hand and improved and changed almost beyond recognition. In their native state they are plants of the Mexican uplands, with a few in Central America and in northern South America. But the modern Dahlia bears little or no resemblance to these Mexican wild flowers. The early hybrids were stiff and unattractive, appearing as if carved out of soap, their colors hard and flat. Today there are innumerable types and varieties, lovely in form, gracious and various in color.

The Dahlia is a tuberous-rooted plant. It thrives best in good, well drained loam. The drainage is important, for while it requires plenty of water after it begins to flower it does not flourish where the soil is moist or water-logged. If the soil requires enrichment, bone meal is the best fertilizer to use. "Dahlias seem to thrive best when fed from the surface, after they have made a good start. It is a good plan to use a top-dressing about August 15. For every ten hills one may apply two pounds raw bone meal and a half-pound muriate of potash, keeping it away about six inches from the base of the plant and raking into the surface" (from "The Garden Dictionary").

Dahlias may not be put out in the open until after danger from frost is past. They are sensitive to frosts and, once killed back, are fatally injured. The roots should be planted at least three feet apart, and if in rows these should be at least four feet apart. The root should be laid so that the "eye" faces upward in a hole at least six inches deep. Three inches of soil will be enough covering at first, but as the plant grows the soil may be drawn in about it. Only one or two shoots should be allowed to develop, and a stake should be driven in behind the root at the time of planting so that as the shoots lengthen they may be tied up without the delay which might

[*203*]

mean that the brittle plant would be injured by too heavy rains or winds.

As has been said, there are now many types of Dahlias. The one illustrated in Plate 187, King Harold, belongs to what is known as the Decorative type, fully double flowers, of a rich dark red with dusky shadings, that fit well into the autumnal hues that prevail as the season draws on.

✠ Dahlia Camille Franchon (Plate 188)

This lovely flower (Plate 188) belongs to the Duplex type. These are open-centered blooms with only two rows of ray florets, or what we should call petals. Many persons like these semi-double Dahlias better than the stiffer and more formal Decorative kinds. This one is especially beautiful both in shape and in coloring, and the flowers are nearly seventeen inches in diameter.

✠ Dahlia Covenander (Plate 189)

The Cactus type of Dahlia is well represented in Plate 189. It is a delightfully informal type and fine for indoor decoration. When the Cactus Dahlia was first introduced, the flowers were heavy-headed and made little show in the garden or as cut flowers; but the modern flowers hold their heads well up and are borne on long firm stems. There are several types of Cactus Dahlias: the Incurved Cactus, having fully double flowers with most of the "petals" or floral rays "turned back for half or more of their length, the rays tending to curve toward the center of the flower"; the Semi-Cactus, like the foregoing but with "the margins of the majority of the floral rays turned back for less than half their length"; Recurved and Straight Cactus, "the floral rays recurved or straight."

❦ Dahlia Elfenprinz (Plate 190)

This is another of the charming Duplex type; its mauve coloring and yellow center are particularly appealing, and the flowers are held well above the foliage on stems long enough to make them available for cutting. (Plate 190.)

❦ Dahlia Mauve Star (Plate 191)

Plate 191 represents one of the very lovely semi-double Dahlias whose pointed petals and irregularity of form make it especially delightful for house decoration.

❦ Dahlia Rose Jane Cowl (Plate 192)

Plate 192 shows a handsome American-born Dahlia of the Informal Decorative type, sometimes known as Scharazad. The flowers are very large and carried on strong stiff stems well above the foliage. It is a type of Dahlia that American growers have been especially interested in. The color is tinged with a golden glow.

❦ Dahlia Jersey Beauty (Plate 193)

There are few Dahlias comparable in handsome coloring with that of the American variety Jersey Beauty, which was originated by W. H. Waite in 1925. It is truly representative of the modern giant or formal decorative type of Dahlia. With proper care and culture it will reach a height of nearly five feet and bear flowers nearly ten inches in diameter, on strong erect stems. Their rich pink coloring is most effective in the garden as well as for cutting.

* * *

Other types of Dahlias recognized by the American Dahlia Society are, Single, many of which are exquisite and especially good for cutting; Mignon, plants no more than eighteen inches high and bearing single flowers in many colors; Anemone, open-centered flowers with tubular disc flowers surrounded by two rows of petals; Collarette, single and usually of two or more colors; and besides these are the Peony-flowered Dahlias, those known as Ball Dahlias, Rosette Dahlias, and the little Miniatures and Pompons. The Pompons are small forms of the show or Ball Dahlias, ball-like in form and producing masses of flowers on the freely branched plants. These and the Miniatures are rapidly growing in popularity. They are very gay and charming in the garden as well as for cutting.

❦ Dahlias Growing Among Annuals in the Autumn Garden (Plate 194)

Here against a background of trees we have one of those mobilizations of many flowers of widely varying types and often antagonistic hues that are tolerable in the autumn only. In fact, at this season of near departures and farewells their exuberance, which seems to promise indefinite continuance, gives us a sense of security. Winter must be far away when flowers can bloom with such splendid vigor.

Dahlias form the mainstay of the border, but between them are masses of Calliopsis showering between the upstanding Dahlia plants. And in front the ruddy Cockscomb defies criticism while the riot of *Verbena venosa*, now at the height of its blossoming, helps to soften the contending hues.

✠ A Border of Dahlias Edged with *Sedum spectabile* (Plate 195)

In Plate 195 is a border of Pompon Dahlias in various tones of pink and red, edged with that reliable plant of many uses, *Sedum spectabile*. Between the Dahlias and the Sedum are a few Petunias, Snapdragons, and other annuals which brightened this strip of border earlier in the season. At that time the broad glaucous leaves of the Sedum are an ornament in themselves and make a neat and seemly edging.

Sedum spectabile is a robust, hardy perennial that grows from tubers somewhat the shape of carrots. It comes from Japan and China and has been long cultivated in the latter country, "but until lately not certainly known there in the wild state." It is one of the noblest plants of its numerous tribe. The flowers are borne in flat panicles four to six inches across, and in the type are a sort of ash-pink. These rest upon the pale leafage with fine effect, beginning to bloom towards the end of summer and continuing well into the autumn.

Under the varietal names of *atropurpureum* and Brilliant, forms with brighter-colored flowers are to be had. The plant is erect and dense and is indifferent, seemingly, to heat, cold, damp, or drought. It is happiest perhaps in full sunshine, but it also thrives in partial shade. It will, like most of its relatives, grow in any kind of soil, but if a choice is to be had it prefers a soil on the heavy side. It is very hardy and comes through the severest winters unscathed.

Sedum spectabile is a good plant to mass at strategic points in borders where there is a necessity for presenting a neat and tidy front. It is delightful as a foreground for the many-toned Michaelmas Daisies and for the bright blue-flowered *Salvia Pitcheri*.

Some attractive Pompon Dahlias are the following: Betty Ann, rose-pink; Bob White, milk-white with yellow cast; Honey, primrose-yellow;

Little David, russet-orange; Atom, scarlet; Yellow Gem, clear pure yellow.

❧ *Colchicum speciosum* in a Rock Garden (Plate 196)

Colchicums are not nearly so much used in the decoration of autumn gardens as they deserve to be. When they begin to spring out of the earth after the first hard autumnal rains, we are taken in thought back to April, for they look like Crocuses, both in color and in shape. But Colchicums belong to the Lily tribe while Crocuses are Irids.

Colchicums have one drawback which might as well be mentioned at once. In the spring they send up a mass of hearty foliage which looks handsome and fresh enough in borders but is too heavy for rock gardens save those of large size; and even in these it must be kept away from small choice plants over which it would flop dangerously when it loses its stiffening in passing away. This should be considered in placing them. The flowers are appropriate anywhere, but the leaves are out of scale with any save large plants. In a rock garden they may be planted in a section given over to rather strong-growing plants: Mertensias, *Anchusa myosotidiflora*, Dicentras, and the like. In a border, in front of some of the lower-growing Michaelmas Daisies now so much used, or with Japanese Anemones, *Chrysanthemum arcticum*, and the sprawling blue Plumbago, *Ceratostigma plumbaginoides*, they add an unusual touch that is most attractive. The colors of Colchicums range through the pinkish lilac tones to reddish violet, and there are some very lovely white ones. Certain of them are quaintly checkered.

They should be planted in August, and then we are sure of enjoying the blossoms the same season. They like a partially shaded situation and rather rich deep soil that is not too bone-dry; where suited, the bulbs

[*208*]

Plate 187. DAHLIA KING HAROLD

Plate 188. DAHLIA CAMILLE FRANCHON

Plate 189. DAHLIA COVENANDER

Plate 190. DAHLIA ELFENPRINZ

Plate 191. DAHLIA MAUVE STAR

Plate 192. DAHLIA ROSE JANE COWL

increase very rapidly, so that, beginning with a few, one soon has fine plantations of them which may be dug up every few years after the foliage has died down in spring and replanted, giving them more space. Place the bulbs just about an inch beneath the soil.

Colchicum speciosum of Plate 196 is found in the Caucasus, Macedonia, and as far east as Persia. It blooms in late September; the flowers are large and, in the type, of a fine pinkish lilac color, the tubes long and pale greenish lilac. It has an odor, but it cannot be said to be wholly pleasant. The white form, *C. s. album*, is one of the loveliest of bulbous plants. *C. speciosum* seeds freely and has produced a number of forms differing slightly from the type. There is a variety *rubrum* which has flowers of a warmer, deeper hue, and numerous others.

⚜ Colchicum Violet Queen (Plate 197)

Colchicum Violet Queen is one of the numerous beautiful new hybrids that have recently been developed. The flowers are very large and of fine form, the color a soft light violet, paling towards the center.

Other handsome hybrids are the following: Lilac Wonder, Conquest, Autumn Queen, the Giant, and a lovely double one named Water-Lily. A border of these large-flowered hybrids presents a handsome spectacle in the autumn garden.

⚜ *Colchicum autumnale minor* (Plate 198)

Colchicum autumnale has smaller flowers than the foregoing kinds, and their effect is somewhat starry, the color a soft uniform pinkish lilac. This species increases more rapidly than any other and should be taken up every third year, the bulbs separated and sorted out as to size and replanted. There are numerous forms of it. One known as *C. autumnale flore-pleno* has handsome double flowers of such substance that they last in perfection despite storms and wind, for as long as two weeks. It blooms late in the season. The white form *album* has even smaller flowers than those of the type, and they appear somewhat later; so freely are they borne that even a handful of bulbs makes a charming show. There is a beautiful double-flowered white form, variety *album plenum*, which E. A. Bowles says is an "old and very beautiful variety. There is an inferior form in which the flowers are neither so double nor so white as in the better. It should show twenty or more long, narrow, white segments, with just the faintest imaginable flush of pink in their heart." This fine form is always scarce and rather expensive, but it is worth searching for. The double flowers last long in perfection.

✤ *Crocus iridiflorus* (Plate 199)

There are many charming autumn-flowering Crocuses but *C. iridiflorus* is quite different from any of them. It is called the Iris Crocus with good reason. It really looks like a tiny Iris. The outer segments reflex slightly and are twice as long as the inner ones, which, when the flower is in full bloom, stand upright; the latter are also narrower and more pointed. The outer segments are a deep lilac-purple, and the inner are quite pale in hue. All this contributes to the Iris-like effect. *C. iridiflorus* flowers early in October without its leaves, and its native home is in Hungary and Transylvania.

This is not one of the most easily grown of autumn Crocuses, and it requires slightly different treatment from many of its fellows. Instead of the bright sunshine that most of them love, it prefers partial shade and a soil that is somewhat more moist than would be thought wholesome for

Crocuses in general. A soil made up of peat and leaf mold is recommended for it.

It is a delightful Crocus to grow in a rock garden, where it may be placed on the north side and somewhat low on the construction, where the ground is not too dry. A rock at its back, which may be covered with some small green creeper, shows its delicate form and color to advantage.

Crocus speciosus (Plate 200)

This is the finest of all autumn-flowering Crocuses. The flowers are large and beautifully shaped; in color they tinge toward blue, which makes them at once conspicuous among other autumnal species. It is the first of its kind to flower, thrusting impetuously through the earth in late September after a day or two of heavy rain. This species has an extended range "from northern Persia through eastern Asia Minor, the Caucasus, and the Crimea to the province of Podolia, and into southern Russia." The corm is large, and when one tucks it away in August one feels that something spectacular will come of it. And so it does.

There are numerous forms and varieties of this fine Crocus, all of them eminently worth while; and, as they flower at different times and vary in their color tone and markings, planting them all adds variety to the garden without repetition. The white form is exquisite, not pure white but with a faint tinge of gray or ashes of roses which serves to make it appear more fragile; as a matter of fact they are quite sturdy and ride out the storms without injury. The variety *Aitchinsonii* is larger and later to bloom, if paler in color than the type. The flowers have pointed segments and open starrily in the bright sunshine, displaying the orange-red anthers that all of this type possess. Atabar flowers a few days earlier than the type; the blooms are very "blue" but feathered darkly on the outer segments. Cassiope is bluer still and has a pale yellow base; the flowers are very large and striking. It blooms in October. *Globosus* has a lovely rounded form, is very blue, and flowers as late as any of these *speciosus* Crocuses. Pollux is magnificent, large with an almost violet-blue interior; the exterior is pale and silvery. It begins to bloom during the first week in October, and because of its coloring is one of the most effective.

The *speciosus* Crocuses flower without their leaves, which appear in spring, and are very effective planted on level plains of the rock garden where there is a covering of *Thymus Serpyllum lanuginosus* or some other slight creeper. Or they may be ribboned along the edges of borders of Japanese Anemones and other autumn-blooming plants. They are very hardy and increase in a satisfactory manner. Like other autumn-flowering Crocuses they should be planted if possible in August.

❧ Garden Scene in September (Plate 201)

In September the plants in the borders seem to sense the coming of the end and redouble their energy in producing flowers. The cooler nights and frequent rains incite them to this generosity, and so we have colorful scenes such as the one depicted in Plate 201. Against an evergreen hedge are massed numerous hardy border plants. The tall yellow-flowered plant at the back is one of the Goldenrods (Solidago) that are so much more used abroad than in this country for garden decoration. We generally think of these prolific plants, that border our roadsides so profusely, as weeds; but the picture shows they have real value in the borders, especially the tall kinds whose plumy flower spikes mitigate the too universally present plants of the Daisy type. Pale pink Phloxes also linger in the background in this picture, and in front of them masses of Rudbeckia, Michaelmas Daisies, and Nepeta, the latter giving an enthusiastic second flowering.

[*212*]

In the back right-hand corner tall *Heliopsis helianthoides*, which has been producing its yellow "Sunflowers" since midsummer, still carries on and makes a good background for the masses of Gaillardia, which also flowers the summer through.

⚘ Aster Nancy Ballard (Plate 202)

Michaelmas Daisies or Hardy Asters have become of conspicuous importance in the autumn garden. There are now many hybrid varieties, and the different kinds cover a long season of bloom—from late August until well into November. Their heights vary from a few inches to many feet, and in color they cover the whole scale of gray, lilac, lavender, purple, violet, blush, pink, rose, crimson, as well as pure white. Whole borders may be planted with these flowers alone without a sense of too great monotony. They flower in billowing masses, and, properly staked with twiggy branches of brush thrust in among them to keep them more or less upright while maintaining their natural grace of pose, produce an effect lovely indeed. There is a new race of dwarfs recently introduced that are fine for edging borders of the taller kinds or for use towards the front of borders of miscellaneous plants. They range in height from six inches to about a foot.

Aster Nancy Ballard, depicted in Plate 202, is one of the best of the mid-season varieties. It belongs to the group known as the *novi-belgii* Asters. It branches freely, and blossoms with such prodigality that the plants are literally covered with the large semi-double flowers of a pure mauve color. The plants grow about three feet tall.

⚘ *Helenium hybridum* Moerheim Beauty (Plate 203)

No flowers are handsomer in the late summer and autumn borders than the Heleniums, or Sneezeweeds. They are native to North America, with a few in South America, but the species unimproved are seldom planted in gardens nowadays; the handsome hybrids have taken their place, and rightly so, for they are much finer than the wild kinds. They are chiefly developed from *Helenium autumnale*, and they range in height from the low stature of *H. a. pumilum*, which grows only about one foot tall, to the soaring five- or six-foot height of *H. a. rubrum*. Their colors are truly autumnal: *autumnale* is a pure good yellow in tone; Riverton Beauty and Riverton Gem, growing four to five feet tall, are respectively lemon-yellow with a purplish conelike center, and rich reddish orange; *rubrum* is a deep terra-cotta in color, a most effective flower, blooming late; Golden Youth—one of the new hybrids, in color a fine pure golden-yellow, in height from three to four feet—begins to flower in July; Windley, flowering later, is two and one-half feet high and bears very large reddish bronze and yellow flowers; Moerheim Beauty, illustrated in Plate 203, a rich copper-red (a most effective hue), with the handsome flowers carried well above the foliage, grows from two and one-half to three feet tall and begins to flower late in July.

The tall-flowering kinds are of the utmost use at the back of the borders; the lower-growing kinds bring their rich coloring to the middle spaces and the foreground. There are numerous other fine hybrids that are not yet offered in this country.

The Heleniums thrive well in almost any soil that is well drained, and they love sunshine. The tall varieties should be staked. Few flowers are handsomer for cutting.

❦ *Helichrysum bracteatum monstrosum* (Plate 204)

The Everlastings, of which Helichrysum is one, are pretty and gay in the summer and autumn garden, though their peculiar texture and rather stiff habit causes them to appear a trifle unnatural among other flowers. But the fact that they may be cut and dried for winter house decoration gives them a special value. The growing and drying of Everlastings is an old-fashioned custom that has been revived of recent years with a good deal of enthusiasm. Florists offer baskets and other containers of the various kinds, sometimes mingled with dried grasses and bright-hued berries; and if these are attractively assembled they are not to be scorned when cut flowers are scarce and expensive.

They have the name of Everlastings because they resist the usual withering process and, if dried properly, last over the winter indoors. There are numerous kinds of Everlastings, among which the Helichrysums are thought to be the most attractive and useful. There are both single- and double-flowered kinds of various colors. The type known as *monstrosum* has double flowers. Fireball and Goldenball are respectively red and yellow, and there is a charming one the name of which accurately describes it—Silvery Pink. And there are white and rose and salmon varieties. The plants grow from two and one-half to four feet high; they are nearly all of annual duration and come from Australia. In texture they are crisp and strawlike to the touch, and they are often called Strawflowers.

Seeds may be sown indoors in March and planted out when danger from frost is past, or they may be sown directly where they are to grow in early May; but in this case the flowers will be very late in making their appearance.

Other Everlastings are Rhodanthe, *Xeranthemum annuum*, various Statices (Limonium) including *Bonduellii, sinuata, Suworowi,* Acrocliniums, *Ammobium alatum* (quaint small white flowers with yellow centers). The Sea Lavender, *Statice latifolia* (Limonium), a true and easily grown hardy perennial, is also a useful and graceful Everlasting, keeping its mistlike prettiness throughout the winter, and lending a certain lightness to these rather stiff bouquets.

One who contemplates the making of winter bouquets will do well to grow some of the ornamental grasses. Of these *Stipa pennata*, the Feather Grass, is very pretty with its silvery plumes; *Briza maxima*, the Quaking Grass, is also useful, and the beautiful Foxtail Grass, *Lagurus ovatus*, as well as *Avena sterilis, Bromus aureus, Agrostis nebulosa, Eragrostis abyssinica*, and *Pennisetum longistylum*. With the exception of *Stipa pennata*, all these are annuals and easily grown. Their attractive greenery is useful with summer as well as with winter bouquets.

The colors of the Everlastings remain almost undimmed if they are gathered just before they are fully expanded and hung head downward in a cool airy place until quite dry. Then they may be made up into bouquets at one's leisure. It is pleasant to keep a stock of Everlastings and grasses on hand and so be able to change the winter bouquets occasionally.

✤ A Wide Border Effectively Planted for Autumn Beauty (Plate 205)

This border (Plate 205) has been not only beautifully planted but well staked. Strong twiggy brush has been thrust in among the plants to keep them from being battered down by heavy rains while at the same time they are allowed to maintain their natural grace of pose. None have been tied tightly to stakes. Such a method of staking would completely have spoiled the showerlike effect of the long wandlike stems.

In the border are the tall Goldenrods (Solidago), Michaelmas Daisies or Hardy Asters in white, mauve, blue, pink and of various heights, the

[*216*]

Plate 193. DAHLIA JERSEY BEAUTY

Plate 194. DAHLIAS GROWING AMONG ANNUALS IN THE AUTUMN GARDEN

Plate 195. A BORDER OF DAHLIAS EDGED WITH *Sedum spectabile*

Plate 196. *Colchicum speciosum* IN A ROCK GARDEN

Plate 197. COLCHICUM VIOLET QUEEN

Plate 198. *Colchicum autumnale minor*

Plate 199. *Crocus iridiflorus*

Plate 200. *Crocus speciosus*

Plate 201. GARDEN SCENE IN SEPTEMBER

Plate 202. ASTER NANCY BALLARD

Plate 203. *Helenium hybridum* MOERHEIM BEAUTY

Plate 204. *Helichrysum bracteatum monstrosum* (STRAW-FLOWER)

richly colored Heleniums, Rudbeckias, tall Boltonias, Japanese Anemones, Anthemis, Snapdragons, and numerous other flowers.

☙ Chrysanthemums and Hardy Asters (Plate 206)

Chrysanthemums and Hardy Asters, or Michaelmas Daisies, are the most important plants in the late garden. September and October find them at their best, and even November offers a number of kinds.

☙ Small-Flowered Chrysanthemums in October (Plate 207)

Throughout October and November the tough small-flowered Chrysanthemums keep the garden gay. Even frosts do not dismay them, and we have them for cutting and for enjoyment out of doors.

The new Korean Hybrids are stronger and more long-lasting in the garden than the older kinds and will winter safely where others fail. They make very bushy plants and blossom with the most amazing freedom. Where hardiness is a consideration they should be used. The flowers are single and semi-double and come in the most lovely colors—pink, flesh, lilac-pink, crimson, tawny scarlet, gold with a bronze overlay, russet, and so on.

Often in driving about the countryside one finds fine plantations of small-flowered Chrysanthemums, and upon inquiry one is told that they have grown there for many years. These varieties are valuable because they have proved themselves hardy, and if a few roots may be secured they are worth having. Drainage is a first requisite in choosing a site for Hardy Chrysanthemums. They may survive cold, but they will not survive a damp bed. When drainage is assured, we may remember that Chrysanthemums are hungry plants and like a soil that is rich as well as light.

[*217*]

Manure, they like; and they should have it dug into the soil before planting. Spring is the best time to set out these plants, for then they have the
summer in which to get settled and gain strength for their autumn efforts,
and are better prepared to survive the winter cold than the autumn-
planted stock that has not had time to take proper hold upon the soil. Set
the plants about two feet apart, and divide the roots every year.

⚜ Autumn Coloring of *Polygonum affine (P. Brunonis)* (Plate 208)

The Polygonums are a vast family whose members are found in nearly
all parts of the world. Many of them are weeds of the most authentic character and must be fought shy of. Some are herbaceous plants of large size
and terrifying spreading ability; some are rampant climbers. The common
name of the family is Knotweed. *P. affine* is a pretty little alpine from high
in the Himalayas, where it is said to grow on stream banks or to hang in
neat cushions from moist precipices. In cultivation it grows into wide
mats, making a good ground cover in the rock garden. During the late
summer and early fall, out from among its narrow leaves spring stems a
foot or more high carrying two- to three-inch spikes of soft pink flowers
that turn to a deeper hue as they age.

In the late autumn the leaves, as shown in Plate 208, turn a nice russet
color and become an ornament in themselves. This is not a choice plant,
but for those who are looking for an amiable tenant for their rock gardens
it is a good thing. Any situation that is open will suit it, and almost any soil.
It may be divided whenever more of it is wanted.

P. vaccinifolium is a choicer plant, also valuable for late flowering. It
is a neat trailer, its wiry stems lined with very narrow leaves. The flowers
are pink in slender spikes, and very pretty. Given a warm slope to spread
over, it should be hardy and will cover several feet of surface. But a
severe winter will sometimes take it off.

[*218*]

⚏ Hardy Asters and Evergreens in the Late Garden (Plate 209)

In November nearly all the color has gone from the garden. The latest Michaelmas Daisies still lend soft and somewhat dimmed hues to the scene, and some of the earlier varieties of *Erica carnea* are flowering freshly in different tones of pink and rose. It is a season when evergreens come into their own, when we notice and appreciate their colors and textures. Plate 209 shows a rocky bank backed by tall conifers and planted chiefly with low evergreens and creepers that at this season weave a pleasant pattern and keep one's mind from dwelling too persistently upon the passing of summer and the approach of winter. Forms of *Chamaecyparis obtusa* are there, numerous low-growing Junipers, and in the foreground Thymes, Hypericums, and other creepers that find a congenial home among the rocks.

⚏ *Saxifraga Hostii* Flourishing in a Dry Wall (Plate 210)

The face of a dry wall makes a happy home for many rock plants; especially well housed in such a situation are certain of the encrusted Saxifrages. There the silvered rosettes may spread from crevice to crevice until wide mats are formed from which the large light panicles of delicate blooms erupt with great effectiveness.

Thus grown in Plate 210 is *Saxifraga Hostii* in one of its numerous forms, *altissima*, which comes from Styria and is somewhat taller and more robust than the type.

S. Hostii belongs to the central European Alps and is one of the easiest of Saxifrages to grow, producing rosetted offsets very freely and strongly among stones or in the chinks of a wall. The leaves are strap-shaped and gray-green, with a silver beading along the round-toothed margins. The flowers come in June in large flat-topped panicles and are cream-color

[*219*]

more or less flecked with red. "Its size, its flattened mass, the *bluntness* of its outspread grey-and-silver leaves, and their *rounded beading*, clearly distinguish *S. Hostii* among its kin." So says Reginald Farrer in "The English Rock Garden." It is indeed a vigorous and amiable Saxifrage, and one upon which the beginning experimenter among the Rockfoils may safely fix his affections.

The encrusted Saxifrages are beautiful, winter or summer, in or out of bloom, and show to especial advantage in the wall face.

⚘ *Oxydendron arboreum* in the Autumn (Plate 211)

Although a deciduous tree growing from fifteen to sixty feet tall, *Oxydendron arboreum* (the Sourwood, or Sorrel tree) is, like the Rhododendrons, Heathers, and Laurels, a true Heath. Its growth is slender, and its branches form into an oblong round-topped head. It is a native tree found growing in the wild from Pennsylvania, Ohio, and Indiana south to Florida, Alabama, Louisiana, and Arkansas, choosing moist woods for its habitat. It is hardy as far north as Boston.

The leaves are alternate, oblong or lanceolate, and both twigs and leaves have a pleasant acid flavor "said to temporarily assuage the thirst of the hunter lost in Southern woods." This little tree, which deserves to be seen more often than it is in cultivated grounds, has several periods of outstanding beauty. In the spring, there is the young bronze-tinted foliage; in June, it bears long racemes of small creamy bells, very prim and neat, and pinched at the mouth, as is the way with so many of the Heaths. And these are followed by small light gray fruits that are conspicuous. But its chief time of glory is in the autumn, when it wraps itself in scarves of vivid scarlet.

A small plantation of Sourwoods would surely be an ornament on any

estate where there is a bit of low ground to accommodate them; or even
one tree will make a gay little festival when the days begin to grow short
and we are so warmed and heartened by the farewell glow of autumn
foliage.

⚘ *Trapa natans* (Plate 212)

Trapa natans is commonly known as the Water Chestnut. It is a floating aquatic plant, native in Europe and Asia but naturalized in the United
States. Its white flowers borne down among the leaves are rather insignificant, but its warmly colored and mottled long-stemmed leaves are so
brilliant in the summer and autumn that it is in demand for use in tubs,
aquariums, or still ponds and pools. It is a self-seeding annual, liking to
root in good rich loamy soil. The seeds, which are said to be two inches
across, and have prominent horns, are also said to taste like Chestnuts;
hence the common name.

⚘ Conifers Against the Bare Trees of Late Autumn (Plate 213)

As winter approaches, we appreciate the rich green of conifers against
the bare trunks and branches of leafless trees. In summer their color is
merged with the greenery of the deciduous trees; and it is not until this
fails us that we realize how gaunt would be the late autumn and winter
landscape without the softening influence of the evergreens.

In the foreground of Plate 213 is a fine specimen of the Tamarix
Savin, *Juniperus Sabina tamariscifolia*. It is a beautiful low-growing, spreading evergreen that, because of its extreme hardiness as well as its beauty,
deserves more frequent planting, especially in cold climates. Its branches
are procumbent or ascending, not often erect; the leaves are needle-

[*221*]

shaped "and often in threes, slightly incurved, free at the tip and sharply pointed, dark green with a white band above, often bluish-green." It is an ideal low evergreen for specimen planting or for covering rough banks among stones, especially where the soil is sandy. It does not like a clay soil.

There is great beauty in the plains of its spreading branches and in its soft color—green in some lights, bluish in others. It is one of the finest of the Junipers. "The native American Juniper known as *J. Sabina* var. *prostrata* and also as var. *procumbens* is *J. horizontalis*." The Tamarix Savin is a native of Europe.

❧ *Berberis Thunbergii*, *Juniperus Sabina*, and *Anaphalis margaritacea* (Plate 214)

Dominating the scene in Plate 214 is a bush of the Japanese Barberry, *Berberis Thunbergii*. It is a universally useful shrub, commonly low-growing but capable of reaching a height of six feet. It is very hardy and is often used to form hedges as it stands clipping well. The flowers, which are yellow faintly tinged with red, are small and not of great importance; the leaves, which are small and oval and remain on the bushes until very late in the fall, turn a glorious red as the season advances; and the brown twigs are strung with oval scarlet berries that frequently remain on the bushes throughout the winter. If twigs are brought into the house in winter and placed in water in a sunny window, the little yellow flowers will often appear, and also the leaves, so that we have leaves, flowers and berries at the same time with which to make a gay table decoration.

With the Barberry may be seen the soft blue-green of *Juniperus Sabina* and a few heads of the Pearly Everlasting, *Anaphalis margaritacea*. This is the prettiest of the native Everlastings and is often used in winter bouquets, sometimes being dyed a bright hue, which is a pity for the white flowers are quite lovely as they are. The stalks are leafy with narrow gray-green leaves, and the flowers almost round, made up of many "miniature petal-like white scales surrounding the central yellow staminate flowers, arranged not unlike the petals of a water-lily." This is a common plant found from Maine south to South Carolina and west to South Dakota, blooming in August and through the autumn in woods and pastures. Thoreau in his diary writes of it: "The Pearly Everlasting is an interesting white at present. Though the stems and leaves are still green, it is dry and unwithering like an artificial flower; its white flexuous stem and branches, too, like wire wound with cotton. Neither is there any scent to betray it. Its amaranthine quality is instead of high color. Its very brown centre now affects me as a fresh and original color. It monopolizes small circles in the midst of sweet fern, perchance on a dry hillside."

This common native plant is quite attractive enough to be brought into the garden, but it is not often so distinguished.

Acer palmatum and Grasses (Plate 215)

The Japanese Maple, *Acer palmatum*, is a graceful shrub or small tree. The leaves have five to nine deep lobes and in certain varieties are "often deeply dissected and skeletonized." These shrubs may grow as tall as twenty feet, and their leaves may be green or yellow or blood-red or purplish red and so on. There are many variety names to choose from.

Needless to say, these small trees or shrubs are much used in Japan. In this land where flower festivals are many, the Maple-viewing, the feast of the Maple leaves, is one of the most popular. "Then all the world makes holiday outdoors again for the last time; up and down the mountain slopes the people go in swarms, climb rugged hill paths, descend rocky valleys, to admire, near and afar off, the glory of the dying Maples. Hot saké

[*223*]

warms their blood, and the blazing leaves their hearts." Mrs. Basil Taylor, whose delightful book, "Japanese Gardens," has just been quoted, says in another place, emphasizing the poetic feeling of the Japanese in the treatment of their flowers and plants, "The Autumn comes from the West, the Japanese say, and on Western-sloping hills there are the Maples set to catch the very last gleam." One of their poets says:

> Like far-off smoke upon the hill-side lies
> The purple haze of Autumn, pale and chill:
> Is it the blazing maples, whose flame dies,
> And trailing off in smoke would linger still?

The Japanese Maples are hardy in New England, but they grow best in partially shaded situations in rich, well drained soil. They are often planted as specimens or set at the back of a flower border to lend their rich autumn colors to those of late-blooming flowers. If it is desired to keep them dwarf, they may be headed in occasionally by cutting back the leading shoots. Autumn Crocuses planted thickly about them make a most beautiful picture.

Some of the hardiest varieties are thought to be *atropurpureum, dissectum*, and *ornatum*, and these are vigorous of growth. *A. Sieboldianum* is hardy as far north as Boston. It is similar to *A. palmatum* but somewhat coarser. The varieties of Japanese Maple with variegated leaves are said to be more tender of constitution than the others.

✤ *Berberis Thunbergii* in Its Autumn Dress (Plate 216)

Here in Plate 216 *Berberis Thunbergii* is shown in the full beauty of its autumn regalia, its little oval leaves all glowing, its dark stems strung

[*224*]

Plate 205. A WIDE BORDER EFFECTIVELY PLANTED FOR AUTUMN BEAUTY

Plate 210. *Saxifraga Hostii* FLOURISHING IN A DRY WALL

with oval scarlet berries. It makes a handsome specimen at the front of the shrubbery border, its slender branches sweeping to the ground.

There are several varieties of *Berberis Thunbergii;* one of them *(B. T. purpurea* or *atropurpurea)* has leaves which in autumn are a brilliant reddish purple. To show at its best and to color well, it must be planted in full sun. Specimens planted in shade are dull-hued and uninteresting. There is also var. *minor,* low and dense and with smaller leaves, which may be used for very small hedges or edgings, five to six inches tall; but they must be kept carefully and severely clipped. The common name, Box Barberry, is misleading, for while it will form a Box-like edging for beds and borders the leaves are not evergreen as are those of the true Box.

Berberis Thunbergii is a favorite plant for making low hedges and may be kept neatly clipped to a formal line if desired.

❀ Pale Tree Trunks Against the Reddening Leaves (Plate 217)

In the autumn a plantation composed of various types of trees weaves a tapestry of color and texture against the pale sky that is both brilliant and beautiful. The dark red-brown of the Oaks mingles with the scarlet of the Maples, the flame of *Nyssa sylvatica* and Liquidambar. Sour and Sweet Gums, the gold of *Liriodendron Tulipifera* (Tulip Tree), of the gray-stemmed Beeches with their yellow autumn-colored silken leaves. The pattern of the twigs and branches shows through the thinning foliage, lending definition to the fabric.

In Plate 217 groups of Birches with their shining white trunks add immensely to the scene.

⚜ A Sweep of Heather Against Evergreen and Deciduous Trees (Plate 218)

Against a close planting of evergreen and deciduous trees, the flowering mass of Heather seen in Plate 218 is very effective. This autumn-flowering Heather is *Calluna vulgaris*. It comes in many colors and forms. The one in the illustration is *Calluna vulgaris rubra*, the Red Heather, and there is a taller form of this called *elata*. Some of the kinds have heavy gray foliage, some golden, some bronze. A good list would be the following: *C. v. alba*, White Heather, with a taller variety known as *elata*; *C. v. Alportii*, flowers deep rose color; *C. v. aurea*, foliage golden; *C. v. cuprea*, Bronze Heather; *C. v. Hammondii*, profusion of pink flowers (there is also a white variety of this); *C. v. hirsuta*, thick gray foliage; *C. v. monstrosa*, twelve inches, flowers purple and foliage tipped with yellow; *C. v. nana*, Moss Heather, growing in thick mosslike clumps.

The height of these various Heathers is from six to twelve inches. They are lovely planted in masses of one kind on rough banks or long slopes in full sun where they bloom in August and September. They require an acid soil if they are to thrive.

⚜ Autumn Garden Scene (Plate 219)

The presence of a little winding stream makes a garden picture of interest and beauty very easy to bring about. In Plate 219 we have such a little stream lending itself to simple but effective treatment. In the background is a bridge and a vine-hung stone wall beneath which the stream flows through a culvert. It is autumn, and the surface is sprinkled with fallen leaves while the clear water reflects the warm hue of the reddening tree that overhangs the left bank. On the right bank a plantation of Bergenia, with its large handsome leaves, appears very much at home, and these, too, acknowledge the advancing season by softly flushing.

卐 Linden Trees in Autumn (Plate 220)

How delightful is this walk shadowed by European Lindens, *Tilia vulgaris*, in their autumn dress. The grass and the walk are sprigged with the rusty gold of the fallen leaves; the graceful branches hang low. In the spring after the orchard blossoms have gone over, the Linden bursts into flower, covering itself with bunches of small yellow blossoms among which the bees hum loudly as they rob them of their abundant store of honey. The scent of these flowers is carried far on the breeze, and walking beneath the trees is a delight. The far-famed honey of Hybla was made from the blossoms of the Lime or Linden trees, and the wood is used for carving. "No wood," says Gilpin in his "Forest Scenery" (1879), "is so easily formed under the carver's chisel. It is the wood which the ingenious Gibbons used, after making trial of several kinds, as the most proper for that curious sculpture which adorns some of the old houses of our nobility."

If allowed to grow freely, the Linden is a graceful and an elegant tree. Throughout Europe, avenues and walks are lined with it; but it is often spoiled by being clipped into "straight bondage" to form the sides of avenues and vistas. In winter the tree is distinguished by its smooth bark and the "lusty symmetry of its frame." It is interesting to remember that Carl Linnè, afterwards known as Carolus Linnaeus, took his name from a beloved Linden that grew close by his peasant father's dwelling.

The American Linden, or Basswood, *Tilia americana*, is also a handsome tree, tall and spreading with a round top and more closely leafed than any American tree. It has two faults: it opens its leaves late in spring,

[*227*]

and its great leaves when mature attract many insect enemies. "Plant lice cover them with patches of honeydew, and the sticky surfaces catch dust and smoke. Riddled with holes and torn by the wind, they fall in desultory fashion. The faded yellow does not please as does the gold of Beech and Hickory leaves." But the American Linden, too, has its period of unusual beauty and sweetness when the branches are covered with the honey-laden, sweet-scented pale yellow blossoms.

⁂ *Liquidambar styraciflua* (Plate 221)

One of the most beautiful American trees in autumn is the Sweet Gum, or *Liquidambar styraciflua*. Then "the tree is not a flame—it is a *conflagration.*" But it is a beautiful tree all the year round. In winter it is hung all over with curious woody seed balls that are conspicuous against the sky. In summer the star-shaped leaves claim the attention and admiration. The bark of the trunk is red-brown and curiously fissured and ridged, while the branches have "warty bark, broken into rough, horny plates." This has given the tree its name of Alligator-wood.

The tree grows tall, from seventy-five to one hundred and forty feet, the trunk straight and with its short slender branches forming almost a pyramid. The largest specimens are found southward in damp woodlands, but its distribution is from Connecticut to Missouri, south to Florida and Texas, also in Mexico and Central America. "Travellers in the Bayou country of the Mississippi Valley can easily verify the statement that a hollow Gum tree is large enough to entomb a man. Giants exist there to-day, standing in rich bottom lands, or on soil that is inundated a part of the year, whose trunks, fifteen feet or more in girth, carry their tops a hundred and fifty feet into the air." In the North the trees do not grow so tall; but they are just as beautiful, and one wonders why we do not oftener see plantations of Gum trees on large estates instead of the omnipresent Oaks and Maples. It is highly valued abroad and freely planted as an ornamental tree in parks and gardens. Here we are slow to make use of it, often choosing in its place some unwilling alien.

Clematis vitalba in Fruit (Old Man's Beard) (Plate 222)

Clematis vitalba, Old Man's Beard, White Vine, Traveller's Joy, as it is variously called, is a rampant woody climber reaching a height of from fifteen to thirty feet. It is found freely growing in the wilds of central and southern Europe and in northern Africa and is also common in Great Britain where the soil is calcareous. It scrambles along wayside fences and walls and swings itself into trees much as *Clematis virginiana* does in this country. The flowers are borne in panicles and are small, greenish white in color and have the scent of almonds. William Robinson says, "Old plants with rope-like stems will cover tall trees for hundreds of square yards if allowed to trail freely in woodland." He considers it too vigorous for garden culture, yet where unsightly objects are to be blotted out it is very useful. It is not, however, perfectly hardy in this country north of Maryland. In the autumn it is made conspicuous as is our own wild Clematis by the shaggy plumose seed vessels, covering the vine like puffs of smoke. It is from these that the name Old Man's Beard is derived.

Taxus baccata (English Yew) (Plate 223)

The English or European Yew is one of the most beautiful of evergreens. All who are familiar with old English gardens have seen it at its best, and there "is no English tree that has gathered round itself so much of historic, poetic and legendary lore as has the Yew." The tall Yew hedges

[*229*]

of English gardens are their glory, and though we may not as a rule care for clipped trees these strong green hedges cannot but be admired. "The Yew is of all other trees," says Gilpin, "the most tonsile. Hence the indignities it suffers. We everywhere see it cut and metamorphosed into such a variety of deformities that we are hardly brought to conceive it has a natural shape, or the power which other trees have of hanging carelessly and negligently."

It has been employed since earliest Tudor times to form the pleached or clipped hedges for which English gardens are so famous, as well as cut into the forms of birds and beasts, cones and pyramids which add much to the quaint charm of a certain type of garden. But the Yew is beautiful also as a free-growing tree. It may reach a height of from twenty-five to forty feet, occasionally even a greater stature. The wide-spreading branches create a broad flat crown; the color of the narrow leaves is a rich, shining green, paler beneath. The cup-shape of the scarlet fruit is well shown in Plate 223.

Taxus baccata is widely spread from England to North Africa and western Asia. At one time it was freely planted in the United States, but of late the hardier Japanese Yew *(Taxus cuspidata)* has largely taken its place. If the English Yew is used it should be planted in situations not open to the south, as late frosts injure the young growths where they are exposed to the sun. There are numerous forms of *T. baccata*, some of them lower-growing and hardier than the upright type. Also their low stature makes it possible to protect them from the cold in northern latitudes.

❀ *Parrotia persica* (Plate 224)

The Ironwood, *Parrotia persica*, is a little known small tree or large shrub, growing from fifteen to twenty feet tall, having smooth flaky bark, the branches spreading, bearing foliage much like that of the Witch Hazel. The purplish flowers with pendulous stamens are not very conspicuous but are extremely pretty when examined closely. They make their appearance in March. The bush or tree often makes a fine specimen, branching to the bottom. In the autumn it shows what it can do in the way of beauty, for then the oval leaves with their coarse rounded teeth create literally a burning bush, turning all tints and tones of yellow, orange, and scarlet, and keeping up this spectacular show for a long time.

It is fairly hardy, at least as far north as New York, but it should be given a situation in well drained soil on high ground or on a slope, in full sun.

This little tree is a single species belonging to the family Hamamelidaceae, and is native in Persia. It was named for F. W. Parrot, a German naturalist.

❀ Fothergilla Amidst Other Coloring Shrubs (Plate 225)

Fothergilla major is another member of the family Hamamelidaceae, this being a native, known as Witch Alder. It comes from Georgia and thereabouts and is probably not reliably hardy north of Philadelphia. But it is a most attractive shrub growing vigorously to a height of six feet and forming a broad bush branching to the bottom. The leaves are rounded, irregularly notched, and somewhat coarse, and in the fall turn a soft orange-yellow that is very effective. In the spring, while the branches are still naked, the bush is covered from top to bottom with brushlike tufts of white flowers that make it a conspicuous object.

F. Gardeni is a lower-growing species, seldom reaching a greater height than four feet. The leaves turn red in the autumn, and the flowers are white with pinkish stamens.

The Fothergillas, it is said, are found at the margins of shady swamps. A light, peaty soil is the best for them.

An Irish writer has spoken of the Fothergilla thus: "When its leaves turn it makes the most adorable little yellow tent, casting a glorious gleam round it of yellow sunlight on a dark day when you think that everything that delights is over in the garden."

❦ *Festuca glauca* (Plate 226)

Nearly all plants used in the rock garden are prostrate or at least spreading. Now and then it is a relief to find one that stands upright. There are certain low-growing grasses that serve this purpose admirably. They appear crisp and fresh throughout the season, and though they do not add flowers to the general scene they are not lacking in color.

One of the prettiest of these is *Festuca glauca*, the Blue Fescue (*F. ovina glauca*), member of a large genus of chiefly agricultural grasses containing more than eighty species. *Festuca ovina* is a valuable pasture grass, but the variety *glauca* is well suited to certain situations in the rock garden. It forms dense tufts of narrow bluegrass about a foot tall and seems to thrive in almost any situation given it. Its suitability as a rock plant is well shown in Plate 226. If it sends up blossoms, these should be cut off, as they spoil its neat appearance. It is easily raised from seed or may be increased by division of the roots. It does not spread too widely but makes a blue, fountain-like mass that is very effective. The Blue Fescue is suitable for edging borders as well as for use in the rock garden.

[*232*]

Plate 211. *Oxydendron arboreum* IN THE AUTUMN

Plate 215. *Acer palmatum* AND GRASSES

Plate 216. *Berberis Thunbergii* IN ITS AUTUMN DRESS

Plate 217. PALE TREE TRUNKS AGAINST THE REDDENING LEAVES

Plate 218. A SWEEP OF HEATHER AGAINST EVERGREEN AND DECIDUOUS TREES

Plate 219. AUTUMN GARDEN SCENE

Plate 220. LINDEN TREES IN AUTUMN

Plate 221. *Liquidambar styraciflua* (SWEET GUM)

Another little grass that is well worth using is the Variegated Oat Grass, *Arrhenatherum variegatum bulbosum*. It grows from six to twelve inches high, and its green and white striped "blades" appear neat and fresh. It grows from a string of little tubers. Like the Blue Fescue, it is a hardy perennial and is often used as an edging for borders, especially in old-fashioned gardens. It is sometimes known as *A. elatius tuberosum*. It also is a member of a large genus of perennial pasture grasses of European origin, but naturalized in parts of the United States.

⚜ *Pieris japonica* (*Andromeda japonica*), Japanese Bog Rosemary (Plate 227)

This is one of the handsomest and most useful of broad-leaved evergreens. Under especially favorable conditions it will reach a height of eight feet, but generally it is lower. The leaves are oblong and of a rich shining green, leathery in texture; and when covered with its drooping spikes of small bell-shaped white flowers in spring it is an object of real beauty. Nor is this all it has to offer, for when the young growths begin to appear after the flowering is over, they are soft pink and buff in color and the bush appears to be blossoming again. It is native to Japan.

Pieris floribunda, growing wild from Virginia to Georgia, is also valuable where a dense broad-leaved evergeen is desired. Its clusters of creamy blossoms are carried upright instead of drooping, and the branches are covered with coarse hair. This species is generally considered to be hardier than the Japanese plant, but it is somewhat less handsome. The thick leaves of both kinds, however, assume lovely bronzy tones as winter approaches, so that at no time of the year are they valueless in the scheme of the garden.

These shrubs dislike lime and clay and thrive best where the soil is definitely acid, and of a somewhat light texture, and the situation partially shaded. They are fine combined with the taller Rhododendrons, with

Mountain Laurel *(Kalmia latifolia)* and *Leucothoë Catesbaei*. Foreground plantings for these handsome broad-leaved evergreens may be made of the Leatherleaf *(Chamaedaphne calyculata)* and *Leiophyllum buxifolium* (the Sand Myrtle).

FRUITING BRANCHES

⚘ *Hippophaë rhamnoides* (Sea Buckthorn) (Plate 228)

The Sea Buckthorn, *Hippophaë rhamnoides*, is a large shrub or small tree native to Europe and temperate Asia, often found growing by the seashore. It is one of the most attractive berried shrubs in cultivation and should be planted far oftener than it is. It is commonly no taller than from eight to ten feet, but it is known to reach a height of thirty feet. Yellowish inconspicuous flowers appear in spring along the gray spiny-tipped branches. The effect of the whole shrub is softly gray except for the flowers and fruit. The young growths are covered with silvery scales, and the narrow alternate leaves are also silvery. The berries, which ripen in September, are ovoid in shape and warm orange-red in color, and they are produced in such profusion that they often clothe long lengths of the branches, as may be seen in Plate 228. These decorative berries often hang all winter as they are not relished by the birds, and branches may be gathered for house decoration when most other berries have been appropriated by the hungry birds.

"The plants are unisexual, the female alone bearing fruit, and this only when a male is planted in close proximity. One male will pollinate several females, and thus grouping should be resorted to where possible."

This is such a valuable small tree from several standpoints that even small places should find room for at least one group. Its gray leaves and branches make a delightful background for flower borders featuring lavender, pink, and pale yellow flowers. Gray-leaved shrubs are not many, but this with Elaeagnus, which it somewhat resembles, and to which it is related, is among the best. While it will grow inland well, it is one of the best shrubs for seashore planting as it thrives in the sandy soil and will sucker there, even serving to bind and hold the shifting sands. In "The Book of Shrubs" Mr. Hottes says, "As a silver-leaved hedge it is very interesting." This is a suggestion that might well be used. We have not too much variety in hedge plants, and a silver-leaved hedge would be a distinct novelty. Mr. Hottes also says the berries are reputed to be slightly poisonous.

❦ Bright Fruits of *Skimmia japonica* (Plate 229)

Skimmia japonica is a low-branching evergreen shrub from Japan. While it may endure over the winter as far north as Philadelphia it is not reliably hardy north of Washington. In the North it is occasionally grown in cool greenhouses. In the South it is a valuable shrub for outdoor planting. It forms a rather dense growth three to four feet tall; the leaves are bright green above and yellowish green beneath. The plants are unisexual, so that both sexes must be planted if flowers and fruit are to result.

The flowers are yellowish white, small, and fragrant, appearing in the spring, and are followed by clusters of handsome bright red berries in the late summer; and these remain on the branches all, or nearly all, winter. *Skimmia japonica* is a neat shrub for a partially shaded corner. It dislikes limestone, and the soil best suited to it is made up of sand and peat. It endures smoke and is therefore advised for city planting.

"Skimmia" is from a Japanese word *skimmi* and means poisonous fruit.

⚘ Fruiting Branches of *Sorbus splendida* (Mountain Ash) (Plate 230)

This showy Mountain Ash, *Sorbus splendida*, is a cross between the American Mountain Ash, *S. americana*, and the European tree, *S. Aucuparia*, commonly known as the Rowan tree, though erroneously.* It is a handsome small tree, and chiefly valuable for its bunches of warm-hued fruits, which are somewhat larger than those of either parent, and which appear in autumn. It is quite hardy far north and is a very ornamental deciduous tree.

⚘ *Malus pumila* x *M. baccata* (Plate 231)

Usually we grow the various species and varieties of ornamental Crab Apples for the sake of their lovely blossoms. Most of them are small trees suitable for use in gardens, where they may be planted at the back of wide borders or as a focal point at the end of a vista. The shade they cast is not heavy enough to interfere seriously with the development of plants beneath them. Also they are delightful set out in groups on a hillside, and small bulbs may be scattered thickly about them. Often the branches are crooked and picturesque in outline, and they blossom so freely that they become veritable bouquets of pink, white, or rose-red blossoms during May. The fruits of most of the kinds are negligible, but now and then one comes across a variety with fruit handsome enough to be considered for its own sake.

The variety pictured in Plate 231 is a cross between *Malus pumila* and *M. baccata*. *M. pumila* is the common Apple, parent of most of our cultivated eating Apples and often crossed with other species. *Malus baccata* is the Siberian Crab Apple, so called, and grows in Siberia, Manchuria, and

*The true Rowan is *Pyrus Aucuparia*, a close relative of the Hawthorn and the Apple.

[236]

China. In time it may make a tree forty feet tall, with a round head. The hard wiry branchlets will be literally clothed in white flowers about a half-inch across on slender pedicels in May, and the fruit that follows is three-quarters of an inch in diameter, yellow or red and somewhat waxlike.

The hybrid here shown has larger fruits, beautifully colored and freely borne, and branches are handsome used for house decoration. The blossoms are pinkish and very attractive.

This tree is very hardy and may be used far north.

Berberis vulgaris, fruiting (Common Barberry) (Plate 232)

Although the Common Barberry grows along our New England waysides and appears in every way a native, it is, as a matter of fact, an introduction from Europe. But it came to us so long ago that it has had time to settle down and appear thoroughly at home. At first it was grown in gardens; but this restricted sphere became too narrow for this wanderer, and it took to the hospitable wild. Sometimes it is found in rocky pastures, but more often along the roadside mingling with the outlaw company that it finds good. In spring its racemes of yellow blossoms may be overlooked by the wayfarer, but in the autumn, when the thorny bushes are hung all over with scarlet fruit, one must be blind indeed not to heed its glowing bid for attention.

Though the Barberry has gone wild, it is still a most desirable bush to plant in cultivated areas. It has a most graceful habit, the shoots bending beneath the weight of the racemes of yellow blossoms and later the heavier fruits, so that it always has a sort of shower effect. The berries have been described as being the shape of little sausages. "They are generally a little curved, and of a brilliant scarlet color, each being tipped with the little black style." They are very sour to the taste, and perhaps that is why the birds leave them alone so that they hang from the branches long after the leaves have fallen, lending to New England hedgerows a most delightful gaiety. But old-fashioned housekeepers made good use of these plentiful berries, and they may be made into a jelly or a conserve, with plenty of sugar; "or they may be gathered while yet green and pickled." In Europe they had many medicinal uses, even being credited by one old writer with the power to "fasten loose teeth."

The common Barberry makes a good hedge plant. It is very thorny and grows rapidly into a close-knit bush from five to eight feet tall. This will stand clipping to a neat line if it is desired so to treat it, or it may be left to grow freely without becoming too untidy in appearance. One drawback it has: in the spring when it is in flower, the dangling yellow blossoms have a delicate scent in the early hours of the day; but towards night this scent changes in character and becomes extremely offensive to some persons. This, however, is only for about a fortnight.

Berberis vulgaris is very hardy and will grow far north, but it prefers a calcareous soil rather than an acid one.

There is a variety *atropurpurea* with reddish purple leaves that is well worth planting.

Viburnum prunifolium (Black Haw) (Plate 233)

The Black Haw is a large shrub or small tree and not a Hawthorn as might be suspected. It is a native plant found in our spacious wild from Connecticut to Florida and west to Michigan and Texas, a handsome round-headed sturdy small tree or shrub decked in spring with white cymes of small white flowers that are followed in autumn by oval dark blue drupes, sweetish to the taste. The leaves are like those of a plum, and the twigs are distinctly reddish in winter, showing brightly against the snow.

[*238*]

The Black Haw is smaller in all its parts than its sister trees, the Rusty Nannyberry, *V. rufidulum*, that grows from Virginia to Florida and west to Illinois and Texas, but which has been found hardy as far north as Boston, and the Sheepberry, *Viburnum Lentago*, that may be found from Quebec to Saskatchewan, south to Alabama, west to Kansas, Nebraska, and Wyoming.

All these trees are valuable for use in cultivated grounds and require little attention. They are attractive in flower, in fruit, and in the autumn when the leaves begin to color.

❦ *Enkianthus japonicus* in Autumn Garb (Plate 234)

There are about ten species of Enkianthus in eastern Asia and Himalaya. They are comely shrubs that have the appearance somewhat of a Pieris or Andromeda. But they are deciduous.

Enkianthus japonicus (E. perulatus) bears little modest white bells in clusters before the leaves in spring; but it is in the autumn that the little shrub flashes into vivid life, the leaves turning brilliantly to yellow and scarlet. It then forces itself upon the attention from all parts of the garden. The bush may grow from three to six feet high with horizontal tiers of twiggy branches; the leaves are narrow obovate "and clustered at the end of the shoot, each from one inch to an inch and a half in length."

A better known and more popular species is *Enkianthus campanulatus*, which in some gardens may grow twelve feet high. In its native country, Japan, it is said to become a tree of the dignified height of thirty feet. It has bell-shaped pendulous blossoms, creamy white veined with red and tipped with red also. The leaves are a good deal like those of an Azalea, and it has the family habit of turning into a veritable conflagration in the autumn. For this reason alone these shrubs should be grown, though pretty enough

[*239*]

are the dangling blossoms and the characteristic flat spreading system of branching common to so many Japanese shrubs "and beloved of the Japanese artist, as one may see on many a screen and fan."

The Enkianthuses belong to the Heath family and so do not like lime but prefer a peaty soil or an open one in which plenty of leaf mold is incorporated. They grow well in partial shade.

⚑ A Fruiting Branch of *Rosa Willmottiae* (Plate 235)

Many of the Rose species have very handsome fruits. Few of the species have a second flowering; but those with decorative fruits are given another opportunity to, as it were, bloom again. *Rosa Willmottiae* was discovered in western China by the late E. H. Wilson and named for Miss Willmott* of Warley Place, who in her lifetime did so much to give the wild Rose species importance. It is a graceful dense shrubby species five to six feet high, and sometimes more, erect-growing with arching branches covered with small gray-green leaves that are a decoration in themselves. This foliage, I understand, has become very popular in England for use with cut flowers, especially with some of the hybrid teas that have not too much foliage of their own.

The Roses of this species are small and single and borne singly or in pairs in some profusion and have a distinct beauty of their own. But perhaps the bush is most attractive when hung all over with its orange-red ovoid fruits in autumn.

This Rose may be grown in the shrubbery border or as a free-growing bush alone. It has three periods of beauty, which is more than can be said of most shrubs. J. Horace McFarland speaks of it in his "Roses of the World in Color" as "a great and graceful shrub with fine foliage and beautiful light pink blooms."

*Author of "The Genus Rosa."

Plate 222. *Clematis vitalba* IN FRUIT (OLD-MAN'S-BEARD)

Plate 227. *Pieris japonica* (ANDROMEDA), JAPANESE BOG ROSEMARY

Plate 228. *Hippophaë rhamnoides* (SEA BUCKTHORN)

Plate 229. BRIGHT FRUITS OF *Skimmia japonica*

Plate 230. FRUITING BRANCH OF *Sorbus splendida* (MOUNTAIN ASH)

Plate 231. *Malus pumila* x *M. baccata*

Plate 232. *Berberis vulgaris* FRUITING (COMMON BARBERRY)

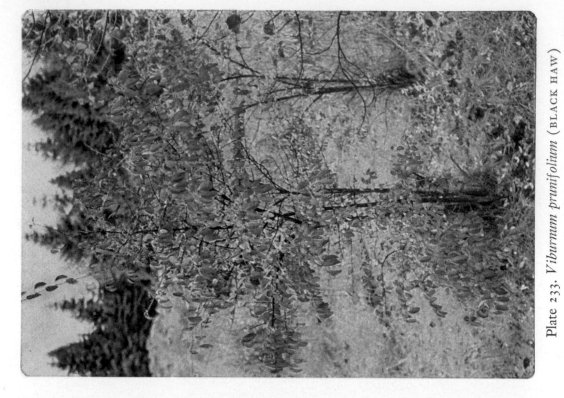

Plate 233. *Viburnum prunifolium* (BLACK HAW)

Plate 234. *Enkianthus japonicus* IN AUTUMN GARB

⌘ *Celastrus articulatus (C. orbiculatus)* (Oriental Bittersweet) (Plate 236)

All who fare countrywards in the autumn are familiar with our native Bittersweet, *Celastrus scandens*, that winds about the fence rails and scrambles over walls making a brilliant show with its scarlet berries after its leaves have fallen. This Bittersweet, or Waxwork, as it is sometimes called, is a fine rampant climber for covering low walls or training over arbors; but it must be borne in mind that the flowers are unisexual and both male and female plants must be set out if the inconspicuous blooms and the bright fruits are to be the reward of our efforts. The fruit is yellow and borne in clusters; the aril is scarlet and only displayed when the yellow outer coat of the "berry" has split. The Bittersweet is very hardy and may be grown far north.

Celastus articulatus, from China, is even more prolific of berries than our native kind and will often climb to a height of thirty feet. Because of these two facts many persons prefer to plant it rather than our native Bittersweet; but it is somewhat less hardy, and as the berries are borne in clusters in the leaf axils rather than in terminal clusters as are those of the native kind, they are less conspicuous until after the leaves have fallen. If Plate 236 is examined, the split yellow berry will be noticed showing the scarlet inner coat (the aril) of the seeds.

The Bittersweets are close relatives to Asiatic and Australian and American trees, the Celastraceae, about thirty species, among them our native Strawberry Bush *(Euonymus americanus)* and the well known Wahoo, or Burning Bush *(Euonymus atropurpureus)*, a gay little tree whose purplish scarlet dangling fruits split to display the brilliantly covered seeds. Like all the family, it holds its fruit until late in the autumn, lending gaiety to the early days of winter.

✤ *Viburnum opulus*, Fruiting (European Cranberry Bush) (Plate 237)

Plate 237 shows a fruiting branch of the Guelder Rose, *Viburnum Opulus*, native to many parts of Europe, northern Asia and northern Africa. It is a handsome bush or small tree, at all times; but it is in the autumn that it especially calls attention to itself. Then the Maple-like leaves turn a fine crimson-purple, and it is abundantly bedecked with bright berries, hanging in heavy clusters, each containing a single seed. The individual bunches of berries will often show several colors, such portions of the bunch as receive the full sunshine being much more richly stained; we may have every tone from pure yellow to pure scarlet in a cluster of berries, even in a single berry. When fully ripe the berries become almost black, and their gay variety is gone. These berries if tasted will be found anything but attractive; they are sour and harsh to the taste, and even the birds do not much relish them.

The Guelder Rose's favorite haunts are somewhat moist situations, in thickets, along the margins of woodlands, and it will be found not infrequently in the wayside hedgerows. It loves the North, thriving upon the asperities of cold climates, and is a very attractive small tree to use in gardens or other cultivated areas. It may reach a height of twelve feet. In early summer it attracts our notice with its masses of wide creamy flower heads. These if examined will be seen to be made up of "two entirely distinct forms; in the centre the blossoms are closely clustered together, individually small, but perfect in structure; while surrounding these there is a ring of much larger flowers that are reduced to a flat disk-like five-lobed corolla, stamen-less, pistil-less. It is this outer ring that is the conspicuous and attractive feature, if not to the botanist at least to the lover of the quaint and picturesque." The outer flowers are sterile; it is the small inner ones that make the berries.

[*242*]

There are numerous Viburnums of great decorative value. *V. trilobum* is closely related to *V. Opulus* and much like it in appearance. It is the so-called American High Bush Cranberry; the variety of *V. Opulus* called *sterile* is the well known Snowball Bush, and there are many others, including the lovely and exquisitely fragrant *V. Carlesii*, from Korea, flowering in April and early May, one of the finest of recently introduced shrubs, and *V. fragrans*, less hardy but said to be even more highly scented.

Callicarpa japonica (Japanese Beauty Berry) (Plate 238)

The importance of planting a well selected collection of berry-bearing shrubs is not always realized; but when the autumn days come and flowers grow fewer the bright berries come to our rescue in making indoor decorations, as well as providing color in the garden and, in the case of many of them, food for the birds. The flowers of many of these berry bearers are less spectacular than the fruits, sometimes; indeed, they are quite insignificant, and this is probably the reason why they are so often overlooked in our plantings. We hate to give up space to a shrub that is not going to give full value in flowers, and we do not look ahead to the short-rationed autumn season when so many of the earlier-flowering shrubs are merely monotonous green units, or an indistinguishable part of the general verdant setting.

The Callicarpas are among the shrubs that should certainly not be neglected. In the first place they are low-growing, and there is room for several of them on the smallest place. True, the little pinkish flowers are not very conspicuous, but they are followed by clusters of translucent amethyst-colored berries, not only unusual in color but very lovely, and the twigs are fine to combine with flowers of the late season, with Dahlias, Cosmos, Japanese Anemones, and others in indoor arrangements.

[243]

Callicarpa dichotoma, which is often sold as *C. japonica* and is superior to it, is a Chinese shrub belonging to the Verbena family. It grows from three to four feet tall, and it with the less showy *C. japonica* likes to grow in full sun in a good rich soil. In very cold climates they sometimes kill back but spring again from the root as do the Buddleias. There is also an American species, *C. americana*, not often seen and strangely called French Mulberry; it is found wild from Virginia to Texas. The leaves are said to be densely rusty and downy beneath. The fruits are reddish violet, and a white-fruited variety is offered. The bushes grow somewhat taller than do *C. dichotoma* and *C. japonica*. It is not generally hardy out of its own territory.

❦ *Cotoneaster Dammeri (C. humifusa)* in a Rock Garden (Plate 239)

Certain of the large family of Cotoneasters make tall bushes and belong in the shrubbery or used as specimens in the garden. But a few are low-growing and may be made to fit the rock garden or be used on rocky banks. *C. Dammeri* is one of these. This is a prostrate species of great merit. It seldom rises more than six inches above the rock or earth but forms big flat mats of very real beauty, the branches rooting as they go, or if planted at the top of a rock, as in Plate 239, trailing down its surface with charming effect. The small leaves are a lustrous dark green and, where the plant is hardy, remain on over the winter. In the spring or late summer it bears small white flowers which are followed by coral-red berries. A berry-bearing shrub for the rock garden is something of a novelty. This one is not, however, recommended for small rock gardens, as its prostrate branches reach widely, covering a considerable area. But where there is a large rock or a rough rocky bank that needs veiling there is the place for *Cotoneaster Dammeri*. It was introduced by the late E. H. Wilson from China.

[244]

Other Cotoneasters that may be used in large rock gardens, on rocky banks, or in retaining walls are the following: *C. adpressa*, *C. thymifolia*, *C. apiculata*, and *C. horizontalis*. The latter has several forms, and all spread so widely that their situation should be carefully chosen. Planted, for instance, near a path edge it soon reaches across the path, and mutilation necessarily follows. All bear handsome red berries in the fall and are nearly if not quite evergreen. They are not particular as to soil or situation and will even thrive very well in partial shade. They self-sow rather freely and little Cotoneaster volunteers, as they say in the South, spring up in unexpected places and may be transplanted to situations where they are wanted.

⚘ Autumn Flowers in Clear Glass Vase (Plate 240)

When the late autumn days arrive, gathering a bouquet of flowers from the garden becomes something of a treasure hunt, so to speak. We are much more easily satisfied than in the spring and summer, and we go about gleaning here a blossom, there a bit of attractive foliage or a twig of berries and are very well pleased with the result, whatever it may be.

In Plate 240 is such a little late-begotten nosegay in a clear glass vase perhaps to be placed on the reading table or desk so as to be where it may be often looked at. Any garden, almost, will yield such a small bouquet, but no two will be alike. This one is made up of Autumn Crocuses, Potentilla Miss Willmott, the late-flowering hardy Cyclamen, *Geum Borisii*, and a number of Primroses, these last flowering, as they so often do, for the second time. One can find a Primrose at almost any season except the hottest and dryest part of the summer.

⚏ Parkland in Autumn (Plate 241)

As the leaves thin in autumn we see the beautiful structure of the trees and realize how various are the different patterns of twigs and branches. Clothed in their lush summer dress, their beauty eludes us; but now with winter drawing on it is displayed for us. More than this, the remaining leaves are red, russet, or golden, sometimes pale yellow, and this rich color scheme is repeated where they have fallen to the ground and also by certain of the grasses and the stems of shrubs. When we rake up the leaves from lawns we deprive ourselves of one of Nature's loveliest effects and the earth of its natural nutriment. The autumn bonfires seen on every hand mean the destruction of this natural food. Wherever possible, the leaves should be allowed to lie on the ground and rot, returning to the earth what it earlier gave forth in flowers and verdure.

AUTUMN FLOWER ARRANGEMENTS

⚏ *Celastrus articulatus* in Jar with Eryngiums and Berberis (Plate 242)

A very attractive decorative arrangement from the standpoint of color and form is shown in Plate 242. Here we have the Oriental Bittersweet (*Celastrus articulatus*), its yellow berries split to show the scarlet arils, some twigs of the Japanese Barberry (*Berberis Thunbergii*), still holding its small brilliant leaves, and some stalks of Eryngium, or Sea Holly, its flowers and bracts a soft steel blue. The Sea Hollies are massed to give strength to the arrangement while the slender twigs of the other shrubs are so disposed as to lend it an especial grace and lightness. The narrow-mouthed jar holds them all in place admirably.

[*246*]

There are numerous kinds of Eryngium, all with the same general form and habit, some with flowers of a deeper tone than others. *E. giganteum* is a tall vigorous species, a biennial, with ivory-white involucrum. *E. Bourgati* is handsome and vigorous, with flowers and bracts a fine metallic blue. It grows one and one-half feet tall. Save *E. giganteum* they are all hardy perennials, liking a sunny situation and good friable soil. The different kinds grow from one to six feet tall.

✿ *Pyracantha coccinea Lalandi* in Jar (Firethorn) (Plate 243)

There are few more beautiful berried shrubs than the Firethorn, especially the variety *Lalandi*. There are six species of Pyracantha natural to southeast Europe, Himalaya to central China. They are evergreen, usually with thorny branches, leaves narrow, and blossoms white in compound corymbs and not very conspicuous, followed by brilliant fruit. Some have yellow berries flushed with orange, some are orange-red in color, others are clear red or clear yellow.

The kind in Plate 243 is *P. coccinea Lalandi*, which may be said to be the hardiest and the one most frequently seen in this country. It is often trained against the north side of a house or wall, where it fruits so heavily as almost to obscure the leaves; or it may be grown as a free bush at the back of a large rock garden or in some other situation where it is sheltered by tall evergreens or by a house or other wall. In Massachusetts it will even then be cut back by the cold, though probably not killed. It is one of the few evergreens that fruit handsomely and freely against a north wall, and as such has a special value. Its fruit is orange-red, and it may grow as high as twenty feet, and with the branches spread out will cover a large space of wall. Needless to say, its sprays of berries are fine for cutting as the days grow short and flowers fewer.

[*247*]

✠ An Arrangement of Vine Branches in a Basket (Plate 244)

If flowers fail in the autumn, we may always turn to leaves for making decorative arrangements for the house. In what an attractive manner this may be done, Plate 244 shows. The graceful basket has been utilized to hold the lax branches of various kinds of Ampelopsis (Parthenocissus), of which there are many to be had. The different kinds are native of North America, eastern Asia, and Himalaya.

Some of the most interesting kinds are *Ampelopsis aconitifolia* (Monkshood Vine), deeply cut leaves like those of a Delphinium; *A. heterophylla* (Porcelain Berry), attractive three- or five-lobed leaves of medium size and many light blue berries in the autumn; *A. quinquefolia* (the well known Virginia Creeper), that bears blackish fruit and brilliant foliage in the fall; *A. tricuspidata Lowii* (Geranium Creeper), with small leaves, purplish while young and turning a warm crimson in the autumn. It is a closely clinging vine. There is a still smaller-leaved form called *A. t. minutifolia.* *A. t. Veitchii* is the well known Boston Ivy that in the late season seems to assume all the colors of the sunset.

The little variety *Lowii* is one of the prettiest and daintiest vines in cultivation and is lovely to use on low walls. The Virginia Creeper is strong-growing and will cling to trees up which it clambers, swinging free here and there, and in the autumn making the tree appear as if on fire.

✠ Chrysanthemums, Asters, Delphiniums, and Leaves (Plate 245)

As autumn draws on towards winter, we are always glad that we have planted plenty of Chrysanthemums, though in the earlier season we may have grudged them the space they occupied. Now in November they are almost the only flowers that may be culled to fill the vases and jars indoors.

[*248*]

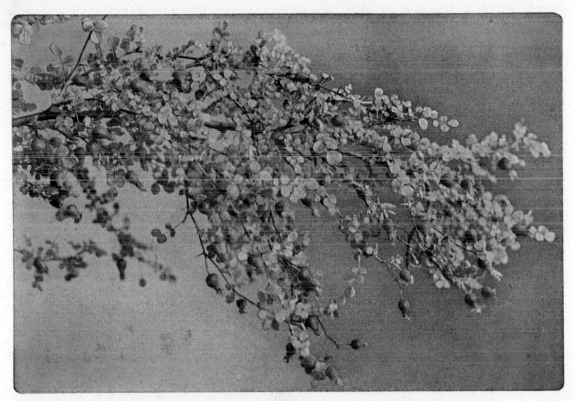

Plate 235. A FRUITING BRANCH OF *Rosa Willmottiae*

Plate 236. *Celastrus articulatus (C. orbiculatus)* (ORIENTAL BITTERSWEET)

Plate 237. *Viburnum opulus*, FRUITING
(EUROPEAN CRANBERRY BUSH)

Plate 238. *Callicarpa japonica* (JAPANESE BEAUTY BERRY)

Plate 239. *Cotoneaster Dammeri (C. humifusa)* IN A ROCK GARDEN

Plate 247. AN ARRANGEMENT OF CONIFER TWIGS

Plate 248. AN ARRANGEMENT OF SEMI-DOUBLE CHRYSANTHEMUMS

Here and there we may find a late second flowering on the Delphiniums that were cut down after their first effort, and these are nice to add to the collection of little shock-headed hardy Chrysanthemums; and there are always leaves, brown, gold, russet, crimson, and scarlet, that blend with the colors of the Chrysanthemums and give variety to the bouquet.

✿ Hardy Asters in a White Jar (Plate 246)

Not only do the Michaelmas Daisies or Hardy Asters create a soft-toned mistlike beauty in the garden where they are planted (as they always should be) in masses, but they furnish splendid material for indoor decoration. Their colors all seem to blend harmoniously with one another, making selection easy, and they last very well in water. Their long wandlike stems and full flower heads practically arrange themselves.

In the attractive white pottery jar in Plate 246 are a number of varieties, among them the deep rose-colored Barr's Pink; the soft lavender-purple King of the Belgians; the delicate crimson-mauve Nancy Ballard, semi-double and borne on branching stems three feet high; Weinholtzi, bright pink and growing to a height of two and one-half feet; and several varieties of German origin that are not at present obtainable in this country.

A good selection in addition to the above would be the following: Skylands Queen, flowering fairly late, about two and one-half feet tall, large single lilac-blue flowers; Red Rover, three to four feet, brilliant crimson flowers with gold centers in immense sprays, also flowering late; Grey Lady, three to four feet, semi-double, opalescent gray; Peggy Ballard, three feet, rosy mauve, September; Queen Mary, immense lavender-blue flowers on stems three to four feet tall in September and October. For white flowers there are Mount Everest, branching pyramidal heads of large white flowers on stems three to four feet tall; Perry's White, flowering

[*249*]

earlier and of lower stature, golden center; and White Climax, growing five feet tall and flowering in September. Also there is the native Upland Aster, a bushy plant bearing a multitude of small white flowers on bushy plants about eighteen inches high. This is *Aster ptarmicoides.* It is very pretty both in the garden and used for cutting combined with other flowers.

Gardeners who have not tried the Yellow Michaelmas Daisy, listed in catalogues as *Aster luteus* or *hybridus luteus,* will be pleased with it. It flowers in August and September in sprays of small yellow flowers, rather like those of a Goldenrod but better in color, from cream to lemon. It grows under three feet high.

✠ An Arrangement of Conifer Twigs (Plate 247)

One need not grow desperate for want of flowers in the late autumn or winter if he numbers among his blessings a collection of different kinds of Conifers. Look them over, and note the variety of form and color, and consider their possibilities for indoor decoration. It will be a soft-toned restful arrangement that will result, greens of many tones, some verging towards blue, some dark, some light; if one cares for the so-called yellow evergreens, these may also be included, but the general effect is better without them.

In the bunch of Conifer twigs shown in Plate 247 some idea of the possible variety is given. They are the following: the Veitch Fir (*Abies Veitchii*), a Japanese evergreen that is one of the most ornamental of Firs, very hardy, and should be given a northern exposure in medium clay loam; *Thuja orientalis (Biota orientalis)*, Chinese or Oriental Arborvitae, native in Korea, Manchuria, and parts of China, which may be hardy as far north as Boston but not reliably so; *Picea orientalis* (Oriental Spruce), a hand-

[*250*]

some tree with dense compactly set "needles," dark and glossy, that is hardy as far north as Ontario; *Picea pungens Kosteriana* (Koster's Weeping Blue Spruce), the foliage bluish white, the branches pendulous, which originated in the Boskoop Nurseries in Holland); *Pinus koraiensis* (Korean Nut Pine), native also on the main island of Japan in certain mountainous districts. The last is hardy North but likes a sheltered situation where rough winds do not reach it. It grows slowly, but Professor Bailey says "It is a very promising species for ornamental purposes. At Ottawa a tree planted in 1896 is about thirty feet in height, and next to the White Pine is, perhaps the most ornamental species in the Arboretum." The foliage is dark and rich in color.

An Arrangement of Semi-Double Chrysanthemums (Plate 248)

The Dahlias have gone down before the nipping frosts, most of the annuals have succumbed, a few stems of late Aconite and *Salvia Pitcheri* remain, a few wands of late-flowering Michaelmas Daisies, their colors dimmed. For it is November. But undismayed the Chrysanthemums still blossom.

Shown in Plate 248 is a collection of single or semi-double varieties that many persons think are more lovely than the fully double kinds. Their colors are exquisite and, combined with ruddy autumn leaves and branches of berries, few flowers are finer for indoor decoration.

Here is a selection that will give the greatest satisfaction: Afterglow, burnt orange; Ann Bartlett, bronze-red with very wide individual petals; Anne Vaillant Dort, superb salmon-bronze; Besse La Roche, Brazil red; Bronze Buckingham, sport of Mrs. W. E. Buckingham; Cleopatra, amber and yellow; Crimson Splendor, early; Donald Geddis, superb apricot-orange; Godfreys Triumph, bright yellow and shaped like a Water Lily;

Helen Page Wodell, yellow with narrow petals; Jeanne Shelly Adams, deep rose-pink with white zone; Last Call, orange-yellow-tinted bronze; Mabel Seymour, fine white; Mrs. David Lloyd George, yellow-suffused pink; Mrs. W. E. Buckingham, fine pure pink; Ruth Adams, old-gold-tinted bronze; Sunburst, intense burnt orange with lavender sheen; Valencis, beautiful pure pink, one of the best.

WINTER

THE GARDEN IN WINTER

WHAT does the winter season offer the gardener? Little, it may at first be thought. And yet this is not the truth. First, and very important, there is during the closed months time to meditate upon our mistakes and failures (which have doubtless been many) and to seek some way to remedy, or at least not to repeat, them. There is time, too, to study the catalogues and to make brave lists to insure future garden glory; leisure also to read and make notes from the garden books that during the busy spring and summer months have somehow gotten tucked away on the lower sections of the bookshelves. And then there is remembering: remembering the bold scarlet of the Poppies in June, the towering spires of the Delphiniums, blue, pink, purple, or ivory, the blue intricacies of the little flower we know as Love-in-a-mist (Nigella) the flaunting ruffles of the Petunias, the perfect beauty of the new Roses, the haunting sweetness of Honeysuckle and the White Tobacco on still summer nights—a thousand delights that come back to us as rude winds rattle the casements, as icicles lengthen along the eaves, or as the snow falls stilly layer on layer, turning all the world towards peace and purity.

And forgetting! Forgetting is perhaps as important as remembering. If we are to start the new season with vigor and enthusiasm, we must forget the backaches, the scratched arms, the loathsome prevalence of slugs and other pests, the superiority of our neighbor's Sweet Peas and Asters, and certain humiliations suffered from the behavior of various sniffy alpines that turned up their small toes and died in the face of our most earnest

[255]

ministrations. Yes, there are numerous things to forget during the winter months. But the new season, the new spring, is a fair page upon which we may write what we will.

Out of doors, perhaps, the gardener's eyes only may be actively employed. He may, of course, draw the blanket closer about the crowns of certain tender plants, shake the snow from the evergreens upon which it lies too heavily, look to his tools, replacing those that are worn out and seeing that all are clean and in place. This will save much time when the busy spring weeks begin. We may also save time, when orders for plants are sent out, by writing labels for them then and there, and by looking up and noting the needs and preferences of each plant, so that, when the packages and bales and boxes begin arriving, we shall have a label ready for each plant and know at once just what it wants in the way of soil and situation. By planning, too, each plant's place in the scheme of the garden, we can enable the various members of our plant family to live harmoniously side by side; and the crimson Phlox will not arise next to the angry orange Lilies, or some great stalwart lean too heavily upon a plant of frail physique. The grapevines must be pruned in February; and this is a good time to clean and sort the seeds we have collected, and to send off neat little packets of them to appreciative friends.

Out of doors there is time to note the beauty of leafless trees, and the lovely handwriting of their twigs against the sky. The colors of their bark come as a surprise to us—reddish, white, gray, all tones of brown, yellowish, and bright green. We realize anew the important place filled by the evergreens, both broad- and narrow-leaved, and resolve to have more of them. There is time to note the different ways snow lies upon the various trees, and the magical way frost and sleet deal with twigs and branches, leaves and old seed heads. There will be a few berries, a few clinging dry leaves, some bushes whose foliage shines as if burnished, the Mahonias,

Plate 249. *Helleborus niger* (CHRISTMAS ROSE)

Plate 250. *Helleborus atrorubens* (LENTEN ROSE)

Plate 251. *Cotoneaster horizontalis* IN THE ROCK GARDEN

Plate 252. *Picea excelsa obovata*
Plate 253. *Pinus excelsa*

Ilex glauca, the Rhododendrons, and Leucothoë Catesbaei. All these things have a significance that is lost in the wealth of summer's graciousness. If we have been thoughtful gardeners, we may also have a few flowers during the winter months—Christmas Roses, the Winter Witch Hazels, *Erica carnea*, a few hardy Crocuses, a Viola or two. That these are more precious than any summer flowers goes without saying.

There will be steel-gray days; iron days when the land is fixed in immobility by the bitter cold; blue and gold days, and days when the world beyond the window is blotted out by falling snow or sharply slanting rain, or when all outdoors is turned to one blinding sparkle by a sleet storm that whips suddenly out of the clouds and gives common things the semblance of rare treasure.

And then there are the sounds of winter, so different from those of any other season. There is the creak of inanimate things squeezed by the frost, the crunch of snow underfoot, the cheeping of winter birds. Sometimes the wind is a penny whistle in the trees, sometimes a shrill scream, again a harsh roar.

The rock garden is full of small lovelinesses in the winter season, as is the flower garden that has not been too meticulously cleaned up and blanketed. The roadsides and woods, however, and the neglected fields offer the most beauty.

Indoors the gardener will have his house plants to cheer him, but there is much out of doors also to tide him happily over the period when flowers do not bloom under the sky.

Said Seneca: "Live they not against nature that in the winter ask for a rose, and by the nourishment of warm waters, and the fit change in the heat in winter-time cause a lily or a spring flower to bloom?" Surely this is a sane admonition, to take the seasons as they come, drawing from each the beauty and interest it offers.

"Would you be well," wrote Thoreau, "see that you are attuned to each mood of nature."

Winter is a season of reserves, a reticent season. It does not throw its treasure into our outstretched hands. We must seek it, watch for it, and learn to appreciate the beauty of the gray and white color scheme, punctuated or banded by the heavy darkness of evergreens.

A little patience, for it will not be long before "the winter's last snowflake"—the Snowdrop—thrusts through the seemingly inhospitable earth its narrow spears of green; "before the Crocus lights its golden fires."

Helleborus niger (Christmas Rose) (Plate 249)

When the short and often dreary days of winter have settled upon us, it is indeed a boon to be able to go out of doors and not only look upon but gather freshly blossoming flowers. It is this boon that the Christmas Rose, *Helleborus niger*, confers upon our gardens. Nor is the Christmas Rose a left-over, or a superprecocious flower of some early-blooming plant. It flowers at its appointed time—a legitimate child of winter.

There are numerous forms of *Helleborus niger*, some beginning to bloom towards the end of November or early in December, others in February, or any time during the winter when they are not actually frozen into passivity; and some types have smaller flowers than others. It is indeed a heartening sight to find on a bleak November day large clumps of thick dark green leaves two feet and more across, and at their base some twenty-five to fifty (eighty have been known on a single clump) round white buds. These open out into wide waxen flowers on stems long enough for picking, and they last well in the house, appearing best if a few of their dark leaves are picked with them.

The Christmas Rose is quite hardy, but in localities where the weather settles down early to steady freezing the plants may be covered with hand frames which may be taken off during the mildest part of the day. This enables them to go on blooming until the last of the round white buds has opened, and it also tends to draw up the stems so as to make them finer for cutting.

These hardy plants do not need to be planted in especially sheltered situations but may be set boldly out in borders or at the edges of woodland; but, except where the soil is clayey, they like a little shade.

If you are preparing to plant a number of Christmas Roses, or even a single one, dig the bed both wide and deep, so that the roots may easily go down to coolness. Make the preparations thorough in the first place, and they will be happy for many years. Choose a well drained situation, and trench it at least three times the depth of a spade. As the digging proceeds, liberal amounts of well rotted farmyard manure should be incorporated with the soil, also some lime. The soil should be sandy, rather than clayey. Spring, when working the soil becomes easy, is the best time to set out the plants. It is also the best time for dividing clumps that have become too large. Growth then begins immediately, and the plants become established before they must endure the strain of extreme hot weather. It is said that the finest blossoms are produced on two- or three-year-old plants. The flowers are pure white when first opened, but turn pinkish as they age.

When dividing the plants, do not chop them to pieces with a spade, but force the clumps apart with two hand forks pressed back to back. Each division should consist of not more than three crowns (two will be enough) and as many roots as possible.

About the end of March a mulch of old manure will be much appreciated, and during the heat of summer the plants should be thoroughly watered, occasionally with weak manure water.

If the hand lights are not used in the autumn and winter, a mulch of strawy stuff or leaves should be drawn up around the plants to protect the blossoms from being disfigured by mud spattered by heavy rains. The Christmas Rose, *Helleborus niger*, is a native of Austria and is sometimes called Black Hellebore, from its blackish rootstock. It is said that seeding weakens the plants; as they are very prolific in this matter, the spent flowers should always be removed.

Ferns are a lovely accompaniment for Christmas Roses and make a show when the waxen flowers are gone.

The Christmas Rose is not particular as to soil but dislikes to grow where water stands.

✿ *Helleborus atrorubens* (Lenten Rose) (Plate 250)

The subject of Plate 250, *Helleborus atrorubens*, is one of the numerous Lenten Roses, or Lent Hellebores, native of Asia Minor, Greece, and other parts of southern and eastern Europe. They are chiefly derived from *Helleborus colchicus, olympicus, atrorubens, orientalis, caucasicus*, with probably some others. They have become, said Miss Gertrude Jekyll, who had a famous Nut Walk bordered with them, "much mixed by hybridization, both natural and intentional, and though they are no doubt kept distinct in botanical gardens, yet those to be found in private places are for the most part hybrids." This is all to the good from the gardener's point of view, for we find among these hybrids many lovely colors—soft, ruddy, purplish tones, greenish tints, cream, blush, even pure white ones and some with spotted flowers, or they may be suffused with other hues. These Lent Hellebores are lovely bordering a shady walk or in wide colonies in the wild garden or in shaded borders. When they are settled down and feel at home, they seed about most heartily and, if the seedlings are guarded, may be utilized to make new plantations in which may appear new hues or combinations of hues.

[*260*]

The so-called Lenten Roses flower in the late winter or early spring—late February or early March if the weather is at all relenting—and with their long stems and handsome leaves they are delightful for picking, though they do not last as long in water as do the true Christmas Rose, *Helleborus niger*. They revel in a rich, deeply dug, cool soil and a shaded situation, and may be planted either in spring or in fall, though in cold climates spring is the better.

Several dealers in this country have good collections of Lent Roses, so that American gardeners may enjoy plantations of these attractive spring flowers if they want them. They are also easily raised from seed, but are slow to germinate and take several years to come to blossoming size.

✤ *Cotoneaster horizontalis* in the Rock Garden (Plate 251)

Even in the drier season, when flowers have had their day and gone in the rock garden or wall face, a pleasant if sober color scheme may be maintained if a judicious selection of plants is made. In Plate 251 is shown a bit of rock garden that does not suffer very much from the loss of bloom. *Cotoneaster horizontalis* spreads flat against the stones, its fishbone branches laterally encrusted with small scarlet berries.

This Rock Cotoneaster, or Quince Berry, as it is sometimes called, comes from western China. In the South the leaves are evergreen, but in the North they turn scarlet in the autumn and drop off, leaving the berry-studded branches exposed. In the spring the little pinkish blossoms are of small importance. *Cotoneaster adpressa* and *Cotoneaster microphylla*, with its variety *thymifolia*, having minute roundish leaves, serve the same festive ends. *Cotoneaster microphylla* keeps its leaves later into the autumn than the other two. Many gray-leaved plants add to the scenic display of the autumn rock or wall garden. Among them are numerous Saxifrages, Sedums, Androsaces, dwarf Artemisias, Achilleas, Arabis, and Cerastiums.

The Garden in Color

Any of these grouped about the bright-berried or bright-leaved little shrubs make a picture that would attract notice at any season.

The Cotoneasters are not especially particular as to soil and will grow well where the soil is on the poor side and even in partial shade, though this does not mean that they will not thrive in good soil and sun. They are most successful in rather open situations, where freely reached by wind and weather.

There are a great many kinds of Cotoneasters on the market, each with its individual type of attractiveness of habit, leafage, or fruit. It is well to see a collection growing in a nursery before buying, so as to choose the kinds that best fit our situations.

Picea excelsa obovata (Plate 252)

The subject of Plate 252 is the Siberian Spruce. It is much like the Norway Spruce, though altogether a smaller tree. Also it is slower growing. The branchlets droop slightly, the cones are small and neat, and it is a very graceful tree but less often planted in North America than abroad. In Europe numerous forms of it are known and used. It is native in northern Europe and in northern Asia and Manchuria, and it is said to be hardy as far north as Canada and probably Saskatchewan, a hardy tree that loves the north lands and, according to Professor Bailey, thrives best in mountainous regions. It should be used more freely in cold latitudes.

Pinus excelsa (Plate 253)

The Pines are perhaps the finest of all evergreens, the most individual, the most distinctive, and no trees grow old with such serene and rugged dignity. There is no time, from seedhood until the end, when a pine tree is not beautiful.

[262]

Pinus excelsa is the Himalayan White Pine or Blue Pine, sometimes known as *Pinus nepalensis*. It is characterized by long and very narrow leaves of a soft blue-green color, sometimes as long as eight inches and as fine as needles, and by unusually beautiful cones. These are very slender and tapering, often nine inches long, and on mature specimens give the tree a very unusual effect. "In this area," says Professor Bailey, "trees more than forty feet tall are not uncommon. In some places it is subject to insect attack." The branches droop slightly, and in autumn, when the long blue-green foliage is punctuated by the slender brown cones, the tree is an outstanding object of beauty.

In its native regions, "in clear stands of mixed forests," it reaches a height of 150 feet, "with spreading and slightly ascending branches forming a broad open pyramid, with a rather loose open habit." It is native in the Himalayas from Bhutan to Afghanistan up to 12,500 feet, and is said to be hardy in sheltered places as far north as Massachusetts, but is apt to be injured in very cold winters.

✠ *Bruckenthalia spiculifolia* (Spiked Heath) (Plate 254)

Rock gardeners are always on the lookout for small shrubs to fit the contours of their miniature hills and valleys. The Spiked Heath is one that may be chosen with assurance of its suitability, and that is quite easily come by. It is a pretty little Heath-like shrub, sole member of its genus. It grows under a foot high, and the little branches are clothed with short, very narrow leaves crowded together. In summer it bears small bell-shaped pinkish flowers deeply four-lobed in short dense spikes. It is evergreen, but in the winter sometimes turns a soft rusty color.

It prefers a gritty soil and a position in full sunshine. In localities where the winters are apt to be very severe a mulch of salt hay or dry leaves drawn about the little plants is a wise precaution. Thickets of the Spiked

Heath on sunny slopes in a rock garden give a very attractive effect all the season through.

Bruckenthalia spiculifolia is a native of Asia Minor and southern Europe.

✠ Rock Garden in Winter (Plate 255)

In winter it is natural that the rock garden should be robbed of its gay coverlet and don a more sober spread. Nevertheless, all attraction is not lost to it. Sometimes it is enveloped in a blanket of snow through which protrude the gaunt shoulders of the larger stones and over which the dwarf evergreens cast their bluish shadows. When there is no snow the hoar frost takes a hand at making beauty, and every least leaf and stem is outlined with silver beads and fringes. The humblest overlooked weed, or fragment of withered foliage, or still standing seed stem becomes suddenly, overnight, outstandingly beautiful.

But there is more than this in the winter rock garden to catch and hold the seeking eye. Here and there will dangle a bright berry; the little evergreens look especially thrifty, and their different tones of green show up clearly in the dour season. The stems of certain Sedums and other plants show color that we had not noted during the summer—coral-red, old gold, pinkish, straw-color. And there will be the bronze leaves of Ajuga and some other plants, few red leaves and many patches of silvery gray. As the winter wears on and mild spells occur, little rash blades and noses will thrust up, and perhaps a blossom or two in sheltered, sun-trapping corners. No, assuredly the rock garden should not be wholly abandoned and ignored in our winter walks about the garden. It is never quite barren of beauty if we have the eyes to see it—a quite different world, but one that is well worth viewing.

Plate 254. *Bruckenthalia spiculifolia* (SPIKED HEATH)

Plate 255. ROCK GARDEN IN WINTER

Plate 260. *Euphorbia myrsinites* (SPURGE)

Plate 261. *Hepatica triloba* IN MORNING FROST

Plate 262. *Hamamelis japonica* (JAPANESE WITCH-HAZEL)

Plate 263. *Hamamelis japonica Zuccariniana*

Plate 264. *Rubus Giraldianus* WITH *Berberis asiatica*

Plate 265. *Cornus alba* WITH BETULA IN WINTER

Plate 266. *Thymus lanuginosus, Saxifraga umbrosa* AND *Veronica Allionii*, ETC.

Plate 267. *Onopordon acaule* (STEMLESS THISTLE) IN THE WINTER ROCK GARDEN

Plate 268. *Betula corylifolia*

⚘ *Saxifraga rotundifolia* and *S. aizoon* (Plate 256)

A sheltered wall face or rocky slope offers warmth and comfort and freedom from standing moisture to many plants in winter. In Plate 256 we see well rooted in the crevices of a dry retaining wall two Saxifrages of quite different type.

Saxifraga rotundifolia, the Round-leaved Saxifrage (above), is found in most parts of southern and central Europe. It starts life by making a tuft of round leaves on fairly long stalks. The stems branch and are headed in May and June, and sometimes thereafter, by small, pretty white flowers, spattered with scarlet dots. In the autumn the round leaves turn a pleasant purplish brown. Catalogues offer numerous named forms of this Saxifrage, but all are very similar. *Saxifraga rotundifolia* belongs to a small group of Saxifrages known as the Miscopetala group, all of which are characterized by rounded leaves and small white flowers that, when growing in masses, produce a soft mistlike effect against the stones. It is a free-growing kind where suited, but not too hardy.

The other Saxifrage in the illustration, *Saxifraga aizoon*, belongs to the large encrusted group; that it is the most variable species of the group, is "due partly to the fact of its wide distribution over the mountains of Europe and in the northern and Arctic regions." Some of the forms make little hummocks of very small rosettes, others are much larger with strap-shaped leaves; and the sprays of flowers vary from scarcely more than an inch in height to many inches. The flowers may be pure white, white flecked with pink, and certain forms have yellow flowers—variety *flavescens* and variety *lutea*. Variety *rosea* has pretty pink flowers.

All the *aizoon* saxifrages are very easy to grow and are decorative in or out of bloom. They quickly establish themselves in cracks and crevices where they are seen to the best advantage. They are happy where they re-

[265]

ceive sun for at least a part of the day. They flower in the early summer. In the winter their silvered or hoary rosettes mounded together add much to the beauty of that sparse season. They prefer to grow on limestone rock but are not set in the matter. They prefer a raised, well drained position between stones and a generous diet of loam, old mortar rubble, or lime siftings, with leaf soil and sand helps them towards the fullest development of their characteristic leaf beauty.

❀ *Asarum europaeum* (European Wild Ginger) (Plate 257)

The European Wild Ginger, *Asarum europaeum*, like the several Wild Gingers that grow wild in this country, makes lovely ground covers in shady places. In England it is called Asarabacca; in Germany, *Haxelwurz;* in Italy, *asaro.* The leaves are large, kidney-shaped, and evergreen, on short stems. It is a strange plant but one of real charm and interest. Its broad leaves spread a canopy of changing green close to the earth, and in May it brings forth a solitary dull greenish, drooping flower on a short tough stem low between two bright shining leaves. The roots are aromatic and have long been used medicinally; "and from its frequent use as a remedy for the effects of excessive drinking," says Anne Pratt, "the plant has acquired in France the name of Cabaret." The leaves when powdered were used as snuff, and were believed to relieve headache. Along a shaded path it is a pleasant companion, winter or summer; but it is in winter that we are most sensitive to the fine form of the leaves and their changing lights and shades.

There are numerous Wild Gingers found growing wild in various parts of North America, all with the same wide green leaves that make one feel cool to look at them on a warm day, and bearing the same solitary bell-shaped blossom of a rather unlovely brownish purple. They are useful

[*266*]

in the same way as the European species for carpeting the ground in shaded places. They thrive and spread about freely in rich moist soil. Some of the best known North American kinds are the following: *Asarum canadense*, New Brunswick to North Carolina; *Asarum caudatum*, British Columbia to California ("blooms prolonged into tails"); *Asarum Hartwegii*, Oregon, California (leaves mottled with white); *Asarum virginica*, Virginia, South Carolina, and Tennessee (leaves mottled, and rather small).

Erica carnea Winter Beauty (Plate 258)

The various varieties of *Erica carnea* are among the best dwarf shrubs for use in the rock garden as well as for clothing rock banks. Winter Beauty, the subject of Plate 258, has little bell-shaped flowers of a good rose-pink hue, and it blooms at almost any time during the winter and early spring when the least softness creeps into the air.

Sedum oreganum in a Winter Rock Garden (Plate 259)

Sedum oreganum is sometimes found in gardens under the name of *Sedum obtusatum*, "an allied plant which is not in cultivation so far as I know." Mr. Praeger, author of "An Account of the Genus Sedum," says, "Among the group of North American yellow-flowered Sedums it may be distinguished by its remarkably long, acute sub-erect petals (resembling in shape and position those of the common *Sedum spurium*) and tapering buds no less than ⅜ inch long." It is a pretty small evergreen perennial, forming a neat mat of rosetted leaves that are sometimes tinged with red. The leaves are thick and shining and often are tinged with red. The flowers are borne about midsummer or a little later, starry, yellow,

[*267*]

and in forked heads. The plant is really more ornamental without the flowers, which are of the usual harsh Sedum yellow.

Sedum oreganum is found from Alaska to northern California. Many of the Sedums are worth winter inspection, and this little westerner especially makes an attractive tangle of leaves and stems among the rocks. Mrs. Rowntree says that in its native haunts it grows "at the bases of cliffs, in the gravel of sloping granite benches and in rocky crevices where pine needles and washed granite have lodged." This is a hint as to the sort of situation that should be given it in the rock garden.

❦ *Euphorbia myrsinites* (Spurge) (Plate 260)

Not many of the Spurges possess real beauty, but some of them have both usefulness and interest. *Euphorbia myrsinites* is one of these. A southern European plant, it will grow in any soil, and is sometimes said to be biennial; however, experience teaches that it is in reality perennial but dies if the plant becomes injured in any way.

Mr. Farrer designates this plant as "choice and even precious . . . creeping along with stems of six inches, set with thick blue-grey foliage and heads of yellow." Its prostrate branches are indeed pretty, trailing over the rocks at any season, and attract the flattering notice of all those who are not familiar with it, especially in the winter.

It has the habit of self-sowing rather too freely, which causes one to have the feeling that it is a little pushing and common; and so we lose our appreciation of its quite authentic attractiveness.

✥ *Hepatica triloba* in Morning Frost (Plate 261)

In Plate 261 we see the beauty wrought by the hoar frost in the garden. There are leaves and grasses and ferns edged with silver rime, displaying a new loveliness, a new character against the dark earth.

Flowers may be gone, but something else has taken their place that makes going abroad on an early morning well worth while.

Hepatica triloba is our own Liverwort or Liverleaf, familiar to all who wander in the woods in early spring. Indeed, the furry buds and fragile white, pink, or blue flowers may often be found nestled among the rusty leaves of last year, beneath the snow. It is a curious fact that most of the flowers that brave the storms and snows of winter or early spring are so delicate in appearance. The Hepatica is usually the earliest of our wild flowers, if we except the Skunk Cabbage, which seems to be able to brave any sort of weather. It blooms without its new leaves, which begin to uncurl after the blossoms have appeared. These rounded three-lobed leaves arise directly from the root and are quite lovely in themselves.

The name "Hepatica" is from a Greek word for "liver" and was doubtless bestowed because of the shape of the leaves. Dr. Prior says that "in consequence of this fancied likeness it was used as a remedy for liver complaints, the common people having long labored under the belief that Nature indicated in some such fashion the uses to which her creations might be applied."

✥ *Hamamelis japonica* (Japanese Witch-Hazel) (Plate 262)

The Winter Witch-Hazels, Hamamelis, have no rivals among shrubs or trees that bear their blossoms during the cold season. They are a small group, but all are worth growing. The structure of their flowers is both quaint and lovely, and they string the leafless branches at a season when we are not expecting flowers out of doors.

Hamamelis japonica forms an irregular-shaped bush or small tree. It usually flowers in February. It grows wild both in Japan and in China. It starts life as a somewhat ungainly shrub, but a little judicious pruning will convert it into a very pretty small tree. The flowers are composed of numerous narrow yellow petals like bits of floss silk; and, while they are inconspicuous in themselves, the effect of the sun shining upon a well clothed tree is striking and very lovely, especially if there happens to be snow upon the ground.

There is a variety of *Hamamelis japonica* called *arborea*, which tends to grow into a somewhat larger and stronger tree; the flowers usually open earlier, and they are somewhat deeper in hue.

The Witch-Hazels are a very interesting and distinctive small group of shrubs or small trees, native of North America and eastern Asia. Their leaves much resemble those of the common Hazel, and their twigs are supposed in some matters to possess magic properties that make them useful as divining rods.

☗ *Hamamelis japonica Zuccariniana* (Plate 263)

The subject of Plate 263 is a very handsome variety of the so-called Japanese Witch-Hazel. Its flowers are a paler yellow, more lemon-color, more prolifically borne, more crinkled, and usually bloom a little later.

Groups of Witch-Hazels about the grounds give one great pleasure during the late winter and early spring, and our own *Hamamelis virginiana* flowers in the autumn.

The finest and showiest of them all is *Hamamelis mollis*, a Chinese species with large soft leaves, and a decided shrublike habit of growth. Its

[*270*]

starry flowers, crowding the branches before the leaves appear, have narrow, almost flat petals curved at the tip, and are of a warm golden color, very brilliant when seen in sunlight.

The two North American species are *Hamamelis virginiana* and *Hamamelis vernalis*. The first is familiar to every country wayfarer. It is found from far north to Texas, "a tenacious coarse bush, very attractive for its late autumn bloom." *Hamamelis vernalis* is found from Missouri to Louisiana and Oklahoma. It is a shrub growing six feet high with long leaves, and the characteristic yellow thready flowers, with a reddish calyx, make their appearance in March in the neighborhood of New York.

The Witch-Hazels will grow in almost any situation, but they like sunshine. They are lovely grouped on a steep slope where we may look up into the clouds of yellow blossoms, and of course a background of evergreens shows them up to great advantage.

⚘ *Rubus Giraldianus* (Plate 264)

In the winter time we have the opportunity to appreciate the beauty of the naked stems of trees and shrubs, which in summer are hidden from us by the enveloping foliage. Many members of the genus Rubus are lovely in their winter state and are far less used for ornamental purposes than they should be.

Crowning the summit of a rock garden in Plate 264 is a graceful specimen of *Rubus Giraldianus*, a Raspberry native to China that is occasionally planted in gardens with a view to decoration. Its rather large leaves are whitish beneath, and it bears small purplish flowers in narrow terminal panicles.

Thus far it is not outstanding in any way; but when the frosts come and the leaves are shed, its whiplike prickly stems show gleaming-white, and stand out against a background of evergreens, or the dark wood of other shrubs and trees, with startling effectiveness. Others of the Rubus clan have purplish or glaucous stems that are equally attractive. When we come to plan gardens for the winter, such plants are well worth bearing in mind.

✠ *Cornus alba* with Betula in Winter (Plate 265)

Groups of White Birches are always lovely in the landscape. In spring the wire-thin graceful twigs are hung with charming dangling catkins; in summer the white trunk and flexible branches show through the small pretty leaves, which in autumn turn the most lovely pale gold color and seem to cover the ground beneath the tree with gold pieces. In winter the white trunks with their delicate tracery of twigs are a delight. The American White Birch is called the Canoe Birch or Paper Birch—the latter name because of its exfoliating bark. This is *Betula papyrifera;* but often planted in this country are two other white-barked Birches, *Betula pendula*, the European White Birch, which has several forms, and *Betula pubescens*, native in Siberia and Europe.

Birches are not long-lived trees and are happiest in cold climates, preferring slightly moist sandy soil.

As shown in Plate 265, nothing could be more effective to plant against a group of White Birches than a thicket of Tartarian Dogwood, *Cornus alba*, with its blood-red stems. This shrub, a native of China and Siberia, in time grows ten feet high. It bears large leaves and small flowers in cymes two inches across. But it is in the winter and early spring that the shrub makes its mark. Against the snow or against the dark earth its stiff branches flame, and as the first hints of spring start the sap running they seem to deepen in color. No more effective waterside planting could be found than White Birches and red-stemmed Dogwoods.

[*272*]

Plate 269. *Allamanda cathartica*

Plate 274. CLIVIA, HYBRID (KAFIR LILY)

Plate 275. *Clianthus Dampieri*

🐝 *Thymus lanuginosus*, *Saxifraga umbrosa*, and *Veronica Allionii*, etc.
(Plate 266)

As is shown in Plate 266, the winter rock garden is not without interest. Many of the creeping and tufted evergreen plants gather themselves into hummocks and close-knit mats seemingly to resist the cold, and their effect against the cold stones is very heartening to the winter-weary observer.

In the illustration numbered 266 we have a number of kinds showing what they can do to resist the onslaughts of winter.

Thymus lanuginosus is known as the Woolly Thyme. It is one of the many forms of *Thymus Serpyllum*, and is lovely and useful as a carpet for the rock garden. Its leaves are small and gray with a covering of silvery hair. It forms thick mats and is a good ground cover for small bulbs. In early summer it bears small lavender flowers that hardly show against the gray background. It likes sun and an open situation and, if desired, may be grown between the crevices of flagged paths.

Saxifraga umbrosa, known commonly as London Pride and St. Patrick's Cabbage, is one of the easier of the Saxifrages to grow. It likes partial shade, where its shining leaves form into little compact rosettes, and from it in the early summer spring slender stems carrying graceful sprays of pinkish flowers spotted with red. In England it is a commonplace in every garden, where it is used for edging beds and in the rougher parts of the rock garden; and in that moist climate it will flourish either in sun or in shade. It is native in Ireland and in southwestern Europe. In this country, however, it is not quite so easy-going; while hardy in the neighborhood of New York City, it likes a shaded position in a soil not too dry, but light and with plenty of humus.

Veronica Allionii is a little creeping alpine, plentiful on Mont Cenis. It

[273]

has small, neat dark leaves and bears, rather sparsely, bright blue flower spikes an inch or two high.

Cerastium Biebersteinii is also here with its thick mat of woolly white stems and leaves. In spring it is submerged beneath a tide of heads of snow-white flowers.

✠ *Onopordon acaule* (Stemless Thistle) (Plate 267)

The Stemless Thistle, better known as *Carlina acaulis*, is a handsome plant that may be used in spacious rock gardens. As the illustration shows, it makes a flat star of silvery gray roughly pinnatifid leaves. It bears solitary heads of white flowers about six inches across, but it is in its flowerless stage that it is the more ornamental.

It is a native of southern Europe, and, unlike the even handsomer Stemless Thistle of the Alps, *Carlina acanthifolia*, is not a biennial. The Carlina thrives in a deep light soil and full sun and prefers some limestone in its diet.

✠ *Betula corylifolia* (Plate 268)

Nearly all the Birches possess grace and beauty. Some have white bark, some gray, some tawny, some almost black. The subject of Plate 268, *Betula corylifolia* is a handsome form of the River Birch, *Betula nigra*, which is widely distributed in this country. *Betula coryfolia*, according to the "Manual of Trees and Shrubs," by Alfred Rehder, grows about sixty feet high and has bark of a pale gray color that shows up handsomely in the winter landscape. It flourishes in a moist sandy soil.

THE GARDEN UNDER GLASS

❦ *Allamanda cathartica* (Plate 269)

Any one who has visited the American tropics has seen the Allamanda, one of the most beautiful of climbing plants. It clambers over walls and houses enveloping their shabbiness with a glory of golden color.

The blossoms of *Allamanda cathartica* are tubular, pure yellow, and about three inches across. The leaves are usually in fours, dark green, leathery, and shining. There are numerous varieties, some with a reddish brown throat. The blossoms are most prolifically borne, and the fragrance is like that of a Magnolia. It is a native of Brazil.

Allamanda cathartica Hendersoni and *A. c. Williamsii* are grown out of doors in southern Florida.

The various kinds of Allamandas are famous as stove plants, for their yellow trumpet-shaped blossoms are borne over a long period of the year. "They are especially useful on account of the many ways they can be grown, succeeding well as trained pot specimens and as roof climbers, planted out or in pots.... They increase readily from cuttings of the young half-ripened shoots, inserted in sand, with brisk heat, in a propagating frame or under a bell glass; they can be struck at any time of the year when cuttings can be obtained in the above condition, but about the beginning of March is the best, and then time is given for the young plants to make considerable progress before the autumn."

The Allamanda blossoms are lovely for cutting, which is another good reason for growing these beautiful climbers.

⚜ Calceolarias (Plates 270, 271, 272)

Calceolarias, commonly known as Slipperworts, are shrubby and herbaceous plants limited to greenhouses in northern regions but grown out of doors in warm climates. There are many species and varieties displaying a great variety of colors and markings.

The flowers are in cymes and are like little pouches or slippers in shape. The greater number of the species are native from Mexico to Chile. There are two types of these gay green house plants—the shrubby and the herbaceous. The herbaceous kinds bear much the more showy flowers and have been greatly improved in recent years, but the shrubby species flower over a longer period. A good strain of seeds of the herbaceous Calceolaria can be relied upon to give satisfactory results. They are usually sown in the late spring or early autumn in order to secure plants for the next winter's and spring's blossoming. From Dr. Bailey's "Hortus" comes this advice about sowing the seeds: "Finely sifted soil should be provided, preferably one containing leaf-mold, and care should be exercised in watering as the seed is very small; sub-irrigation is the best method. A temperature of 60° is recommended and no direct sun till the plants are quite large." After the soil in the flats is prepared, it should be watered and allowed to stand a day before the seed is sown thinly on the surface and pressed lightly into the soil with a flat board. When the plants appear they should of course be kept fairly moist. They should be given some air in the daytime, and the atmosphere of the house should be kept moderately moist. Further instruction comes from "Greenhouse and Stove Plants," by Thomas Baines: "When they are large enough prick them off to two inches apart in pans, or boxes, in soil like that in which the seed was sown, and treat as before with the exception that the sun's waning influence will make further shading unnecessary. When the leaves are about an inch long, move singly into three- or four-inch pots; keep them growing through the winter, and for

[276]

this purpose a night temperature of about forty-five degrees will be sufficient." If they are stood on a moist bottom it will help to maintain the degree of moisture that these plants like. "About the end of February or the beginning of March move them into eight-inch pots, using the soil a little more lumpy and with one sixth of rotten manure in addition to the leaf-mold and sand as before." As the days become warmer they may have a little more air; but draughts must be avoided or the leaves will be injured and the fine appearance of the plants marred.

The plants will grow rapidly during the warm weather, and a light shade of some kind should protect them from the too ardent rays of the sun. The plants should then be lightly syringed at the end of the day. If very large specimens are desired, they may be moved into still larger pots.

Calceolarias are heavy feeders, and a good drink of manure water is greatly appreciated once or twice a week after the plants have been put into the eight-inch pots and gained a firm hold upon the soil. Each plant should be carefully staked, for the burden of blossoms, as will be seen in the illustrations, is a heavy one. When the flowers open, it is wise to continue to keep them lightly shaded.

For the shrubby kinds the treatment is the same, but they may also be grown from cuttings. These are "usually taken when the plants are trimmed in late summer or early autumn, choosing firm wood and cutting down to two joints, giving a temperature of 45-50° and protection from the sun." These are the directions given in "Hortus." What seems to be exactly the opposite advice is found in Mr. Baines' "Greenhouse and Stove Plants." Cuttings may be made at almost any time of the spring or autumn, he says; "about March will be the best. Take the young side shoots whilst the wood is soft and they consist of about three joints; remove the lowest pair of leaves; and put four or five together in six inch pots filled with sand. Keep quite moist, moderately close, and shaded in a temperature of about fifty degrees. They will root in two or three weeks, when give more air, and move singly into four inch pots, drained and filled with soil similar to that advised for the herbaceous kinds." Thereafter the treatment is also the same "except that when the plants begin to move freely the leading shoots should be stopped to cause them to grow bushy."

Aphides are very partial to a diet of Calceolarias, and must be guarded against.

Among potted plants for spring blooming in the greenhouse none can touch for beauty and variety the Calceolarias, which offer constantly new colors and forms. Red and yellow are perhaps the predominant colors, but there is a vast number of tones between the two and much spattering of contrasting color and other markings on the pouchlike flowers.

The modern race of Calceolarias is the result of much cross breeding, covering many years, under intensive culture.

The Calceolaria shown in Plate 270 is a hybrid of the Chilean Slipper-wort. It is thought that *Calceolaria canna* and *Calceolaria Pavonii* may have had a part in producing this cross. The plants are immensely free flowering.

Calceolaria Clibranii (*Calceolaria profusa*), shown in Plate 272, is a large and graceful form, a hybrid form of *Calceolaria Burbidgeii*, the latter being a cross between the Peruvian *Calceolaria Pavonii* and *Calceolaria deflexa*.

✠ *Lithops mundi* (Plate 273)

Belonging to the enormous Fig-Marigold family (Mesembryanthema) are the curious little Stone and Windowed Plants of South Africa. In Mrs. Sarah Coombs' "South African Plants for American Gardens" is a good description of these curiosities of the plant world: "The Windowed Plants long ages ago retired into the ground leaving as their only communication

[*278*]

with the upper world, the flat, translucent tops which let in the light to the underground plant."

They do bear handsome big flowers above ground, "but for most of the year are hidden from all but the sharpest eyes." Mrs. Coombs says that these plants may be grown in our country quite easily, "under glass in the North and outdoors in warmer parts of the country, though many of them will do better for a little protection from summer rains. The Windowed Plants may not, away from their native habitat, be grown entirely submerged, for even under our dryest conditions, our atmosphere is damper than their desert home. They will rot if planted as deep as they grow normally, and must have more than their tops out of the ground." The Windowed Plants, as may be seen in Plate 273, are much the color of the surrounding ground, and often all but disappear in the dry season, "shrinking so that their tops are below the level of the old sheath, and dust blows over them, hiding them completely." They are said to be among the most remarkable "mimicry plants" in existence. "They are very small, averaging an inch and a half across before they begin to cluster." They are such pygmies that any one, however small the space he has to devote to plants, has room for a few of them; and a complete set of them could be grown in the space of a foot square. There are more than fifty species available from dealers, and so one has a wide selection. It has been said that they "are as handy to collect as postage stamps and grow so slowly that once 'mounted' they are nearly as permanent. Besides this they are friendly and quite willing to live under greenhouse conditions." The Lithops usually have some decoration, lines, or dots of contrasting color or rounded protuberances or wrinkles.

Lithops mundi is very close to *Lithops pseudo-truncatella*, one of the best known of the Lithops, and is thought by many authorities to be merely a form of the latter.

[*279*]

⚕ Clivia, Hybrid (Kafir Lily) (Plate 274)

The beautiful and showy Clivias, or Kafir Lilies, belong to the same family as do such other splendors as Amaryllis, Hippeastrum, Crinum, Hymenocallis, Eucharis, Sprekelia, and the dainty Zephyranthes. They are Amaryllids and close kin to the true Lilies, which they somewhat resemble.

They are South African plants "with fleshy roots, the expanded leaf bases forming bulb-like parts," bright green strap-shaped slightly drooping leaves and terminal umbels of warm-hued substantial orange- and apricot-colored Lily-like flowers set at right angles to the rather stiff stalks.

These plants are splendid subjects for the greenhouse, or they may easily be grown in the window or "in pots and tubs in the garden in summer." They have a long period of blossoming which makes them especially valuable. Mrs. Coombs, in "South African Plants for American Gardens," says: "Once established they will not fail for many years to send up their annual quota of beautiful flowers. This is true even under indifferent treatment." And she adds, "Good friends and faithful."

The species most usually seen is *Clivia miniata*, which has tubular erect flowers almost scarlet outside and yellow inside, followed by bright red berries. It is easily raised from seed, and numerous fine hybrids have been obtained in this way. The plants may also be increased by division, this operation being performed in the spring, though it is said that plants left undisturbed for several years give the best results.

The pots should be filled with rich, fairly heavy but well drained soil. "During the growing period water freely and feed with liquid manure. During the resting season keep the plants in a cool greenhouse and give little, if any, water."

The glowing flowers look as if they would be fragrant, and it is a disappointment to find that they have no scent.

Other valuable kinds are *Clivia nobilis*, with reddish yellow flowers; *Clivia Gardenii,* with flowers in shades of apricot and orange ("this species like a little shade and a good deal of moisture"); *Clivia cyrtanthiflora,* "an especially fine hybrid with large clusters of drooping orange and green flowers."

These are pot plants that the amateur may approach with some assurance of success. There are always beautiful and striking displays of Clivias at the winter flower shows.

✠ *Clianthus Dampieri* (Plate 275)

The subject of Plate 275 is the Glory Pea of Australia. It is a lovely vinelike plant of the pea family that does not grow over four feet high. The stem is pale and slightly hairy; the leaves are compound and arranged along the stems like the parts of a feather, numerous and without stalks. The flowers are most interesting in shape, as may be seen in the plate. They dangle in a cluster of four to six blooms, each flower nearly three inches long. They are pinkish scarlet, with a gleaming black velvet blotch on the lower part of the standard, which gives them a very smart and striking appearance. They are borne with great freedom, and are followed by a hairy, silky pod.

Another species, *Clianthus puniceus*, inferior to the last, is called the Parrot's-Bill. It is a taller plant, and the stems are without hairs. The flower cluster is longer, about eight inches, and each flower is three to four inches long. They are crimson, streaked with white at the base of the standard, and soon fade. There is a white-flowered variety. *Clianthus puniceus* belongs to New Zealand.

The Clianthuses are evergreen plants grown in greenhouses in the North, where they are much used for covering back walls or training on posts, either planted out or grown in a large pot. Training and tying must be carefully attended to, or the plants will become straggly and present a poor appearance. They "are easily increased from cuttings of the young shoots taken off when four or five inches long, with a heel—these may usually be had in the right condition about May." They are happiest in a cool greenhouse. In the greenhouse they are said to bloom in April or May. The best soil is good sandy fibrous loam, and if grown in pots they appreciate an occasional watering with manure water. The Glory Pea is often grafted on a stock of *Colutea arborescens*. In the southern part of Florida these showy plants are grown in the open air.

Clianthus Dampieri is found on the northwest coast of Australia, in the interior of New South Wales, and in other localities. It is far superior to *Clianthus puniceus*, indeed is one of the brightest of all leguminous plants, though seldom seen grown to perfection. Well grown plants are occasionally seen with over a hundred and fifty spikes of their brilliant blooms. Watering in winter should be attended to very carefully to prevent damping off, to which they are prone. In its natural habitat *Dampieri* is said to grow freely in dried-up cracks or small water courses. One of its not too far-fetched names is Lobster Claw.

A writer in an early number of *Curtis' Botanical Magazine* stated that he had once seen a striking tiara made of the single blooms mounted.

✿ *Hydrangea macrophylla* (*H. opuloides, H. hortensis*) (Plate 276)

The Hydrangeas, strangely enough, belong to the family of the Saxifrages, many of which have sprays of such tiny flowers. They take various forms, the majority being deciduous shrubs, but some are climbers *(Hy-*

[*282*]

drangea petiolaris), climbing by means of rootlets to a height of as much as fifty feet if support is provided—otherwise making a straggling, lax bush. The climber commonly known as the Hydrangea Vine is *Schizo-phragma hydrangeoides.*

Other Hydrangeas assume almost treelike proportions. The one under consideration grows to a height of about ten feet. Its leaves are elliptic, eight inches long and nearly as broad as long, slightly pubescent beneath, and more or less thick and shining. The showy flowers are blue, pink, or white "in flat or roundish cymes" that may be eight inches across.

Most Hydrangea species are hardy, but the numerous forms of *Hydrangea macrophylla* are somewhat tender and need special culture. It comes from China and Japan, "where it has been cultivated for centuries and where there are many named varieties." It is now one of the important plants forced by florists in pots or tubs for the spring trade.

It is said to be perfectly hardy along the coast from New York southward, "and north of this if protected with straw and bagging." Visitors to Nantucket Island will remember the magnificent specimens of this Hydrangea that decorate all the little yards, their huge globular clusters of sterile flowers, blue or pink, coming to great perfection in the moist sea air. "Pink-flowered globe-shaped specimens may sometimes be changed to blue by putting bits of iron or alum in the soil."

For winter or early spring flowering under glass cuttings are made late in the previous winter. They are in pots or pans of sand, placed over gentle heat until rooted, when they may be moved into small pots of a somewhat richer soil mixture. As the plants increase in size, they may be moved to larger pots which, during the warm weather, may be plunged outside. These stripling plants should not be allowed to dry out under the heat of summer, and an occasional dose of liquid manure is of great benefit to them. "By September they are ready to be put into eight inch pots, and after the first frost they should be brought into the cool greenhouse and kept there until January. Then increase the heat to fifty or sixty degrees when they should be ready to flower by Easter."*

⚘ *Chrysanthemum indicum* Brilliant (Plate 277)

Chrysanthemum indicum is a Chinese species very little known in cultivation, that is believed nevertheless to have played an important part in the origin of the magnificent race of florists' Chrysanthemums that we enjoy today. *Chrysanthemum indicum* is a perennial plant growing from two to three feet high with the usual much divided leaves, lined with a sort of felt on the undersides. The flowers are yellow, borne on short stems in numerous clusters.

Today there is a vast number of florists' Chrysanthemums differing widely in form and color, and every succeeding year adds to their number and variety.

The Chrysanthemum is the most important flower of the autumn, both in the garden and under glass. It is said that it comprises "over a hundred and fifty species of the family Compositae, nearly all from the temperate or subtropical regions of the Old World." These species include many plants that we do not call Chrysanthemums—the herb Costmary, the gay Painted Daisies (Pyrethrum), the Moonpenny and Shasta Daisies, even the common Daisy of the fields, among others.

The handsome specimen illustrated in Plate 277 called Brilliant, is one of the florists' Chrysanthemums, and like most of these, is probably the result of a union between *Chrysanthemum indicum* and *Chrysanthemum morifolium*, a Chinese plant with strong-scented large flowers.

In China and Japan the cultivation of Chrysanthemums has been almost

* See *The Garden Dictionary*.

a religion for over three thousand years. "Since the hybridizer began his work in the United States," says "The Garden Dictionary," "about three thousand varieties have been grown and listed. . . . Every year new varieties are grown and disseminated, while others are discarded, and not over seventy-five or eighty varieties are now actually in cultivation."

✤ Gloxinia Meteor (Plate 278)

The Gloxinia is, rightly, the florists' pride. It is a beautiful showy plant, one of a small genus of Brazilian plants formally known as Sinningia. They grow from tuberous, cormlike roots and have large velvety oblong-oval toothed leaves, opposite and long-stalked.

One species only is cultivated, *Sinningia speciosa*, and this is the beautiful plant we buy of the florist or admire in greenhouses. The flowers are solitary or borne a few in a cluster. They are large, tubular or bell-shaped, nearly stemless. Their colors are rich, some shade of violet and sometimes reddish spotted with white; but the pure white ones are the most lovely. When we have a well blossomed white Gloxinia planted in a white pot we have something that is indeed worth looking at.

Gloxinias, we find, are "plants of the warm humid rain-forest and need during their growing season a warm greenhouse, seventy or eighty degrees. Because they are plants of the lower canopy of the forest floor," says "The Garden Dictionary," "they must have shade and this must be provided by painting the greenhouse glass or by the roller type of shades. Also after blooming, which corresponds with the beginning of a dry season in their natural environment, they need a resting period." The tubers may then be dug up and stored in a dark place at a temperature of about 47° until February or March, when they may be potted up and again started into growth.

In watering the plants, care should be taken not to wet the leaves; but they need plenty of water on the roots. The best way is to water them from the bottom. Gloxinias make excellent house plants, being very ornamental; and the buds continue to open week after week.

Plants may be propagated by seeds or by leaf cuttings.

⚘ *Begonia elatior* (Plate 279)

There is so vast a number of Begonias and their hybrids that a society has been formed to deal with and further the interests of the many species and varieties. They were named for their introducer, a French botanist, Michel Begon, and they are probably the most satisfactory (and long-suffering) of all house plants.

They are a genus of tropical plants found around the world and are remarkable for the beauty of their flowers and their long-blooming habit, their handsome foliage and interesting and various forms. The flowers may be white, pink, scarlet, or yellow, and the leaves are usually as ornamental as the flowers, often being elaborately variegated, banded, spotted, or of a curious metallic appearance. "Begonias have given rise," says Dr. Bailey in "Hortus," "under cultivation, to numberless forms and hybrids and many of them bear Latin names as if they were species, thus adding to the confusion of the nomenclature." In the tropical lands in which they grow, the majority of them are perennial, but there are a few annuals.

Very little attention is required to keep the Begonia plants happy in your window garden. It had best be a window, however, that does not get the full force of the sun for long hours during the day. The earth in the pots should be kept damp, but not too damp, not really wet, and the leaves appreciate an occasional spraying; also the air of the room or sun porch where they grow should be occasionally sprayed in order to maintain a moist atmosphere.

There are so many kinds that it is useless to advise a selection. Visit the glasshouse of a botanical garden or a florist who specializes in Begonias, and see them in all their infinite variety. Then select the kinds you most admire.

If you are going in for Begonias on any scale, whether as a window gardener or as a florist, it would be well to join the Begonia club. Its literature is interesting and helpful, and as there are over four hundred species known, besides the countless hybrids, you are sure to want accurate information about them.

The Begonia in Plate 279 is probably one of the many hybrids, and a very handsome one. *Elatior*, its specific name, means taller.

Begonias do best in pots filled with a soil composed largely of good fibrous loam and a little well rotted manure, or leaf-mold, with enough sand to provide free drainage; for, though because of their quick habit of growth they require a good deal of water, they will not tolerate stagnant moisture in the soil.

Streptocarpus Hybrids (Plate 280)

The Cape Primrose, Streptocarpus, is a genus of South African plants of great interest and beauty. The flowers, which are shaped somewhat like those of a Gloxinia, grow on slender stalks and nod slightly. "They are generally," says Sarah Coombs ("South African Plants for American Gardens"), "of exquisite shades of pale blue or deep blue or mauve, though there are red-flowered ones, the species *Streptocarpus dunni* being described as bright rose-red and as pink to yellow. I think it is rather red than pink though it may vary. There is a yellowish one, *Streptocarpus lutea*."

Streptocarpus is a tender plant grown much in greenhouses abroad, but little in this country. It is said that it thrives in a cool greenhouse and is of easy cultivation. European seedsmen offer packets of mixed seed, as well as separate colors, which may be easily raised. Mrs. Coombs says: "The growth of the plants is attractive. They are stemless or nearly so. Some have a growth of leaves from the root with much the look of a Primrose plant. Another group has stems and opposite stem-leaves, but the most interesting ones to grow are those of a third type where the flower stalk grows from the one leaf that lies flat on the ground. This leaf is really an enlarged seed-leaf, the other not enlarging."

Though Streptocarpus seeds are very tiny, the "seedlings bloom in from eight to fifteen months . . . and they may be grown rather easily from leaf-cuttings."

It is strange that plants so easily grown and so lovely for house decoration are not more commonly grown in this country.

⚘ Begonia, Gloxinia, and *Achimenes longiflora* (Plate 281)

In Plate 281 we have a group of greenhouse plants effectively arranged. There are the large-striped, somewhat metallic-looking leaves of Begonias (see Plate 279), the lovely flowers of the Gloxinias (see Plate 278), and *Achimenes longiflora*.

Achimenes are branching plants, one to two feet high, with "thickened tuberous or scaly roots," usually grown under glass. The flowers are showy and somewhat like those of Gloxinias. They are tropical American plants. There are about forty known species, only two of which are common in cultivation, but there are many hybrids.

The plants should be grown in pots or hanging baskets in a cool greenhouse.

After they have finished blooming the tubers are removed from the soil, dried off, and stored in cool sand, without watering, in a cool cellar or apartment, where the temperature, however, does not go much below

[*288*]

Plate 276. *Hydrangea macrophylla (H. opuloides, H. hortensis)*

Plate 277. *Chrysanthemum indicum* BRILLIANT

Plate 278. *Gloxinia Meteor*

Plate 279. *Begonia elatior*

Plate 280. STREPTOCARPUS, HYBRIDS

Plate 281. BEGONIA, GLOXINIA AND *Achimenes longiflora*

Plate 282. AMARYLLIS WITH VARIOUS FLOWERS IN A GREENHOUSE

Plate 283. AMARYLLIS HYBRID

Plate 284. DIANTHUS (CARNATIONS)

Plate 285. DIANTHUS (CARNATIONS)

Plate 286. *Naegelia zebrina*

Plate 287. *Mesembryanthemum emarginatum*

Plate 288. LAVENDER-COLORED PELARGONIUM

Plate 289. PELARGONIUM

Plate 290. CYCLAMEN

Plate 291. PELARGONIUM (GERANIUM)

45°. They are quite easily propagated by division of the rhizome or tuber, "or by cuttings in summer in a moist greenhouse." The roots are also sometimes purchased from seedsmen and planted out for summer decoration after danger from frost is past.

The flowers are very attractive and are borne in the axils of the leaves. They come in various tones of red, violet, and white.

Achimenes longiflora (*Achimenes Haageana*) is from Guatemala. The leaves are toothed and pale beneath, the flowers long-tubed and violet in color. There is a white-flowered variety. Those in the illustration are probably of hybrid origin.

⚛ Amaryllis with Various Flowers in a Greenhouse (Plate 282)

A small greenhouse will hold a great variety of plants. In Plate 282 we find a group containing numerous Orchids, a handsome tall red Amaryllis, some pots of double Daffodils, some Azaleas, and several plants useful for their foliage.

No less care should be exercised in arranging potted plants so that they will harmonize and set each other off than is taken in the garden.

⚛ Amaryllis Hybrid (Plate 283)

Amaryllis is a South African bulb sending up a stout scape two feet high bearing very large Lily-like flowers. Many of the plants in cultivation under the name Amaryllis are Hippeastrums and other genera. In "Hortus," Dr. Bailey gives a list of these impersonators which is useful to one who wishes to be accurate. Among them besides several Hippeastrums and Lycoris are Sprekelia, Brunsvigia, *Crinum longifolium*, *Sternbergia lutea*, *Vallota speciosa*, *Nerine sarniense*, and *Zephyranthes Atamasco*.

Amaryllis is said to be technically a genus of one species, belonging to the family Amaryallidaceae.

The strong stalk arises and bears its showy flowers usually before the strap-shaped leaves appear. These showy plants are very handsome for growing in window or out of doors where the climate is suitable, or in a greenhouse. They require a long period of rest. The bulbs should be dug up and stored in a dry, frost-proof place during the winter in cold climates, "then repotted in a mixture of fibrous loam, leaf-mold and sand and placed in a warm position. Liquid manure should be applied when the flowers develop."

Amaryllis Belladonna, the Belladonna Lily, is a beautiful and fragrant flower, about three and one-half inches long, and borne in close clusters. The typical Belladonna Lily is a fine rose-red, but there are many forms from palest pink to deep rose, and there are numerous other colors as well. In the South it is easily grown out of doors, and even in northern climates it is said to winter if planted deeply, from nine to twelve inches down, and given a heavy covering of straw or leaves. For outdoor use it may also be planted in a tub and wintered in a cool cellar, in which case the bulb should be set with its tip even with or just below the surface.

It prefers a light soil and free drainage. When the plant first begins to grow, water moderately, "increasing the amount as growth is well advanced and decreasing it as the leaves turn yellow."

Mrs. Coombs says that tub culture is better for it "since it is then easier to give the bulb the long ripening which most South African bulbs must have to succeed in the northern hemisphere. Even in warmer climates look well to ripening."

There is a recently formed Amaryllis Society, that is devoted to the culture and study of these beautiful plants and their many related genera.

⚜ Dianthus (Carnations) (Plates 284 and 285)

Our choice of winter florists' flowers would be sadly depleted were it not for Carnations. They are the most cheerful, the most fragrant, and the most long-lasting of flowers; and happily they are less expensive than many of the florists' wares.

The Carnation, as we know it today, has come a long way. Its Latin name is *Dianthus Caryophyllus;* but this name, which is seldom used in connection with the beruffled creations that we buy in the winter, is a relic of the days when it was a simple wild flower, growing wild from southern Europe to India, as it does today, cheering the wayfarer on his way, by its spicy scent and bright color, as it rises from the grasses or hangs from crannies of old walls.

This little flower became the favorite and the concern of florists many years ago. It was one of the first of what we call florists' flowers; that is, it was among the first to be taken in hand and changed out of all memory of their former state—though not always improved—by the green-fingered gentry.

But the Carnation is one that has been really improved. We would not exchange the beautiful double flowers of today for the modest wild Pinks that were their parents. Early writers called them Gillyflowers, and old horticultural works contain long dissertations upon how to make the seed come up double, and much other strange and conjectural lore. Later came the books giving long lists of named varieties of Carnations with exact directions for their culture and more exact rules of points by which they were to be judged. Today the Carnation is well in hand, and though books and articles are still devoted to it they are of a less experimental nature.

In Europe, Carnations are much grown out of doors, and much sweetness they add to both cottage and estate gardens. But in few American gardens do we find them though Dianthus of many other varieties and species are freely grown, both in rock garden and border. In California and elsewhere in mild localities, Carnations may be successfully grown in the open. "The Garden Dictionary" gives a list of favorites grown out of doors in California. They are: San Remo, yellow; Villa Franca, white; Cannes, pink; Beauty of Nice, rose-pink; Mentone, scarlet; Monaco, crimson. They are fine for cutting.

There are now great numbers of named greenhouse varieties, and almost every season new favorites make their appearance and old ones are cast aside. They come in white, in all tones of blush, pink, scarlet, and red, in yellow and salmon. The "green" carnation often predicted has not yet appeared, and how short would be its vogue if it did!

"Anyone with a greenhouse that can be kept during the winter between fifty degrees (at night) and sixty during the day can grow the ordinary florist's Carnation if the following directions are adhered to."

The advice is that cuttings be made in November and December from plants flourishing in the greenhouse: "They should be taken from prolific-flowering stems, cut about halfway between the swollen joints and potted in potting mixture I i.e., two parts sharp sand, one part loam, one part leaf mould." When securely rooted the cuttings should be transplanted to a slightly more nutritious mixture—the three foregoing ingredients in *equal* parts. "After all danger from frost is past," the directions continue, "the potted cuttings should be planted outdoors in rows sixteen to twenty-four inches apart and the plants set eight to ten inches apart in the row." During the summer the plants are treated much as any other outdoor plants—weeded, cultivated, and watered when necessary. They will probably not attempt to bloom; but if they should, the buds must be removed as all strength is to be conserved for later effort.

[292]

Some time before frosts are expected, the plants should be carefully lifted and "planted out directly in the greenhouse bench. The bench should have been filled several days or a week or two before with a rich garden loam. . . . Space the plants six inches apart in the rows and have the rows about twelve inches apart. If you want all the flowers you can get from each plant, they can be grown without further attention except plentiful watering and an occasional dose of liquid manure." (For further directions, varieties, and pests, see "The Garden Dictionary," edited by Norman Taylor.)

ꕤ *Naegelia zebrina* (Plate 286)

Naegelia is a small genus of herbaceous plants found in tropical America. They belong to the family Gesneriaceae, and are sometimes referred to as Gesneria. They are grown in greenhouses in the North in the same mild temperature as Gloxinias and other tropical plants. They are tuberous-rooted, and propagation is effected by division of the roots, offsets, or by means of seeds. The leaves are heart-shaped, with a soft velvety surface, and are very ornamental. The flowers are tubular and red or yellowish white, carried in terminal panicles. They are followed by fruit in a dry capsule.

Liquid manure should be given about once a week upon the appearance of the flower buds; but after flowering, water should be given less often until the foliage dies down. Then the plants should be kept in a dry place without water during the winter.

Naegelia zebrina (*Gesneria zebrina*), the species illustrated in Plate 286, grows about two feet high. The leaves are hairy and clearly marked by veins of purple, red, or dark brownish. The flowers are red and yellow and one and one-half inches in length, the tube pinched at the base.

[293]

The plant comes from Brazil and is said to be particularly good for fall flowering.

Two other species are *Naegelia cinnabarina* and *Naegelia multiflora*, both natives of Mexico. The flowers of the first are cinnabar-red spotted with white; those of the second are white or cream color, and drooping. *Naegelia cinnabarina* is considered a first-class winter-blooming plant. The leaves of both are hairy.

⚜ *Mesembryanthemum emarginatum* (Plate 287)

Mesembryanthemum is a vast genus of mostly South African plants. More than a thousand species have been described under this genus, according to Bailey, but recently the group has been restudied and broken up into a number of genera. Plate 287 now represents *Lampranthus emarginatus*, not Mesembryanthemum, though it is closely allied to it.

It is an erect plant, spreading, with a branched, rather zigzagged stem, narrow long leaves "with a bloom roughly dotted." The flowers are very long-stemmed, in three, the petals notched at the top. The flowers are pinkish lavender. It is native to South Africa.

The Mesembryanthemums have the common name of Midday Flowers, many of them opening in bright sunlight, "but there are many which open at different times, sometimes not till rather late in the afternoon."

Mrs. Coombs says the culture of most of this genus is very simple, the great secret of success consisting in exposing the plants to the full sun at all times, and in not using too rich a soil. A compost of lime rubbish, yellow loam, sand, and decayed manure in equal proportions suits them well. Several species constitute very charming plants for window gardening, and many others can be grown with great success in the open from May until October.

[*294*]

⚑ Lavender-colored Pelargoniums (Plates 288 and 289)

There are many types of garden and greenhouse plants that have the common name of Geranium that are not true Geraniums. They are properly Pelargoniums and they belong to the family Geraniaceae. Most of the Pelargoniums come from South Africa, where they grow luxuriantly.

Mrs. Coombs says: "*Pelargonium inquinans* is a parent of most of the garden Geraniums. It was introduced into England as early as 1714, and has become naturalized in many of the warmer countries." There are a great many species, and a vast number of hybrids that have been developed from them, including the well known Zonal, the plant of every window ledge and many a garden bed, the plants we know as Sweet-leaved Geraniums—the apple-scented, nutmeg-scented, lemon-scented, rose-scented, peppermint-scented, and so on, and the Ivy-leaved Geraniums, so much used in hanging baskets and window boxes. And then there are the splendid Show or Fancy Pelargoniums, usually called Lady Washington Geraniums, specimens of which are shown in Plates 288 and 289.

All the Pelargoniums are tender (though many of the true Geraniums are hardy) and can only be cultivated under glass or out of doors where frost does not fall. The Lady Washington Geraniums have been worked over by hybridists until there are now many beautiful varieties. They have the largest flowers of any of the Pelargoniums and make exceedingly showy plants for the greenhouse. Many of the individual flowers are beautifully frilled or ruffled, and a majority display more than one color. There are lilac ones edged with white, purple with a white center, combinations of rose and maroon with a white center, scarlet with a violet center, pink with white center, bright scarlet with black spots on the petals, and innumerable other combinations as well as plain colors. One variety, Mrs. Layle, displays the remarkable combination of black, pink, purple, and white.

[*295*]

The Lady Washington Geraniums are very popular at the present time, and dealers offer long lists, though not, perhaps as long as those of a generation or so ago, when they burst upon an astonished and welcoming world in all their glory.

They are prodigal of flowers, and no greenhouse is completely furnished without a selection of Lady Washington Geraniums; they grow very well in the house or on a sun porch, indeed the amiability of the race is proverbial.

They are "propagated from cuttings or from shoots three to four inches long in July, inserted in a mixture of one half sand and one half soil in two inch pots, watering well after planting. They should then be placed in a cold frame or greenhouse in an airy position and shaded from strong sun."

When they are securely rooted, transfer them to four-inch pots in a more nourishing soil mixture, keeping the plants near the glass to bring about a strong, healthy growth. "When six inches long pinch out tip of shoots to make branch, more flowers being obtained by this method. In early January re-pot into six inch pots, keeping in a cool, airy place, and water sparingly during winter months. Temperature should be forty-five to sixty degrees. Water well from March to June and when flower buds appear give small quantity of a general fertilizer once a week until first flowers open." The directions from "The Garden Dictionary" continue: "After flowering prune back to within four inches on the base, stand plants outdoors in full sun until new shoots appear, then take out of the pots and remove most of the old soil. Re-pot into smaller pots, placing them under glass in September.... Firm potting and good drainage are essential."

Plate 292. *Anthurium Scherzerianum*

Plate 293. *Strelitzia Reginae* (BIRD-OF-PARADISE FLOWER)

Plate 294. *Aechmea fasciata* (BILLBERGIA RHODOCYANEA)

Plate 295. *Aechmea fulgens*

Plate 296. *Medinilla magnifica*

Plate 297. *Billbergia pyramidalis*

Plate 298. *Arum maculatum* (CUCKOO-PINT, LORDS-AND-LADIES)

Plate 299. *Nertera depressa* (BEAD PLANT)

Plate 300. CROTON

Plate 301. *Beloperone guttata*

Plate 302. *Aloe mitriformis Xanthacantha*

Plate 303. *Lachenalia tricolor* (CAPE COWSLIP)

❦ Cyclamen (Plate 290)

Among the most delightful plants for growing indoors in winter is *Cyclamen indicum (Cyclamen persicum)*. The roundish or kidney-shaped, long-stalked leaves arise directly from the fat corm, as do the flower stalks which are a foot or less high. The flowers are solitary on the stalks and come in exquisite tones of pink, salmon, and soft red as well as white. It has been much improved of late years, and there is great variety in the horticultural forms. The one illustrated in Plate 290 is of a strain called Rococo, a charming novelty in Cyclamens, "which presented many difficulties to the breeder before it was accomplished."

The plants are most decorative in rooms, and the flowers cut are lovely placed in small clear glass vases.

Cyclamen indicum is native from Greece to Syria. There are hardy species of Cyclamen that may be grown out of doors, especially in a rock garden, and while these have the quaintest charm their blossoms are tiny in comparison with those of the plants we buy of the florist or raise from the large corms ourselves. In southern California the charming varieties of *Cyclamen indicum* can be grown out of doors. In more severe climates they require the temperature of a greenhouse or warm room.

If we are to grow them ourselves it is necessary to secure good fat corms of blossoming size and plant them in five- or six-inch pots filled with good loam and sand, with the fleshy corm just protruding from the soil. They require plenty of water but not too much. It is best to water them by placing them in a vessel of water and allowing them to soak up sufficient to moisten the soil. They object to extremes—too much water, too much heat (a temperature of 50° is about right), or too much shade; nor do they like a moist atmosphere. It is said also that they do not like too much room, but grow best when the pot fits them snugly—in other words, when they are somewhat pot-bound.

After they have stopped blooming and the leaves have begun to turn yellow, water may be withheld for a week or two and the pots placed outside in a frame or in a shaded place. They object to great heat in summer; so keep them out of the sun. Some growers advocate placing the pots on their sides during this resting period, and they must be given just enough water to keep the corms plump; too much will cause rot to set in, nor is it desirable to encourage growth before we are ready to bring them indoors again for winter blossoming. In August, when small new leaves will probably begin to appear, the corm may be transplanted to a slightly larger pot in fresh soil.

The two most usually grown hardy Cyclamens are *Cyclamen europaeum,* which has purplish red flowers and the scent of Violets—it blooms in August—and *Cyclamen neapolitanum,* which flowers considerably later and without the leaves. The flowers may be pink or white. These small treasures like a partially shaded position. It is sad that they are so difficult to procure in this country.

⚘ Pelargonium (Geranium) (Plate 291)

This is undoubtedly the best known of all pot plants and is almost equally well known as a bedder. It is what is known as the Zonal Pelargonium or Geranium, and like the Lady Washington Geranium comes from South Africa.

The first Pelargonium introduced from South Africa to England was *Pelargonium triste,* which was brought from the Cape in 1632—a plant with cut leaves and quiet brownish yellow flowers with dark spots. A few more were introduced in the seventeenth century, but it was not until

[*298*]

the eighteenth century that the most important were brought in, including the Zonal Geranium.

Perhaps no flower in the world has been more widely grown than the Zonal Geranium. During the period when bedding out was the fashion, it was the prime favorite for lawn beds and was seen everywhere. Hybridizers soon took it in hand, and lovely frank colors made their appearance—all tones of pink, salmon, scarlet, blood-red, crimson, white, both double- and single-flowered. Even today no window box or indoor window garden is complete without its quota of Zonals; and though now it is rather looked down upon as commonplace, it is doubtful if any one plant has given so much pleasure to so many persons.

It is not generally regarded as a cut flower, yet a white pottery jar or bowl filled with scarlet or pink Geraniums is an ornament in any room where the colors do not clash.

Its specific botanical name, *zonale*, was given because of the zone of dark color that ornaments the leaves. The common name of Horseshoe Geranuim was given for the same reason. In some localities it has been known as Fish Geranium because of the leaves, which some imaginative persons believed to have a fishlike odor.

The name Pelargonium comes from *pelargós*, a stork, in allusion to the fruit, which has the shape of a stork's bill. The true Geranium has the common name of Crane's-bill; and another member of the family, the Erodium, is called Heron's-bill.

Because the Zonal Geraniums are so amiable and easy to grow, they are often subjected to gross neglect. They are overwatered or the reverse, or stood in dark corners. But as a matter of fact, if planted in good soil, watered moderately, and placed in a sunny window, they will bloom all winter, especially if the room is not overwarm.

In frost-free climates they may be grown out of doors the year round and may be trained against the walls of houses or trellises, where they will grow from eight to ten feet high.

Some varieties of Zonal Geraniums have white or yellowish edges or markings (silver and gold) and these were at one time much in demand for bedding and window boxes, though far less showy than the handsome large-flowered Horseshoe Geraniums.

✿ *Anthurium Scherzerianum* (Plate 292)

The Anthuriums are a very large genus of tropical American perennial plants grown in the greenhouse for the sake of their handsome arrow- or heart-shaped leaves and variously shaped and often very showy flowers. They belong to the Arum family. In the greenhouse, according to Dr. Bailey, they "require high temperatures, never below 55° in winter, and a humid atmosphere. They thrive in rough fibrous loam and the roots should be kept well covered. Repotting is necessary only every few years with older plants. Propagated by suckers or root-cuttings placed in pots over bottom heat; also by seeds under a bell-glass in a temperature of about 80°."

This Anthurium is one of the most popularly grown of florists' plants and is very decorative. The flowers are of curious form and may be red, like the one in Plate 292, rose, or white, according to which of the numerous horticultural varieties is grown; the spadix, which is coiled in a spiral form, is yellow. This is the flower; the more or less oval and much larger red, rose, white, or spotted portion is the spathe. It is native in Central America.

[*300*]

✠ *Strelitzia Reginae* (Bird-of-Paradise Flower) (Plate 293)

The beautiful and strange Bird-of-Paradise Flower belongs to the Banana family. It is a tender South African plant. Florists offer it in winter, and it is frequently seen in floral decorative arrangements. Mrs. Coombs's description of it is a good one: It is exotic-looking, she says, even in its own home, "with an air of some wild creature caught. Few flowers are more striking. Their two lower petals are joined, making a pointed boat-like base, the sepals prominent above it, the colors blue or white and yellow or orange. They do resemble a tropical bird poised for a minute on a tall stem."

Strelitzia Reginae grows about three feet tall with long Banana-like leaves, oblong lance-shaped, up to one and one-half feet long and four inches wide. The spathe is green, edged with purple; the sepals are orange-yellow. The petals are dark blue.

The plants are large and look somewhat like banana plants. It is said that they thrive in a cool greenhouse where they are grown in tubs. The night temperature should be about 50°. "For warmer parts of the country, where they could stay in the ground and make large clumps, they are greatly to be recommended," writes Mrs. Coombs, "for they have a long blooming period and are always an interesting sight." They are propagated by suckers or division of the roots in spring. They like to grow in full sun in good rich soil.

✠ *Aechmea fasciata* (*Billbergia rhodocyanea*) (Plate 294)

These are curious South American air plants belonging to the Pineapple family, grown for ornamental purposes in the greenhouse. The leaves are stiff and form a basal rosette; the flowers of the various species are borne in spikes, panicles, or racemes. One description reads, "The plants have a graceful vase-like form produced by the peculiar elegant curvature of the leaves."

In *Aechmea fasciata* the leaves are about twenty in a rosette. They are toothed, the face plain green, the back banded or marbled with white. The flowers are pink with red bract-leaves and arise out of the leaf rosettes on a long stalk. They are followed by a berrylike many-seeded fruit. It is native in Brazil.

"Although many of the cultivated kinds are variously epiphytic in their native habitats, they are usually grown in pots, wire baskets or wooden cribs, in a soil of fibrous material. Growth is mostly in summer, when plenty of water should be supplied; bloom is usually best in the following late winter to early summer." (See "Hortus," *s.v.* Bromeliaceae.)

Aechmea fulgens (Plate 295)

The species of Aechmea figured in Plate 295 also comes from Brazil. It has the long Banana leaves about two and one-quarter inches wide, and occasionally sharply toothed. The flower stalk is longer than the leaves, and the flowers are borne in long-branched panicles tapering towards the top. They are red tipped with blue. There is a variety *discolor* with leaves that are brownish or reddish violet beneath.

Though the Aechmea are a very large group of plants, *Aechmea fulgens* is considered as the handsomest and a very valuable foliage plant in the greenhouse. The variety *discolor* is perhaps more often cultivated. It is called the Coral Aechmea.

Many of these Bromeliads are very effective used in the greenhouse or window garden and require little attention to grow in perfection. They are very tenacious of life and robust in character. The flowers continue in good condition for several weeks. They are easily propagated by offsets from the old plants, started in small pots, which may be given gentle heat until they are well rooted.

Medinilla magnifica (Plate 296)

The Magnificent Medinilla is one of a large group of tropical Old World shrubs most of which occupy the volcanic islands of Asia, within the tropics, and require a damp forest climate. Bailey says that *Medinilla magnifica* comes from the Philippines. It was once a very popular "stove plant" but is less often seen today, perhaps because it is a vigorous plant and requires plenty of space. They are not suitable for small greenhouses, but should be grown in "roomy well-lighted structures such as the Lily house at Kew. The pot may even be stood in water in summer time as the Medinillas enjoy an abundance of moisture during their growing season." Moreover, the plants are greatly benefited by copious supplies of liquid manure.

The leaves are very large and handsome, oval, and about a foot long on angled or winged stems. The flowers are an inch long in large pendulous panicles a foot in length. They are coral-red with great showy pinkish bracts.

The Medinillas were named for José de Medinilla, Governor of the Ladrones.

Billbergia pyramidalis (Plate 297)

The Billbergias are stemless air plants belonging to tropical America. They have stiff clusters or rosettes of leaves out of which arise the flower stems bearing spikes or panicles of rather showy, mostly blue, flowers. Bailey says they are "grown for ornament and as oddities under glass or as house-plants."

Billbergia pyramidalis (Billbergia thyrsoidea) is native in Brazil and has finely spiny-toothed leaves three feet long and two and one-half inches wide. "A simple scape rises from the bosom of the leaves clothed below the flowers with large, concave, oval, lanceolate spathe-like entire bracts, of a fine rose color, which turns brown with age. Above the bracts the flowers grow in a thyrse-like spike." The flowers have bright red petals. The spike is about four inches long.

It is said that this plant holds a great quantity of water "in the bottom of the leaves."

Billbergia pyramidalis used to be called *Bromelia pyramidalis.*

❦ *Arum maculatum* (Cuckoo-Pint, Lords-and-Ladies) (Plate 298)

The plant illustrated in Plate 298 is an oversea relative of our Jack-in-the-Pulpit. The Arums embrace about twelve species of tuberous-rooted plants native in Europe, having mostly arrow-shaped handsome leaves and "unisexual flowers borne on a spadix surrounded by a spathe which is often colored." Dr. Bailey goes on to say that "many plants once named in Arum are now transferred to other genera."

The Arums like the same sort of soil as does our handsome "Jack," rich with plenty of moisture and a shaded position. Some species will stand the winter out of doors even in cold climates, others must be grown under glass and make good pot plants. They are propagated by offsets of the roots or by seeds, which some of them bear in quantity. The best time to divide them is just when they begin to make their new growth, having as many roots as possible to each division.

Plate 304. *Euphorbia pulcherrima* (POINSETTIA)

Plate 309. *Oncidium varicosum Rogersii*, WITH *Cattleya Mantinii*

The Cuckoo-Pint has a perennial root and is native in Great Britain. It has arrow-shaped leaves and a club-shaped spadix, reddish purple and shorter than the spathe.

Anne Pratt, in "Flowering Plants of Great Britain," writes: "Every rambler in the lane, by the thick hedgerow, or the sunny banks which border the meadow, delights in early spring, to see the bright green glossy Cuckoo-Pint, spotted often with dark purple stains, and commonly four or five inches long. . . . Scarcely an English hedgerow but has, in March, its store of the glossy handsome leaves, while in April the tall spadix rears its head to a height of about three inches, sometimes being a yellowish green, at others greenish purple, and often a deep rich violet colour. A ring of glands surrounds the middle of the spadix, and below this is a circle of sessile anthers, which, as the year advances, develop into a cluster of brilliant scarlet berries. Long after the leaves have withered, the stalk, about a foot high, thickly covered at the top with these fruits in a conspicuous mass, may be seen glistening among the sober-tinted wintry leaves beneath the woodland boughs."

The berries are said to be highly poisonous.

The Cuckoo-Pint is well suited to corners of the wild garden as our "Jack" is in North America.

Nertera depressa (Bead Plant) (Plate 299)

The curious little plant portrayed in Plate 299 is sometimes called Fruiting Duckweed because of a fancied resemblance to a tiny floating aquatic, Lemna, which infests the surface of stagnant pools, and which also bears the name Duckweed, though no relation botanically. But this minute plant is a landlubber, native in South America, New Zealand, and Tasmania.

It is a quaint and pretty little plant when well grown and closely set with its tiny reddish orange berries, as shown in the illustration.

It forms densely matted tufts, creeping over the ground if it is grown in the corners of rock gardens, as it is in mild climates. It is used as a ground cover in California, where the ground is moist and shady, and somewhat sandy.

But its most usual use is in greenhouses as a pot plant; and it looks very pretty making mounds of its small leathery leaves and bright berries, which it keeps for a long time. The flowers are green and of no account.

It is easily propagated by seed or division.

Early works on gardening have a good deal to say about this little plant. It seems to have been a favorite, and one book says it always excites interest. Another book, a French one, says, "We do not know of any vegetable growth which is better than this for making the background foundation in a basket for adorning the table." This is surely an echo from another day.

❦ Croton (Plate 300)

Crotons belong to the Euphorbia family and are a large genus of more than five-hundred species of trees and shrubs—rarely herbs—"differing widely in habit and general aspect dispersed all over the warmer parts of the world."

The Crotons of the garden and florist are referred to Codiaeum. Most persons know them as showy foliage plants that are very variable.

"Any good soil," says Dr. Bailey, "is suitable for crotons. They develop better coloring if planted in sunny situations." There is an enormous number of kinds, and those who have a fancy for colored foliage have a wide choice.

[306]

The word "Croton" is from the Greek *króton*, a tick, referring to the appearance of the seeds.

☫ *Beloperone guttata* (Plate 301)

Beloperone guttata is a not very well known or very spectacular plant of tropical South America. There are about thirty species known. The genus, says "The Garden Dictionary," is separated only by technical characters from Jacobinia. "Leaves opposite, without marginal teeth, flowers tubular but irregular and two-lipped, crowded in close spikes and from relatively showy overlapping bracts."

In the South *Beloperone guttata* is used occasionally as a border plant, but in the North it is grown as a pot plant. It is not, however, of great importance, and the cone-shaped clusters of flowers are not very striking despite the brownish bracts. These flowers are white with purplish spots. The plants are native of Mexico.

☫ *Aloe mitriformis Xanthacantha* (Plate 302)

The Aloes are perennial succulent plants having spiny-toothed leaves and bright red or yellow flowers in a raceme on a stout scapelike stem, "sometimes grown in the greenhouse or out-of-doors in the South for their unusual stiff and fleshy aspect." Dr. Bailey adds: "Aloes are well known pot subjects and are likely to be conspicuous about public buildings and parks in countries not subject to killing frost. They commonly do well in the same pot for some years when not grown for bloom."

The subject of Plate 302 was introduced from the South African coast region at the beginning of the eighteenth century. It does not remain, as do some species, a flat rosette, and "the stem or trunk can be seen between the leaves which are thick, green, spoon-shaped with white thorny, triangular teeth at the edges. The scarlet-red flowers form a full, short and rather broad truss." There is a yellow-flowered variety with larger thorns or spines. Gradually the lower leaves fall off, while the stem sometimes attains a height of from two to six feet, "when the greater part becomes woody or naked."

Lachenalia tricolor (Cape Cowslip) (Plate 303)

The Cape Cowslips are small bulbous plants native to South Africa, usually two basal leaves and "red or yellow flowers in racemes or spikes terminating the scape, the perianth-segments partially united" ("Hortus").

The variety *tricolor* has leaves between six and nine inches long, "often spotted purple or darker green." The flowers are long and tubular, the lower ones on the spike nodding. They are yellow tipped with red, "the outer segments much longer than the inner." There are numerous color varieties of *Lachenalia tricolor*. A dealer says of this variety, "The curious combination of colors, green, yellow, and maroon, makes this variety particularly attractive." Another dealer says, "It is odd indeed that such an attractive and easily grown bulb should be so little known in America."

They are not at all fussy about soil, but are satisfied with a turfy loam mixed with leaf-mold, a little old cow manure, and sand. They are handled like Freesias. Planted in their pots in August and kept in a cold frame until growth is well up, about the end of November, when they may be brought into the cool greenhouse or window. It is important to bring them on slowly. The flowering season under glass is March and April. As they approach their time of flowering they should be given plenty of water. After blossoming water should be withheld gradually, and the bulbs allowed to dry and ripen thoroughly. The pots may be laid on their sides in the greenhouse until the bulbs are well ripened, and then stored.

[*308*]

Ten to twelve bulbs may be put into a five-inch pot, with the tops of the bulbs one-half inch below the surface of the soil. They are increased by offsets. If cared for, the bulbs will continue to flower from year to year.

In the *Botanical Magazine* (Vol. III, Plate 82) it is said of *Lachenalia tricolor* that only at the middle of its flowering are the three colors that give it its specific name noticeable: "as it advances the brilliant orange of the top flowers dies away; the spots on the leaves also."

❦ *Euphorbia pulcherrima* (Poinsettia) (Plate 304)

The Poinsettia is generally acknowledged to be the Christmas plant. It is sold in all the florist shops at that season in thousands and reproduced in paper and other materials; and its likeness appears on Christmas cards, and the like.

The Poinsettia is another of the vast and various Euphorbia clan, the Spurges. It is native of Central America and Mexico.

In an article that appeared some time ago in *Horticulture*, David Rust of Philadelphia had this to say about the Poinsettia:

"At the first exhibition of the Pennsylvania Horticultural Society held in Masonic Hall, Chestnut Street, Philadelphia, on June 6, 1829, *Euphorbia pulcherrima* was exhibited by Colonel Robert Carr, proprietor of the Bartram Botanic Garden, Philadelphia.

"This plant was sent to the Bartram Botanic Garden by the Hon. J. R. Poinsett, United States Minister to Mexico, in a collection of Euphorbiaceae. Stock was given to Robert Buist, who was then the leading florist and nurseryman of Philadelphia, who sent a plant to Professor Graham of the Royal Botanic Garden, Edinburgh, Scotland. Professor Graham suggested the name of Poinsett. Later it was exhibited as *Euphorbia poinsetti* and finally as *Poinsettia pulcherrima*."

Few persons but are familiar with the appearance of this plant. In its native habitat it grows to be a shrub ten feet in height. The leaves constitute the showy part of the plant. In the kind best known they are bright red; but there are now a white variety and a pink variety. There is also a variety with a double series of bracts, or colored leaves, that is very showy.

Poinsettias are lovers of the sun and never form their bracts if shaded even in a slight degree. In warm sections of California they grow freely out of doors.

✠ *Calanthe vestita Regnieri* (Plate 305)

Calanthes are terrestrial Orchids "sometimes having pseudobulbs with broad plaited leaves, and white, rose or yellow flowers on erect or nodding scapes . . . mostly deciduous and require rest after flowers are past in winter" ("Hortus").

Looking at *Calanthe vestita Regnieri*, one might well be under the illusion that he is looking at a swarm of fantastic tropical insects. In the type the flowers are white or creamy; in the variety *Regnieri* they have a rose-colored lip and purple markings in the throat, which gives them a very brilliant effect. The type comes from India and Malaya. They are easily brought into bloom in the greenhouse in December and January.

"Calanthe" is from Greek words meaning beautiful flower.

✠ *Cattleya gigas* x *Laelia cinnabarina* (Plate 306)

A great number of crosses have been made between the Orchids Laelia and Cattleya. The one illustrated in Plate 306 is especially beautiful because of the vivid contrast displayed in the colors of its blooms.

The Cattleyas, of which there are a vast number of species and varieties, are native of tropical America. They have very thick leaves and flowers usually in terminal clusters, rarely solitary. They are pseudobulbous.

[*310*]

The Laelias are also native to tropical America, have "showy flowers solitary or in racemes, the sepals and petals nearly equal, the lip three-lobed." Both Laelia and Cattleya thrive in the greenhouse in an intermediate temperature.

⚑ *Cattleya Harrisoniana* (Plate 307)

Cattleya Harrisoniana, one of the vast number of Cattleya Orchids, is from Brazil, and very beautiful. Dr. Bailey's description (see "Hortus") follows: "Leaves oblong-lanceolate, to six inches long; flowers to four inches across, two to five together, rose-lilac, the middle lobe of lip purple with yellow spot, July to October."

⚑ *Miltonia vexillaria* Lyoth (Plate 308)

Miltonias are considered the daintiest and most attractive among the Orchids. Like butterflies, the flowers seem to float in the air about the plants. They are South American epiphytes "allied to Odontoglossum and requiring similar treatment, with one- or two-leaved pseudobulbs and sheathing leaves at base and flowers solitary or in loose racemes, the sepals and petals nearly equal, the lip expanded and not three-lobed" ("Hortus").

There are a great number of Miltonias. *Miltonia vexillaria* has flowers about four inches long in a three- or four-flowered raceme. The sepals and petals are pink; the lip is pink with a white base and edges. It is native to Colombia.

There are many new varieties which have been derived from crosses with *Miltonia vexillaria*. One of these, "Lyoth," is shown in Plate 308, and gives proof of their exquisite daintiness.

 🏵 *Oncidium varicosum Rogersii,* with *Cattleya Mantinii* (Plate 309)

Like the Miltonias, the Oncidiums are tropical American air plants (epiphytic Orchids) with one- to two-leaved pseudobulbs. The flowers are usually in panicles or lateral racemes, which show many tones of brown, yellow, and various shades of red. They are extremely decorative and beautiful.

Both flowers in the illustration are hybrids. The golden-flowered one is from *Oncidium varicosum,* which is the type, has many-flowered panicles to a height of five feet occasionally, and flowers with sepals and petals greenish yellow spotted with russet and a golden-yellow lip.

The other Orchid in the illustration is *Cattleya Mantinii,* a profusely flowering hybrid between *Cattleya Bowringiana* and *Cattleya velutina.*

 🏵 *Echinocactus Graessneri* x *Haselbergii* (Plate 310)

At one time and another a thousand names have been set down to this genus. It is now greatly reduced (in fact to about nine species), but it is still a somewhat confused genus.

The plants are "thick, sometimes very large, many- or several-ribbed, cylindric, the large areoles very spiny; flowers on the crown, yellow or pink, often immersed in wool; axils of scales on ovary and fruit woolly; fruit white-woolly." These Cacti belong to the southwest United States and Mexico.

The handsome hybrid shown in Plate 310 has flowers of a most unusual hue. They are flame-colored and seem to burst from the body of the Cactus like jets of flame. It is a cross between *Echinocactus Graessneri* and *Echinocactus Haselbergii,* which resemble each other. The first produces flowers ranging in color from yellowish green to emerald-green; the flowers of the

Plate 310. *Echinocactus Graessneri* x *Haselbergii*

Plate 314. *Cereus flagelliformis*

Plate 315. *Phyllocactus kermesinus roseus*

Plate 316. *Mammillaria longissima*

Plate 317. *Rhipsalis Gaertneri*

Plate 318. *Echinocactus Haselbergii*

Plate 319. PHYLLOCACTUS JUPITER

Plate 320. CACTUS IN CALIFORNIA

second are flame-red. The variety which resulted from this fortunate cross shows in its lovely flowers the blending of the colors of both parents into a warm and beautiful shade.

✤ *Echinocactus ingens* (Plate 311)

The subject of Plate 311 is another of the species of Echinocactus. It grows five feet high and four in diameter, and is grayish and somewhat woolly. The spines are straight and very sharp—not a nice thing to run into in the dark.

The flowers borne at the apex of the adult plant are reddish yellow on the outside and lemon-yellow inside, with shining surfaces and toothed petals.

It is native in Mexico.

✤ Phyllocactus Hybrid Latona (Plate 312)

The proper name for Phyllocactus is Epiphyllum. Botanists are active in changing and exchanging the names of the Cacti, so that the mere amateur is unable to keep up with them.

Dr. Bailey says of Epiphyllum: "Mostly epiphytic cacti, branches usually flattened and leaf-like and sometimes three-winged; mostly no spines on mature plants; flowers large and showy, with many long stamens, white, red or yellow, nocturnal or diurnal." And he says that many of the Epiphyllums are good for window and greenhouse plants, "and are frequently seen in summer on porches. They propagate readily by cuttings and are of simple requirements."

There are numerous species of this Cactus and many hybrids. The one shown in Plate 312 is a hybrid named Latona. The curious and unusual shape of the flowers and their beautiful color should make it popular.

✠ *Phyllocactus elegans* hybrid, Red Legion (Plate 313)

The great popularity over other Cacti of this type is readily understandable because of the profusion and beauty of its blooms. This is a most lovely hybrid, both in color and in form. The flowers are large and of an exquisite pink. It is a truly magnificent form of Epiphyllum.

✠ *Cereus flagelliformis* (Plate 314)

The genus Cereus of the Cactaceae has been until recently a large one, but according to Dr. Bailey has now been greatly reduced; "as now defined, it has about two dozen species in South America and West Indies." They are for the most part treelike, columnar plants ("but sometimes spreading or prostrate") strongly built, angled, ribbed, or spiny, with short hairs. The flowers are funnelform and usually white. They flower at night.

The famous plants known as "Night-blooming Cereus" are now placed in other genera—"particularly," says Dr. Bailey, in "Selenicereus, Nyctocereus, and Hylocereus."

The plant illustrated in Plate 314 is now called *Aporocactus flagelliformis* and informally known as the Rat-Tail Cactus or Whip Cactus, and it is said that it deserves first place among the Cacti of easy culture. It presents no cultural difficulty even to the most inexperienced Cactus enthusiast, but grows readily and blooms with happy profusion. When it begins to fall off in its blossoming, it should be repotted in fresh soil, and the old growth in the center removed. It will at once take heart and return to its former vigorous state and continue to give untold pleasure.

❦ *Phyllocactus Kermesinus roseus* (Plate 315)

This Phyllocactus, or more correctly, Epiphyllum, is one of the numerous varieties of this type of Cactus and is characterized by the profuse blossoming common to the Phyllocacti. There are many Cacti celebrated for the beauty of their flowers, but none can compete with the beauty of the pink blooms that are shown in Plate 315. This is a reliable old form and a generous bloomer though the flowers are not of the largest size.

❦ *Mammillaria longissima* (Plate 316)

The Mammillaria are small, low depressed members of the Cactus family sometimes rounded or oval or cylindrical and elongated. They have a watery or milky sap, and they are usually woolly or hairy on the encircling tubercles about the tip of the stems. They are a large genus of more than two hundred species found in Mexico and a few in southwestern United States and a few in Venezuela.

They are very popular as window or greenhouse plants. The flowers are small bell-shaped but very pretty, and may be red, pink, yellow, or white. They are borne in the axils of the old tubercles. In addition they display small club-shaped red fruits protruding beyond the tubercles, usually forming a circle around the apex of the plant, and these last for a long time.

These little plants usually grow in clusters and make attractive pot plants. Their culture offers few difficulties. They like a moderately rich soil, and as many of them grow naturally in cold localities they are able to stand a quite low temperature; but none like an excess of moisture in the pots. Their preferences, however, differ, and some are best suited by a sandy or even stony soil. They prefer full sunshine, but a few will stand half-shade, especially during the extreme heat of summer.

⚜ *Rhipsalis Gaertneri* (Plate 317)

Rhipsalis Gaertneri belongs to a group of epiphytic Cacti found mostly on rocky ledges or on the mossy stems of trees, including some fifty or sixty species. They make interesting pot plants, and many of them are grown in greenhouses. Their habit is "hanging or clambering or sometimes erect and more or less rooting or emitting aerial roots, the stems branched, terete, angled, or flattened and leaf-like, sometimes as slender as strings, the areoles on the edges or angles and bearing hairs, wool and bristles." The flowers are small and usually solitary but sometimes borne in clusters. They are very attractive and remain open day and night for more than a week.

The various species range from Florida, Mexico, the West Indies to Argentina.

A mixture of sand and loam suits them well. The species of Rhipsalis are said to be quite easily grown, and they are most effective.

⚜ *Echinocactus Haselbergii* (Plate 318)

This form originates in southern Brazil and is very attractive, blossoming in spring and early summer. The plant is globose but slightly depressed on top and light green. It is about five inches in height and as much broad. The coloring of the flowers is exquisite, as may be seen in the plate; the outer petals are deep rose-red; the petals around the center shade to flame- or orange-color at the edges. It is altogether a most brilliant small thing.

[*316*]

☗ Phyllocactus Jupiter (Plate 319)

Nearly all the many kinds of this type of Cactus are worth growing. Jupiter is a most brilliant hybrid with irregular large flowers and flattened leaf-like branches. It makes a showy window or greenhouse plant. There are usually no spines on mature plants.

☗ Cactus in California (Plate 320)

It is rather staggering to read that there are "about thirteen hundred known species of cacti, now arranged in more than one hundred genera." They are all American plants, North or South, "the few that occur wild in other parts of the world being probably spread from the western hemisphere." They are strange plants exhibiting widely varied forms, cushioned, spiny, forbidding, often bearing barbed bristles or fish-hook spines. It is always a surprise to find them bursting forth with beautiful and delicate flowers, exquisitely colored. Some of them bear a fleshy berry that is edible. The plants assume the oddest shapes, as may be seen in Plate 320, and a collection of the various kinds always excites interest. The body of the plant may be globe-shaped, columnar, or barrel-shaped, and there are delicate climbing forms; and any one who has crossed the American deserts has looked with wonder upon the great treelike forms with angular, reaching arms.

A cactus garden was exhibited some years ago at the New York Flower Show, and such gardens may easily be made in climates where the plants may live out over the winter. They are always interesting, if too strange to be exactly beautiful, though the flowers are nearly always lovely. Where grown out of doors they like a low annual rainfall and a very warm summer temperature. A few species are hardy enough to grow in the

[*317*]

North, and the species Opuntia has a wide distribution and is hardy in sandy districts as far north as Massachusetts.

Many persons have collections of the small kinds indoors where they make an entertaining exhibit. The mixture in the pots for most of them should be two parts sharp sand, two parts sandy loam, one part crushed brick or potsherds, a little leaf-mold—and to each bushel of the mixture a five-inch flower pot full of bone meal, and a five-inch flower pot full of limestone. (This mixture is taken from "The Garden Dictionary" and is recommended for most succulents.)

There should never be any dampness or stagnant water at the roots. A little watering about once a week is all that is required by the majority of the plants grown indoors. If given too much water they will rot very quickly. They need the fullest light and sunshine and should be placed in a sunny window.

Looking at Plate 320, one may easily be under the illusion that he is looking at a natural scene. But it is the picture of a Cactus planting on an estate, with a painting of Death Valley in California used as a background. It shows, however, the great variety of forms assumed by these plants.

INDEX

INDEX

NOTE: Italic numbers in this index indicate plates, while regular Arabic numbers represent text pages. For example, "*Acer palmatum, 216, 223*" indicates that this plant is illustrated in Plate 216 and is described on text page 223.